AVID

READER

PRESS

ALSO BY TOM COYNE

FICTION

A GENTLEMAN'S GAME

NONFICTION

PAPER TIGER

A COURSE CALLED IRELAND

A COURSE CALLED SCOTLAND

A COURSE CALLED AMERICA

QUIET, PLEASE

A COURSE CALLED

HOME

ADVENTURES OF AN ACCIDENTAL
GOLF COURSE OWNER

TOM COYNE

AVID READER PRESS

NEW YORK AMSTERDAM/ANTWERP LONDON TORONTO
SYDNEY/MELBOURNE NEW DELHI

AVID READER PRESS
An Imprint of Simon & Schuster, LLC
1230 Avenue of the Americas
New York, NY 10020

For my crew

I will arise and go now, and go to Innisfree,
And a small cabin build there, of clay and wattles made . . .

—W. B. Yeats, "The Lake Isle of Innisfree"

PART 1

NUNCHUCKS IN THE ATTIC

TUESDAY MORNING

Hands caked with mud, fingertips diced by a thousand tiny cuts, and my wheels were spinning again.

It had been the wettest Catskills summer in memory, and Shaun had warned me to throttle down as I drew closer to the green. I killed the engine and slid out of the seat, got back down on my knees, and ripped clumps of soggy grass from the reels—right, middle, left, then the rear units beneath the chassis that I struggled to reach. If we had the money or time to sharpen our bed knives, I'd have lost a digit by now; instead, I shaved away my fingerprints as I felt for jams and tore chunks of wet earth, pulling hair from a clogged drain, until I could turn each cylinder by hand. This was the ninth time I'd had to clear the reels on this run, eight piles of discharged mud lined up in the rough behind me, and my favorite morning job looked like it would become that afternoon's job, too.

I've come to believe that golfers should know what it's like to ride a mower or cut a hole or water a green before they play. Not as punishment, but to better know our playing grounds and appreciate the big and small things—like freeing wads of vegetation from an undercarriage—that turn a field into a stage. We'd not only understand our good fortune as golfers, but we'd earn the answers to questions we may have long pondered. We'd know why our tees and fairways have rounded corners (because the mowers turn on a certain radius) and why someone let the rough grow on that hillside (because the mower tips over up there) and why we can't have those vertical bunker faces we see on TV (because trimming them costs a day's worth of manpower, fuel, and gear we don't possess and can't afford).

We'd know why tall fescue is fashionable (no cut, no work), why we should pick up our tees (they dull mower blades, and resharpening robs hours), and why benches, cart signs, and tee markers are a blight (cut the engine, hop off, move them, restart, mow, move them back—if your legs are as stiff as mine, you daydream about blowing them out the back of your machine). We'd know that nobody asked a greenskeeper whether wall-to-wall fairways was a trend worth pursuing, and we'd learn how a course's maintenance budget can be halved if the course has been designed for simpler upkeep, or if its players accepted brown as a firmer shade of green. We'd likely never leave a pitch mark or bare divot again, understanding that those banal scorecard requests aren't about manners or even playing conditions—they're about simple respect for the people whose job it is to grow grass, and a gentle nod to their existence. And if you're like me, you'd enjoy the art of upkeep. Maybe even more than your golf.

It's hard and early work, and at places like ours, it doesn't pay that well, either. I used to wonder why they do it, the greenskeepers who might get thanked once a year at the member-guest, but who mostly pass by in hooded sweatshirts and heavy brown boots, working through a checklist that started before dawn. They're a unique breed, the turf types, but those who get it in their blood tend to stick with it, and after a few months among them, I now had some understanding of why. Getting up and going to work for most people is coffee and a commute, shaving or some makeup, dressing appropriately so you can stare at your phone for an hour. Asking and answering questions in as few words as possible, creating tasks and passing them along, and maybe noticing whether the sun is shining or not.

In the work out here, the weather is all you notice—your day is dictated by sun and seasons and a rain gauge that's inspected every morning. The forecast tells you when to fire up the mowers and where to take them, and each morning is a chance to know satisfaction before most people have finished deleting their overnight emails. It's just you atop a humming red rig, tracing lines into a field shining with dew, the fog still spinning in your blades, and your only company a few deer who hardly look up when they see you anymore, and soon every tuft is trimmed and you've got the mow lines to prove it and can look back and see what you've done—it's a kind of work I'd never known before this summer, work that gives you clear beginnings and endings and doesn't ping you after dinner, the sort of job you still feel that evening as you fall asleep, bones sore with effort but your mind clear for having answered what the day asked.

This day's aches and scrapes might last a little longer. We typically welcome the rain because we lack a working irrigation system for our fairways, and our method for dousing the greens is something we try not to discuss, let alone use. We have nine garden hoses wrapped around hubcaps on posts that stand guard beside each green, but the pump meant to send them water from the pond is old and irritable, and the pipes that run to each hose are a patchwork of red iron and PVC held together by putty and tape, and only half of them remain buried anymore.

Where they cross streams or change grade in the woods, we built tiny rock towers to support their weight and keep them from snapping, and with so many leaks, they deliver a mere trickle to those hoses. After a bone-dry May and June, we were praying for rain, forgetting that Noah probably prayed for a drizzle, too.

Not only do we lack the pipes to spray water on the golf course, we don't have pipes to drain water off it, either. Occasionally I'd spot a rusty drain buried in a fairway, relics from our course's heyday, but when the water comes now, puddles form in all our low spots (at a course beside a mountain, we have plenty of those). Rain pushes the weeds higher, then shelters them on turf too soft for the machines meant to clip them.

We often tried when we shouldn't have, and that's when we felt the agony of tires lurching and spinning, stuck dead in a wet patch. Ever try to slide a piece of old furniture and feel a nail gash your wooden floor? It's close to that, and then it gets worse when you hit the gas hard because your only way out is forward as platter-sized pieces of fairway come loose beneath your wheels. On your next pass, you see the mess you've made and wonder what kind of asshole would do that to a golf course.

Sometimes you can't motor through it, and that's where I found myself on number eight, my twice-a-week nemesis. Not only is it big—a runway par-five of almost all fairway—but its approach is an awkward cut, where your lines squeeze into a tight funnel as you approach a narrow, raised plateau with a collar that's tough to trim without dropping clippings all over the green. It sits beside a hidden spring in the greenside rough, and today I'd found the heart of it. I looked around, hoping to find one of my comrades, but it was just me and the deer. They'd been watching me stall out all morning, happy to nibble the grass I was failing to shorten.

Bearded Chris was responsible for trimming the rough on his Ventrac, an eight-wheeled beast that could handle our most unreasonable slopes. Shaun mowed the greens, sometimes pushing by hand or, when the triplex was working, atop his riding mower. Fairways were my job, but maybe not much longer, I thought—I'd cleaned my reels, but the tires were buried in three inches of soup. I rocked from forward to reverse with no luck. Shut it down, started it back up. The ignition was shot so we had to hotwire our fairway unit, pressing a wire against the battery with a wrench we kept in the cupholder. No joy. I pulled out my phone and called Shaun, who was cutting greens on the other side of the property. I don't know how he heard or felt his phone vibrating while his machine was roaring, but when I was working the course, he never failed to pick up. He knew his staff (all two of us) and probably suspected that his fairway guy might be calling.

"I'm stuck. In the spring on eight."

He laughed a tired chuckle. "On my way."

I knew the water was there and should have been more careful, but I was so damn close to done—three hundred yards of fairway cut back-and-forth in perpendicular passes. Cut, loop around, drop the blades, cut, lift again, loop back—and rather than steer my way around the spring, I rolled the dice on turning here and lost.

We varied our fairway cuts to keep the grass from getting too comfortable lying in one direction. On the chalkboard in the maintenance shed, Shaun would draw the design he wanted me to follow that day. Start with a stripe down the middle, then mow in a figure eight to get that half-dark, half-light tuxedo look, or, my preferred method, loop around like a Zamboni until you're done. Shaun didn't love it, but it was easier than trying to set a perfect center stripe the way he could—miss the middle, and you left yourself with more grass left or right, circling back and hunting for ribbons until you lost all sense of where you'd been. The short, perpendicular paths I was tracing today (the dark track is what you just hit; keep it close) ensured a good cut, even if it meant less blade time with all the turnarounds, and what I liked best about this job was that I now used terms like "blade time" and phrases like "That was a good cut" and felt like I had earned them.

As I waited for Shaun to finish up whatever green he was working, I licked the dirt from my fingertips, rubbed my thumb against them, and felt the razor rash from brushing my fingers over bed knives.

Stuck in the mud atop a lawnmower three times the size of anything they sold at Home Depot, waiting beside a green in the Sullivan County Catskills, for a moment, I felt like a fake from afar. I was not a greens-keeper. My new role as course operator had not been earned; I was a measure of last resort. It would be a daydream sort of fun to play my own golf holes, sure, but there was no bucket list in my drawer with Run a Golf Club or Mow a Fairway or Raise Money and Buy a Golf Course scribbled upon it. So how had I landed here? I was a writer and a spoiled golfer—my career had taken me to first tees at some of the world's most wondrous places, where I played golf, jotted down a few paragraphs, bought a shirt, and went looking for the next.

But this place didn't sell shirts. It didn't even have a logo. And *wondrous* wasn't a word a visitor might have used to describe this nine-holer. Sporty and charming with views for days, but not a destination you'd come to write about. This was rural, local, community golf, and as with most golf courses fitting that description, it was failing. If we didn't find a way to turn that around this summer and plot a new path, the course would be sold for land and closed two years shy of reaching its one hundredth anniversary. And from my viewpoint, my wheels still spinning in the slop, that new path was anything but clear.

Truth was, the wheels at Sullivan County had been spinning for quite some time.

•   •   •

THE ORANGE COUNTY TIMES-PRESS, FEBRUARY 17, 1925

LIBERTY RESIDENTS BUY OLD HULL FARM

Plan Construction of Nine Hole Golf Course on Place; Hope to Start Playing in Another Year

Liberty, Feb. 16—Taking prompt advantage of a rare opportunity to acquire lands for a golf course near the corporation of Liberty, a dozen business men last week negotiated the purchase of the Gaylord Hull farm west of Liberty. The large farm, containing about 160 acres, of improved land ideally suited to the purpose for which it was bought, was sold to the group of local men for $120,000.

The deal was put through with surprising promptness. A tentative offer was made and accepted and the moving spirits in the deal hastily gathered together a number of other available business men to sign the contract of sale. Twelve men constituted the original signers.

Final transfer of the property will come on April 1, and immediately thereafter, work will be started on the construction of a nine hole golf course. The property is located just outside the corporation line on the road to White Sulphur Springs and covers a large area.

The ground is in excellent shape, having been carefully cultivated for many years. It is free from serious topographical obstacles and contains a number of natural hazards. Water and sewer have been laid to a part of the property and water could be easily piped to all greens. In time, it was said, a presentable club house might be erected and facilities for other sports, such as tennis, etc., would be provided.

According to a representative of the original 12 men on the contract, action to secure the property was required at once and opportunity to include all local people who would be interested was not offered. Accordingly only those men who were immediately available were asked to join.

The new golf club will not be an exclusive organization, it was said, but opportunity will be offered to all to join at the discretion of the directors. It is understood that some 18 additional names have been secured to the list and constitution and bylaws will be drawn and officers chosen. As soon as this is done, application will be made for incorporation and the membership will be built up.

The acquisition of the Hull property as a golf course located within easy distance of the village will undoubtedly increase popular interest in this game. Aside from that, the business men believe that its use for this purpose will operate to make that end of the village a highly attractive residential district. With the ownership of the property in the hands of men interested in the community, the village will be protected and any new industry seeking to locate in Liberty will be offered a site ideally located at far less than the land could be bought for if it were owned by private properties.

MARCH 2023

SULLIVAN COUNTY GOLF COMPANY
CHECKING ACCOUNT

Beginning balance: $0

Additions: $0

Subtractions: $0

Ending balance: $0

The clubhouse was going to be a problem. Its paint-chipped exterior was more chip than paint, and what color was left was a urinal shade of yellow. Flakes of neglect surrounded the building on all sides—it was as if the house had shaken loose its dandruff—and through smudged windows and torn screens I peered into the long, dark space of a dining room that had not seen a meal in years. The roof was worse. Cheap repair work had nailed one layer of roofing on top of the last, revealing a thick sandwich of shingles around the edges, and nowhere did a gutter find union with a spout.

Within minutes I knew I'd wasted a day to be here. And I'd missed Swamp Night in the process.

Until a few days before, I could not have found the Catskills on a map. I would have pointed at New York, but north, south, east, west—I hadn't a clue, and Vermont wasn't out of the question. As a concept they existed in my imagination as a young Jerry Lewis doing stand-up—a poor man's Vegas, or Brooklyn meets the Poconos. My older sister played our VHS of *Dirty Dancing* on a loop, thus initiating her twelve-year-old brother into the Catskills holiday while educating me on the intricacies of trysts between slick city heartthrobs and teenage girls on vacation with their parents. It was, quite simply, a place people used to go, and it might have remained as much if I hadn't received a message on social media from a person I didn't know.

He went by the handle @gorsenod, which was a clever enough golf name to pique my interest. He explained that he was the superintendent at a nine-hole course in the Sullivan County Catskills, not far from New York City. He described it as a little golden-age gem (the golden age being an era of golf course architecture in the early twentieth century when America's great designers were building courses to meet golf's booming popularity) that was slated to close this year, and he wondered if I might know anyone who might be interested in buying it, restoring it, writing about it—anything to help keep their doors open. It was set to turn one hundred in 2025, and it would be a shame to close two years prior to that milestone. "It has really good bones," he said, which had me recalling the good bones of my last home in Philadelphia, a brownstone/construction site that my wife and I spent most of our thirties making livable, just in time to sell it and move to the suburbs.

I told him I'd love to help if I could. I'd started a small golf architecture firm with my friend Colton Craig, whom I'd first met when he caddied for me at Southern Hills, prearranging our loop so that he could bend my ear about possibly going into business together. He was probably the hardest worker I knew, and in a few years we had turned our partnership into an actual business, but buying and restoring a failing golf course was well beyond our means and modest scope of work. I forgot about Gorsenod until he pinged me again a month later.

"Have you thought any more about coming up to see the course?"

I hadn't, and my schedule wasn't allowing for much more travel, but Google told me Sullivan County Golf & Country Club was just three hours away. I'd also recently been made the editor of *The Golfer's Journal*, and we'd never done a story about golf in the Catskills (we'd never wondered whether there *was* golf in the Catskills), and a greenskeeper trying to save his local nine-holer had feature appeal. We liked to showcase places nobody had ever heard of, and Sullivan County Golf & Country Club had that going for it in spades.

The only slot for fitting in an overnight trip to research what might be a worthwhile magazine piece fell on a date that had been pinned on my calendar for weeks: my daughter's homecoming Swamp Night (her high school mascot is an alligator). Her resilience inspired me; somehow she managed the disappointment of not having her dad at her high school pep rally and encouraged me to head north. My wife, Allyson, was accustomed to my golf comings and goings, but packing a bag in January usually meant Florida. When I told her I was going to look at a golf course in the Catskills, I'd finally surprised her with a destination.

"The mountains? In January?"

"There's a golf course for sale," I said. I let it hang there in the air of our bedroom, fishing for a reaction. I'd married a woman with an exceptional tolerance for golf nonsense, but we'd been married awhile now. Why not keep things spicy.

"Oh, we're buying a golf course. Fun."

We weren't buying anything, I explained, but there might be a story there worth writing. Plus, I was curious about the Catskills. *Dirty Dancing*, all those old resorts. "It's right near where they had Woodstock," I told her. "I hear they have all sorts of hippie shops up there." I expected the dormant Deadhead in her would approve of this detail, which it did.

"Sounds cool. Bring me back a T-shirt," she said. "Tie-dye! No more golf polos, please."

• • •

I would soon learn how the Catskills' fortunes moved through time like the peaks and valleys of its horizons, and how its ups and downs hinged around a particular few months of staggering prosperity that they called the perfect summer.

For eight weeks during the tourist season of 1952, every room in the Sullivan County Catskills was booked. Not an empty bed to be found anywhere; not in a hotel, boardinghouse, or bungalow. It was the height of the American Plan and a time before Disney World and cheap flights to Miami and ubiquitous air-conditioning, when New Yorkers fled the heat of the city by the thousands and climbed hills just to their west in search of cool air and big pools and, of course, a little golf.

Prejudice played no small part in the perfect summer. It wasn't that long ago when East Coast hotels advertised for their desired clientele by an un-subtle code: *Conveniently located near Protestant and Catholic churches* to court one sort of visitor; *Hebrew management* or *dietary laws observed* to attract another. At a time when Jewish guests were not welcome at many American resorts, the Sullivan County Catskills opened their arms and their golf courses to Jewish families and offered them reliable getaways accord-ing to a pricing structure that revolutionized midcentury American vaca-tions. The American Plan offered rooming, meals, and entertainment at one price. Pay your fee and enjoy it all—around-the-clock meals, nightly comics and big band extravaganzas, and days free for tennis or playing bridge or learning the Pachanga. It made for affordable luxury and kept guests in one place for extended summer stretches, at resorts like Grossinger's and Kut-sher's and the Concord, behemoth all-inclusives at the heart of an area that took its name from a classic Eastern European Jewish dish: the Borscht Belt.

In 1952, there was barely enough borscht to go around. With ho-tels bursting at the seams, resorts underwent massive expansion plans before the 1953 season, and by 1960, it's said that little Sullivan County possessed more guest rooms than any county in the United States. Over five hundred hotels and fifty thousand bungalows—it was the highest of times in the not-so-high mountains.

Mention "bungalow colonies" to anyone who didn't grow up in Sullivan County, and they'll think you're referring to some sort of yonder island cult. They were unique to the Catskills, an area once dominated by agriculture, where farmers got wise to the influx of visitors and began taking on boarders, then erected outbuildings for guests that multiplied into communities of small family residences. It was Airbnb well ahead of its time.

And at the center of it all was a town called Liberty, with a bustling main street of Jewish bakeries and theaters and shops transplanted from Fifth Avenue. With the tourist trade came builders and plumbers and roofers and chefs, all settling in and around town, a booming community built on servicing a stream of swim-trunk-toting tourists.

And then it stopped. That stream of guests dried up, the hotels and bungalows closed their doors, and Liberty slipped into a long, cold Catskills winter. It was during one of these winters that I visited Liberty for the first time and, by a string of circumstances I still don't fully understand, came to call it home.

In hospitality terms, the Catskills decline was an extinction event, a seismic and nearly overnight shift that saw an area that once couldn't grow quickly enough turned into a vacation punch line of demolished resorts and shuttered cottages. This collapse has been thoroughly studied and debated, and the tourism literature points to the three A's: airfare, air-conditioning, and anti-Semitism (or the lack thereof).

With new airports in New York City making air travel more convenient and affordable, city folks weren't tethered to their cars when planning their vacations. Air-conditioning made the Catskills' cooler temperatures less appealing, and with changing attitudes and the Civil Rights Act of 1964,

Jewish families felt empowered to seek experiences elsewhere. But local historian John Conway points to a fourth *A* that might have been most responsible for the downfall of Sullivan County: arrogance. The good times would never end, the resorts thought, and so they failed to upgrade and innovate in the face of their guests' new alternatives.

It was the sort of great bust known only to great booms; once the Catskills weren't in, they were out. Once your neighbors had somewhere better to go, so did you, and what was left behind were the people who had made the Catskills go—its suppliers and servers who had come for the work, not the vacation. Schools shrank, home values plunged, and all those rooms and amenities were razed or sold for land—including most every golf course. Twenty or so courses that had served the summer population simply disappeared, some of their hole outlines still visible in satellite photos, the ghosts of golf past.

Most every golf course, aside from one.

The first drive into new territory always feels longer than what the GPS claims. The sky was cold and gray as I headed up the turnpike, surprised to find that only the first hour of my journey to Liberty, New York, was going to take the toll road. The next two wound me along narrow mountain lanes, through farmland and forest where mailboxes became scarcer by the mile. Holiday homes gave way to boarded-up motels and small one-stories with chain-tired pickups parked on lawns and short driveways. This wasn't a route populated by Starbucks or McDonald's, but by the occasional biker bar, then maybe a shopping center all but vacant save for the tanning salon and the childcare center. I'd never heard of Agway, but whatever they were selling, people seemed to want it.

As I rolled past shooting ranges and gas stations advertising hot pizza and fresh bait, I recognized this America from a cross-country journey

I'd made in 2018, when I'd learned to rely on the local gas station/restaurant/grocery store/pharmacy. The farther you wandered, the more likely you could sit down for chicken parmesan after topping up your washer fluid. I'd enjoyed some of my best meals while waiting for my tank to fill, so I wasn't faulting these new environs, but I was understanding that I had not traveled all that far, yet had arrived somewhere very far away.

Shaun had asked me to meet him in the diner above the main street in Liberty, which sounded like a proper and quaint introduction to the Catskills. I was expecting a mountain hamlet of sorts, perhaps with Austrian touches and A-frame buildings and pedestrians in stocking caps, waving hello to their neighbors and stopping to chat about an early spring. I rolled slowly along the central avenue and found that most of the stores were closed—some permanently, it seemed, and some waiting for tourists who may or may not return this summer. A dark supermarket advertised its name—Lemonade—on a temporary banner that had come unstuck in the wind, and a sign identified its offerings as kosher. I saw a dollar store and a vacant ice cream shop; a bank and a theater that looked like its restoration had been paused halfway. The boxing gym looked quiet, but I was excited to see that Liberty's main street still featured one. The sweet science had a proud legacy up here: Joe Louis, Sugar Ray Robinson, Rocky Marciano, and Muhammad Ali had all used Grossinger's Resort as a summer training camp (the same hotel where a young Lew Alcindor waited tables and dominated guests in pickup games), and it felt reassuring to find a remnant of the only Catskills history I knew. The street's liveliest spots were its half-dozen Mexican restaurants, plus a tattoo shop and a small Liberty museum that was only open on Fridays and Saturdays from twelve to four. Lucky for me, I'd landed on a Saturday and made a note to return later as I turned up the street to the New Munson Diner where the parking lot was crowded at noon.

It was a vintage place with silver cladding that might have once fit on a railway car, and I'd later learn it had been transported from Manhattan all the way to Liberty and had once been a location for an episode of *Seinfeld* (the Bizarro episode where Jerry finds himself in an alternate coffee shop). Shaun was waiting by the hostess stand when I stepped in out of the cold. He was tall and thin with short hair beneath a baseball cap, and a slight hunch with pointy shoulders that hinted at a cool, city edge. He'd told me he was forty-five but he seemed younger—wearing a hoodie and black Dickies pants, a skateboarder lingered beneath the surface—with a disarmingly nervous energy. He introduced me to the diner's Greek owners who welcomed me like a long-lost Philadelphia cousin, then seated us at a booth in the back where we ordered burgers and made the awkward conversation of not-quite-strangers, two guys who knew one another through two-sentence exchanges on Instagram.

Shaun had moved to Liberty from Queens, where he'd worked as a horticulturalist in high-rise buildings. If you've ever wondered who plants and maintains those twelve-story gardens inside the lobbies of Manhattan's skyscrapers—Shaun did, and his workday consisted of hopping from one corner of the city to the next to juggle watering and planting and feeding (good preparation for trying to water nine greens without a functioning irrigation system). He'd grown up outside of Kansas City where he played more hockey than golf (his dad loved putt-putt, but that was the extent of his golf as a kid), then relocated to Dayton where he got work on the grounds crew at Moraine, a top-ranked private club with an open policy on staff play. Most afternoons he could sneak out for golf after his shift, and he fell hard for the game, reading as much about agronomy and design as he could and plugging into the nascent online golf community. Then his guitar took him to New York for what was supposed to be two weeks of singing for his supper. It turned into years, and a hard-partying lifestyle he'd learned in Ohio fully blossomed in the Big Apple.

He told me that that the city's music and art scene got into his blood. "I was a kid from Kansas City living in New York, playing music, getting into trouble," he said. "I'd get locked up for hopping a turnstile with a six-pack in my bag. Stupid shit. For a while I was pretty much living out of a backpack in lower Manhattan. Drinking too much and not listening to anybody, your basic alcoholic lifestyle. That's how I found this area, actually, when the state sent me up here for rehab."

When you go and get sober, they tell you there aren't any coincidences, that all the signs pointing you toward a different life mean something if your eyes are open to them. Some might dismiss such talk as self-help twaddle (and was it a coincidence that those boxes of wine were always on sale when I tried to quit drinking?), but I choose to believe that something larger than myself thinks it would be a good idea if I didn't drink today. Maybe it's God, maybe the universe, maybe the Force about which Obi-Wan opined, but I do trust that it places certain people in our lives for certain reasons. Shaun and I being fellow drunks (like other rude labels in our culture, you can use them when they apply to yourself) didn't mean we were suddenly blood brothers, or that we could even trust each other (I've met plenty of sober scoundrels), but there is a bond between those of us who have leaned out over the edge and somehow leaned back. I noted our mutual interest in not being homeless and divorced, and I asked him how he went from vertical gardens to fairways and greens.

"I got cleaned up and met a girl," he began. "Got my shit together, got married and had a kid, moved into a place in Queens. I started thinking about golf again and was following the golf architecture stuff online and hitting balls at Chelsea Piers and playing the city courses. Then the superintendent at Moraine recommended me for a job at The Creek. They were looking for a horticulturalist and said I could come try it out, and I fell in love with it."

The Creek on the north shore of Long Island is one of New York's more coveted tee times. Founded by J. P. Morgan, Vincent Astor, and Marshall Field among others, and designed by the grandfather of American course architecture, Charles Blair Macdonald, it's a rare résumé builder. But after a season making a three-hour afternoon commute back to Queens, Shaun and his wife Marisol decided to look for greener pastures in which to raise their daughter. They moved to Liberty and bought a home with a yard, while Shaun kept his eye on what was happening a half-hour away at Inness.

Rob Collins and Tad King had exploded on the golf scene in 2014 when they designed a nine-holer in Tennessee called Sweetens Cove. Its wild greens and old-world-turned-new architecture broke the country club mold, turning nine holes on a floodplain with no clubhouse or restaurant into a pilgrimage site for golf's soul-seekers. It became an unlikely model for pure golf of unstuffy fun where a season's worth of tee times now sell out in a single day. Word had spread that Rob was building another nine holes not forty-five minutes from Liberty at the Inness resort, a course billed as the back nine to Sweetens, so Shaun reached out and got himself on the greens crew for the grow-in. Buoyed by some agronomy experience, he then turned to the nine-holer down the street from his house, a course for which even his abbreviated golf résumé made him overqualified.

"I remember the first time I played Sullivan. It was still coming out of winter and it was wet and I thought it was fun and a cool place to have right around the corner," he said. "But the more it dried out and I got to know the bounces and the character of the place, it started to feel special." It was being maintained by a retired couple, Tony and Mary, and a few years ago they went down to Florida and decided to stay, so the owners asked Shaun if he could mow it and keep the course from going to seed. "That's basically all we could do with the machines we had, just try to keep the fairways a reasonable length and the greens puttable. But the place has a lot more to offer," he told me. "I mean, I know what we have here. We aren't Augusta. It's not fancy golf and it's not ever going to be that. But it's good. It's good country golf. I would hate to see it go on the market and turned into houses or a shopping center. It's got a lot of history and the place matters to people. You've got families that have played here for four generations. The owners get that. They're good guys. They're willing to give me one more season if I can find a partner who wants to give it a go."

The waitress dropped our check and I grabbed it. Shaun wanted to go halves, but if I couldn't offer him a partner on his golf course, I could at least buy him a cheeseburger.

We paid up at the counter and a large man in a starched white button-down thanked us for coming in and asked us to please, come back soon. As we walked out to our cars, I wondered what reason I might ever have to take the man up on his invitation, but if I was being truthful, an old feeling was returning. Unwelcome and unacknowledged, but there nonetheless, that sensation of holding something warm and bright in my hand, something with a power to alter my trajectory. The fear and impatience and allure of a start. The jumping-off point. My mind might not have seen it yet, but something inside me did, because when I politely said that we would be back, I more than half believed it.

THE SUN (NEW YORK), MARCH 20, 1925

A NEW UP-STATE GOLF COURSE

Sportsmen Up Liberty Way to Have Layout
Presenting a Variety of Holes.

By P.C. Pulver

There's a golf course in the making at Liberty, N.Y., that some day may come in for a deal of attention. Maurice McCarthy, the course architect, who recently returned from a trip upstate, where he left plans for an eighteen hole layout, was impressed with the exceptional possibilities of the land and also surprised that the game had been so long neglected in that locality.

The land, consisting of 165 acres, lies on the edge of the town and one of the fairways will extend 175 feet above the floor of the valley. In fact, play will be along five different levels, and in addition to this unusual situation the architect has been able to take advantage of three streams which wind through the property.

An exceptional condition presents itself at the outset. To the first hole, some 350 yards, the drive will be down hill, followed by an approach over a running stream to an island green. This island, plentifully covered with trees, will be cleared so as to leave an opening in front. In other words, the approach is to be through a crescent-like formation.

The brook on one side will be enlarged by a dam, so as to form a lake, and it is across this hazard that the golfer will drive on his way to No. 2, where the second shot will be to a plateau green at an elevation of fifty feet. This is to be a 340 yard hole, but not so the next, where the line of play extends for more than 500 yards along a ridge.

PLENTY OF LENGTH

Other holes of similar type have been planned for the Sullivan County Golf and Country Club, which is the name of the new organization, and so keen are the founders to get started that work will be concentrated upon nine holes to cover a playing length of 3,250 yards, the idea being to have these ready for play by July. This feat, they claim, is possible because of the cleared nature of the land, most of which was old pasture. Another point favorable to quick action is that turf is available for sodding the greens.

During the off season Liberty, situated in Sullivan county, 120 miles from New York, is a comparatively small town with a population of about 2,500, but during the summer the influx enables Liberty to touch the 30,000 mark. The club has already applied for membership in the United States Golf Association and to the Green Section.

And then I saw it.

I'd been fortunate to survey a gluttonous number of golf holes, but in all those studies of seaside and landlocked and desert and forest and hilltop and valley courses, I'd never eyed one through the lens of a potential course partner (I still wasn't sure what that meant). And I didn't care for this lens. Not at all.

I prided myself on spotting potential and rooting for the routing underdog, able to spot flecks of gold in the most meager links. No clubhouse? No problem. No pro shop? Points for simplicity. No grass? Firm and fast will do. But examining a golf club as an individual who might become invested in it, its every wart and wrinkle stood out in chastening relief.

Two unsteady posts bridged by a stained piece of plywood announced that I had arrived at SULLIVAN COUNTY GOLF & COUNTRY CLUB, faded words beneath it welcoming me to *The Oldest Golf Course in the Catskills*. I wasn't sure if that was true, but this being the oldest sign in the Catskills seemed indisputable. I tried to keep an open mind, reminding myself that there was good old and bad old, but as I caught sight of the clubhouse's crumbling exterior, I feared I was about to tour the latter.

The building itself had some homespun charisma—two gabled roofs on either end, with a low stretch of windows between, the whole structure not much larger than a four-bedroom home. But inside—I hoped peeking through the windows had been enough to satisfy Shaun.

When it came to abandoned buildings, I'd decided that churches and clubhouses were the saddest of the lot. Their refuge had been deemed worthless or ineffective; their neglect suggested a menacing lack of hope. And this one was strangled by snow in the dead of winter, a clear signal to leave it undisturbed. But Shaun had brought the keys, and he began with the least abandoned bit.

The current owners had refurbished the pro shop a few years earlier, and as we passed through the doorway, we found a surprisingly functional space. It was slightly smaller than a shipping container and roughly the same shape, with a bright wooden bar occupying most of the room. The walls had been painted white with beadboard paneling along the lower half. A large TV hung behind the bar, and against the opposite wall were a few high-top tables and chairs. It was sort of perfect, I thought—pro shop and a small hangout in one space, with French doors that opened toward what I guessed was the first tee. The only thing I wasn't sure about was whether this was really a pro shop. Of course there was no pro on staff—this was mom-and-pop golf and I appreciated that—but I didn't see a shelf or hanger or hat anywhere, just a red plastic French fry basket holding a few dirty Dunlops and a handwritten note, "Used Balls: $1."

"Do they sell anything in here?" I asked.

"Not really," Shaun said. "Not the kind of stuff you're thinking of. They collect greens fees and sell drinks, and the league guys will come in here and drink after they play on Monday nights. But there isn't any kind of merchandise. We do have scorecards, and these yardage books," he said, handing over a plain white card with green numbers, and then the yardage book. The golf snob in me bit my tongue. First, why does a community nine-holer that doesn't have hats or shirts or new golf balls—or customers, for that matter—have a yardage book? And second, why is it so awful? It was mostly advertisements with some rudimentary outlines of the holes, and on the cover—good Lord—artwork to break the heart of any golf collector.

"Is this the logo?" I asked, pointing to a Crayola cartoon of a red flag on a green with a mountainous blob in the background.

"I'm not sure," he said, smirking. "I hope not. I don't think we have an actual logo."

"That's probably where I'd start," I said. "If I were you," I added, feeling my parking lot revelation slip with each discovery. Scorecards cost money. Shelves cost money. Merchandise costs money. Logos cost money. These weren't issues I'd ever considered when stepping into a clubhouse before, so even if today was a waste of gas, I'd at least gained a new perspective on the price of our game.

"So this is the good part," Shaun said. "You ready for the rest?"

The question presupposed my answer, and he was right: I wasn't. Shaun swung open a glass-paneled door, and we stepped into the former restaurant. There was no heat anywhere in the building, but this room felt far colder than the one we had just left, and after one look at the cobwebbed fixtures and the leaking drop ceiling and the broken tables and the dusty curtains hiding a service bar that looked like some sort of horrifying puppet theater, plus a pile of clothes in the corner and—are those Barbie dolls?—I wished for Shaun to return us from whence we had come.

"Keith was living here, in the apartment upstairs. This is his stuff. Can't imagine what the apartment looks like," he said.

"Don't show me."

"Don't worry. Nobody can find the key," he said as we surveyed a strange collection of sundries: jeans and sweatshirts, a towering pile of old mail, cans of Heinz beans and packages of Tayto crisps. And the Barbies, still in the box, some sort of evening-gown collector's edition, from what I could tell.

"He's Irish," I said.

"How'd you know that?"

"The Taytos. And the beans," I explained. "What's up with the Barbies?"

Shaun chuckled. "Who knows? Maybe for his grandkids. Keith's an interesting cat. He kind of looks over everything here, but he's been sick in the hospital for a while now. I doubt he's coming back for this season."

If there is a "this season," I thought, a possibility that seemed less likely with each new room. He showed me the bathrooms toward the back—glorious—and, just off the Barbie room, a bar that had potential. Its wooden floor was painted with OSCAR BROWN's in huge lettering ("That was one of the restaurants that tried to make a go here," Shaun explained, "after the members sold the club") but its far wall revealed the first sign of a real golf club that I'd yet noticed: a club championship board dating back to 1925.

"This is pretty cool," Shaun said, pointing out some of the names. "Check out this guy: John Coughlin. Won it thirteen times."

"Damn. That's good playing."

"The Yauns. Deckers. All these names still play up here. I like this one: E. B. Grossinger, from the Grossinger's resort. The place they based *Dirty Dancing* on. All the resorts up here had golf courses, but they were for hotel guests, so everyone who worked the resorts played their golf here. This place was for the locals."

"Very cool. This room isn't bad," I said, and I meant it, because even though the bar was filthy and looked like the kind of place guys like us came to drink ourselves to death—dark, cold, empty—the long window behind the bar perfectly framed a snow-covered golf course, and a romantic bar view cured a lot of ills.

The kitchen did not. Brown ooze dripped from the edges of the coolers; the stovetops looked like someone had been cooking without the aid of pot or pan, and in the refrigerator moldered Keith's groceries from however long ago. I felt inclined to correct myself—*Forget the logo, Shaun. I'd start back here.*

I could only assume he overestimated my lunchtime enthusiasm when he decided to take me down to the men's locker room, a place golf course partnerships went to die. There was no forgetting it and no unseeing it: Sullivan County Golf & Country Club's ninth ring of hell.

"Watch your head," Shaun warned me as we descended a steel set of stairs. A flickering light bulb half illuminated a cold, dank jungle of metal and rot, and I imagined slow players and fence jumpers chained to these walls, begging for the king's mercy. There were trash cans full of old clubs ("Our lost-and-found—some classics in there"), tables piled with broken trophies and cans of spray paint and insecticide, rows of rusted metal lockers tipped over and piled at impenetrable angles. Outing signs from the 1990s. An empty cash box and busted chairs. The concrete floor was coated with a slime of neglect, and the mildew—you could pluck spores from the air. I pulled back a decrepit shower curtain to find a bathroom that had regurgitated upon itself. One sink, one seatless toilet, both caked in foul blackness.

We pushed our way through the mess to a shower stall around the corner—packed with trash bags of empty beer cans—and to another doorway, a dungeon off the dungeon, where I braced myself for whatever sins this place might yet confess.

"This room is kind of cool," Shaun said, and when he flipped on a light that worked, it kind of was. Granted, it was piled floor to ceiling with a tangle of red upholstered chairs, but along the walls there were rules posted for poker buy-ins, along with angry notes about who owed twenty bucks to whom.

"Some wild shit probably went on down here," Shaun said, and I agreed. A hidden basement poker room in the New York Catskills, straight out of *Rounders*, where bottom-dealers lost fingers and fish surrendered small fortunes.

We ascended the stairs and emerged from the locker room to the bright light of day. It was as if I'd never felt the sun before, the rays warming my bones. Before walking the course, Shaun wanted to detour through the cart barn and the maintenance shed. The barn was corrugated steel and Shaun said it sounded like the blitzkrieg in here when it rained. It wasn't in bad shape, and the vehicles parked along its walls in neat rows gave the space a museum quality. They didn't seem capable of moving, but they were fun to look at. Some of the first ever golf carts had found a home here, from bogus-sounding companies like Fairway Go and Royal Electric.

"We need to clean this place out. Half of these don't run," Shaun said. "That's one of the problems here. The carts that do run are in rough shape. They give you whiplash when you hit the pedal."

Golf carts cost money.

"Check this out," he said, pointing to small wooden placards nailed to the wall in front of each parking space. "These are members' names. They owned their own carts. Some still do. They would just come up to the course, take their cart out of here, and go. I think they used to mow the course once during the week and close the clubhouse and just let the members do their thing."

Provided such evidence, it did not take a forensic accountant to uncover why the club had struggled financially. No cart revenue? I was a dedicated walker, but even I understood the nature of cart fees and bottom lines. And it got worse. Shaun told me that a few years ago, a previous operator had tried to raise some cash by offering three-year memberships for the paltry sum of $200. All your golf for three years for two hundred bucks—a death sentence for any semiprivate course. Those memberships had just expired, he said, so he was hoping that might help turn a corner.

All I'd seen of the course so far was a long white field dipping over the horizon, then shooting back up the side of a mountain. "We'll get there," Shaun said. "Come look at what I'm dealing with first."

Calling it a shed was a slight to proper sheds elsewhere, but Shaun's maintenance shed fit its club context. On one side, a sliding garage door that probably hadn't slid in some time, and a doorway on the other, in front of which a thick board covered a hole of unspecific depth.

"Watch your step there."

Inside was Shaun's workshop where the tools were neatly organized along the back wall, adjoining an old steel desk and a couple 1970s bouncy leather chairs likely taken from the patio at Grossinger's. The wall to my left was decorated with cool course signage from yesteryear, 1950s cart directionals, some tie-dyed outing signs, and a wooden plaque advertising $2 greens fees. Everything else was a dark mess of grease and leaking hydraulics. Shaun went around the room, pointing at tractors, mowers, blowers, and machines whose purpose I could only guess.

"That doesn't run. That doesn't run. That doesn't run. That doesn't run. That doesn't run. That runs. That runs," he explained. "I'd love to get this cleaned out and sell this stuff for scrap. I know a scrapper who would pay for it."

He said his maintenance-to-mowing hours were about even—not a good ratio when you have a two-man crew. They spent as much time fixing their gear as they did riding it, and if this course had any hope of surviving, this room's stalled loiterers needed to be swapped out for a whole new fleet.

Mowers *really* cost money.

I noticed a chain hanging from the ceiling and asked about its purpose.

"They must have had a lift in here at some point, for servicing the mowers. But this one," he said, grabbing the frayed end of a thin rope, "I've only been up here once. Want to check it out?"

I didn't come all this way to not follow the mysterious rope in the ceiling. Shaun gave it a pull, and a ladder crashed to the floor, opening an overhead hatch I had not noticed. I slowly followed him up, one creaking rung at a time, until we were standing in a small attic loft beneath the rafters, not large enough to fit one of Shaun's mowers, but big enough for a cot and a wooden chair, both untouched for decades. Newspapers from the 1980s were strewn about the floor, and other than the bed and chair, the loft's only treasures were a trout fisherman's basket, a Polaroid camera with an old flashcube, and a set of leather nunchucks.

"Somebody lived up here," I said, stating the obvious because it was shocking nonetheless.

"I have no idea who. Had to be a while ago. Maybe someone used it to dry out or something."

"If you developed the film in that camera," I said, "you'd probably solve half the cold cases in New York."

He laughed and picked up the nunchucks. "Want these?"

I thought about it. As I kid, I'd owned a set of foam ones purchased from a sporting-goods store, and in my quest to wield them with the deadly proficiency of Bruce Lee, had practiced with them for ten minutes before knocking myself in the balls enough times to abandon the martial arts. I declined and told Shaun he should save them to hang above the bar.

We roamed out back to find another garage occupied almost entirely by a behemoth rusted-out tractor. Shaun had never seen it run and didn't know what he'd do with it if it did. Packed around it were antique golf course goodies—old ball washers and busted benches, giant golf ball tee markers and wire trash baskets, and former hole signs with advertising from businesses that Shaun said no longer existed. The temptation returned—if I did get involved in this golf course, I could fulfill my life's dream of planting a ball washer beside our front door. I had not informed Allyson of this ambition, but I could think of no better way to tell her we'd bought a golf course in a town she'd never seen nor heard of than with a surprise ball washer posted by our front walk.

We didn't step inside the garage—its back wall was cracked, the cement blocks gently folded along a zagging crease but somehow holding on. He did show me the rear of the shed, where golf carts were piled atop golf carts, three-wheelers and stick-steerers that would have been worth some money had they not been left out in the snow for fifty years. An axle here, a steering column there. More dead mowers poked their noses out of the woods, and a blue pickup sat stalled beneath a tree, its rounded wheel wells too far gone for restoration. A giant steel grease box was tipped over, not too far from a rusted gas tank that Shaun said they still used. I'd ceased tallying up the dollars it would take to make this place functional, and I just tried to enjoy this as a trip to a golf world few ever get to see.

I hadn't brought boots to battle the snow, but Shaun wasn't letting me leave until I saw the property from number three.

"Up there?" I said, pointing to a strip of tilted white that topped the mountain like a ring of icing.

"That's it. Come on."

We passed the stream that fronted the first green, where Shaun sometimes caught trout in the morning; he kept his rod strapped to a work cart that wasn't really a work cart. They had no work carts. He had a retired golf cart with a hitch welded to the back bumper, a busted five-iron shaft used as the pin to hook on the blower, when he could get the blower to start. Shaun said Sullivan County was to fly-fishing what Long Island was to golf courses. Knowing nothing about fly-fishing but plenty about Long Island golf, I appreciated the analogy, and he claimed that was one sector of the tourism market that had held on through the years: the trout fishermen.

Fishing and golf on the same property, I thought. Not a bad combination. And the stream, unlike everything else I'd seen today, would cost nothing to get running.

We climbed fairways and Shaun pointed out this hole and that hole— the place certainly had movement and elevation, but under so much ice, who knew what I was witnessing?

And then, I did know. We reached the peak of the course, the heart of what Shaun said was the third fairway, and the wind went still and quiet around us. I could see for miles in every direction, the sort of vantage point designers would die for, a view golfers can't quite believe as they watch a world of green and water unfurl from their feet. Well, white and water in this case, but I could tell—unless you had a bottomless budget, this wasn't the kind of golf course you built anymore. The land was too severe, the angles too unkind. Shaun explained that when the fairways dried out up here, they had to line the bottom of this hole with chicken wire to keep balls from falling off the mountain. I loved every word of that idea. A hole so wild that it introduced chicken wire to golf. Absolutely brilliant.

Our correspondence had revealed the course architects as Len Rayner (one letter off, for the golfheads out there) and Maurice McCarthy, two area pros who built courses all over New York and Pennsylvania. Rayner had led construction at Leatherstocking in Cooperstown, under the eye of the estimable Devereux Emmet, where he'd go on to be the longtime head pro, and McCarthy was responsible for the original course at Hershey Country Club where Byron Nelson lifted the Wanamaker Trophy at the 1940 PGA Championship. Born in Ireland, McCarthy designed 125 layouts over the course of his career and passed along some rare golf genes to his son, Maurice Jr., who won the National

Intercollegiate Championship and played on a winning Walker Cup side. In the 1930 US Amateur at Merion, where Bobby Jones completed his Grand Slam, McCarthy Jr.'s run lasted to the round of eight, but more impressive was how he got there: He aced the thirty-fifth hole during qualifying to take the last spot in the match play field.

Most of McCarthy and Rayner's work in the Catskills had disappeared, but design lineage didn't really matter here. Not from where I was standing, anyway. What mattered was when they built it—1924 into 1925, when like all the great architects of the time, they lacked the machinery and technology to do anything but take the land as they found it. They probably shaped some greens and flattened out some tees, and the rest they left to the slopes of Sullivan County. It was unpretentious, indigenous, unreasonable golf, the sort you can't shape but can only hope to find, and having found it in what might be its final days was as tragic as this view was humbling.

Shaun explained that this entire property was once a horse farm— he'd dug up some horseshoes—and pointed down into the valley where you could just make out the banks of what once was a track.

"We had a plane take off from over there," he said, pointing to a long, flat stretch that looked like a par-five. "It was the first transatlantic flight to Denmark."

"Seriously?"

"Yeah. There's a plaque by the first tee that talks about it. Otto Hillig. Sort of a local hero back in the day. He called his plane *The Liberty*. We have a big model of it somewhere that I want to fix up."

We climbed back down across the property, not speaking very much. I wasn't sure what to say. Shaun had talked about wanting this course to be here someday for his daughter to enjoy, a place for her to grow up, and I wanted that for him. People all over the golf world were building their own courses or pumping money into new properties, and I knew some of those people and could maybe help with introductions. But I feared they'd see the state of the town and the clubhouse and the short Catskills golf season, look at the price the owners were asking for the land, and take their money down to a blank slate in Florida. In fact, I was sure they would. This place required a real dreamer with real money, and I didn't know any of those.

Shaun walked me to my car and asked if I was coming back up tomorrow. I told him I was going to cut it short and head back home, score some points with Allyson and maybe catch some of my daughter's event at school. I'd pretty much seen everything and felt like I had an idea what the place needed. I didn't mention that I wasn't the one who had it.

He said he understood and thanked me for coming up to see the course. "Honestly, I've asked a lot of people if they'd come up and have a look, and you're the only one who took me up on it, so I appreciate that," he said. "I'm not giving up on it. If I have to go to the state to get a historical designation or something, or get the town to buy it . . ." His voice and his glance drifted off. I believed he wasn't quitting, but we both knew those avenues were unlikely, and took more time than this golf course had left.

I told him he shouldn't give up. This place mattered, that was clear, and it deserved to be around for another hundred years. But I was honest with him: It was going to take an investment that I simply couldn't make. I knew some people who might, and I'd be happy to put him in touch with them.

"That would be great. Thank you," he said. And then he changed my life, and my family's.

"I think the owners might kind of just give it to you, for now, if you wanted to try running it."

The jumping-off point. And by the time I got home the next morning, Allyson could tell that I'd already leapt.

THE BINGHAMTON PRESS, MONDAY EVENING, MAY 25, 1931

RAIN, SOGGY GROUND HOLD HILLIG'S TRANSATLANTIC PLANE AT LIBERTY

Big Crowd Sees Ship Christened on Golf Links

Elsie Gerow, 16, Daughter of Sullivan Sheriff, Does Honors

IS NAMED "LIBERTY"

Owner and Pilot Plan to Take Off as Soon as the Weather Clears

By a StaffWriter of The Binghamton Press

Liberty, May 23—Liberty's "Flying Dutchman" is still grounded.

Driving rain this morning caused another postponement in the start of the transatlantic hop which Otto Hillig, 55, wealthy photographer, and Holger Hoiriis, 27, Danish pilot, will attempt with Copenhagen, Denmark, 3,100 miles away, their destination.

The take-off on the first leg to Roosevelt field was set for Sunday afternoon from No. 3 green of the Sullivan County Golf and Country club, but rain during the night made the green spongy and the pilot was unwilling to make the attempt.

It was planned to hop off at 9 o'clock this morning.

Mr. Hillig, much disgusted with the repeated delay, said this morning that the "Liberty" would get underway as soon as the weather cleared and the greens dried up. After arriving at Roosevelt field, the plane will be taken to the Teterboro airport, official testing field for Wright motors, where the final tests will be made under direction of Richard Naffel, chief mechanic. This may take a week.

There is little possibility of getting to Harbor Grace, Newfoundland, for the last take-off before the thirty-first, Mr. Hillig said. Once there, he said, they will have to wait for a favorable prediction from Meteorologist Kimball in New York. The present forecast is unsettled weather for several days.

Liberty turned out in force Sunday afternoon for the christening of the plane. Flags flew from residences and even the weather and his worries failed to take away the "transatlantic smile" from the face of the "Flying Dutchman."

The whole town came out to see it, and in Denmark, a crowd of 100,000 awaited his arrival. It was the biggest thing to happen to Liberty since tuberculosis. A nineteenth-century outbreak sent scores of city dwellers to the Catskills in search of clean air, ushering in the area's first great age of tourism as a health retreat. That boom would end when it was discovered that TB was communicable through one's breath and New Yorkers lost interest in crowded train rides to the mountains. But Otto Hillig was no Catskills tourist. Born in 1874, he emigrated from Germany to America at the age of seventeen. Handy with a camera, he set up a studio on Liberty's main street and made a business of photographing families on vacation. He married but it didn't last—he was an untamed spirit, always on the move. He was likely the first Liberty resident to own a car and locals called him "The Flying Dutchman" for the speed at which he tore around town, crashing into carriages, telegraph poles, and the second story of a barn. He drove from one end of America to the other, writing dispatches from the road and garnering celebrity that would reflect well on his adopted hometown. But the light on Liberty shone most brightly when Otto took to aviation—first for his aerial photography, then as a means of satisfying his wanderlust.

Otto bought a plane he named after the town that had provided him such a rich life, and in 1931, he and partner Holger Hoiriis used the eighth fairway (the paper claimed the third; local knowledge says the eighth) at the Sullivan County Golf & Country Club as their runway for what was to be the first transatlantic flight to Denmark. No matter that they were pushed off course and had to make a pit stop in Germany first—*The Liberty* arrived in Denmark to a hero's welcome, where Otto was knighted by the king, and when he returned to America, he was welcomed with a ticker tape parade in New York City. He tinkered as an inventor and built a castle above Liberty (not a very large one, and the inside resembles a workshop or hunting lodge) and lured thousands to Sullivan County through bucolic postcard photography that captured the region's best side. And when he wasn't snapping shots in and above Liberty, he was killing Nazi saboteurs. Obviously.

The legend speaks of two Germans who hijacked Otto's plane in 1942 and ordered him and Holger to fly them to New York City where the Nazi sympathizers intended to buy explosives with a large cargo of cash, then use the dynamite to blow up the railway trestle in Liberty. The details of that flight are fuzzy (as is the entire historical basis for this story), but some daring maneuvers caught the hijackers off guard, giving Otto enough time to grab a revolver that had been hiding in the cockpit and foil the saboteurs' plot with two bullets.

What to do with a pile of Nazi booty? Hide it, of course. In 1992, the local paper published stories about Otto's lost treasure and shared his twenty-five clues for finding it (or finding a bronze coin which would entitle one to the cash he'd left at the bank in Liberty). It still hasn't been located, and in case you're considering a Catskills treasure hunt:

1. The witch cannot see.

2. The arch of the roots is by your boots.

3. She is as beautiful as her closest sister, who once left Skee-
   tersburg.

4. William Ayers mourned Liberty's first death.

5. The fish won't bite at the Western part but begin the hunt,
   it's OK to start.

6. "Foul wrinkled witch, what makes thou in my sight?"

7. Blue Mountain Cemetery looks over Otto's treasure.

8. Broadhead Points to.

9. Dr. Blake Wales knew it as two log houses.

10. Lucky me, I'm in the Queen's back yard. If you can't find
    me, you haven't looked hard.

11. The Lennon Building holds a clue.

12. Grady's horse kicked the spot.

13. The coin is in the open.

14. Liberty Public Service was there in my time.

15. From the inside of Manion's Store the Mongaup will roar.

16. Mr. Manion's home plate.

17. Ugly Acer rubrum on the rade, then 30 paces and you will
    have it made. Turn to the right if going at, turn to the left if
    walking back.

18. The municipal corner is basically nutty.

19. What once was Hortonville, now is not.

20. You are very close at number one, the plaque is a spot which
    you should plot, go in and eat, and count the feet, from
    there to here, let's have a beer.

21. The lens of my camera has revealed the spot.

22. Now in its place is a restaurant which has food that is fine.

Descramble the words on the bar and you will be one step closer to being the star.

23. As you pass by behold and see in a restaurant across from the old "Big G." My works live on and hold a clue to find the coin now known to you. Enjoy the food and have a ball, examine all the pictures on the wall.

24. O Tsuga Canadensis, protect me!

25. This is it, you have all the clues. If you do find me call the news. Fred will know what to do, he has the treasure to give to you.

I'd probably skip the list and focus on finding this Fred character, but I've never hunted real treasure. The veracity of the entire scheme is questionable—some consider it a stunt to drum up tourism, one that apparently worked. It drew metal detectors from around the world to Sullivan County. Yet one of the clues had me thinking that maybe I should give treasure finding a go—the easiest and most obvious on the list: *You are very close at number one, the plaque is a spot which you should plot, go in and eat, and count the feet, from there to here, let's have a beer.*

It's a finger pointed directly at the plaque beside the first tee at Sullivan County Golf & Country Club, the one that commemorates Hillig's flight, close to what would have, at the time, been a functioning restaurant and tavern. Maybe this was the windfall the course needed, right under our noses, Nazi booty buried on the golf course, and Shaun's solution had simply been waiting for his shovel. The more I considered it, the more I returned to *The Goonies* and their quest to save their town with pirate's gold. Were we Goonies? Could we be? It was the best option on my list of ideas for saving Sullivan County, which seemed a clear commentary on the quality of those ideas.

In the end, I didn't drive home that evening after meeting with Shaun. I booked a room nearby and planned a morning meeting with the course's owners, Sims Foster and Chris Monello. Shaun's proposal was worth investigating, and I wanted to know whether I'd be making this trip back to Philadelphia once, or maybe time and time again.

It was easy enough for Sims and Chris to come by the guesthouse where I was staying—they owned the place, after all. Sims was a decade younger than me and had grown up in Livingston Manor, the next town over from Liberty, while Chris was a few years younger than him and hailed from New York City. I might have guessed their origins from their attire—Sims clad in a denim button-down and jeans (at home we called this double-denim look a Canadian tuxedo) and Chris wearing a gold chain and smart leather jacket ill-suited for a Catskills winter. They seemed excited to meet me; anyone willing to come see the course they were hoping to unload was a win.

Their development and hospitality companies (Foster Supply Hospitality/Western Sullivan Properties) owned restaurants and boutique hotels all over the county, old Catskills inns they'd stylishly refurbished for New Yorkers on weekend retreats. The vibe was rustic luxury—their Arnold House felt Catskills enough to make you feel like you were on a mountain adventure, but one you could tackle in nice loafers. They'd bought the Sullivan County course when it had gone up for sale three years ago, mostly out of Sims's nostalgia for playing there with his dad when he was a kid. They had planned to develop the course as a destination with a 160-room hotel and a subdivision of vacation homes. The property was 180 acres in total, and the golf course only used 70 of those, so the real estate potential was there, but Covid intervened, they got involved in other ventures, and as the golf course continued to lose more money with each passing year, their plans lost steam and they couldn't justify carrying more red ink for another season. They confessed that they played golf but had no prior experience in the golf business, and while they were deeply invested in the county's success and its future, they didn't know how to make this golf piece go.

They knew the land was valuable and that it would be scooped up on the open market, which, given the area's struggles, took me by surprise. Much of Liberty had been designated as an economic opportunity zone, an officially "distressed area" according to the US tax code. And Foster Supply Hospitality ran its own food charity, A Single Bite, to help combat food insecurity in a county that ranked near the bottom—fifty-seventh out of sixty-two—in the statewide health rankings. Yet the course's land would make for an attractive listing because of the latest turn in county tourism: When mainstream Jewish families stopped coming up to Sullivan, the New York City Orthodox and Hasidic population took their place. Thus, that kosher supermarket in downtown Liberty, and the lines of men I saw walking the roads in long black coats and large fur crowns balanced atop their heads. It was Saturday when I was cruising up to the course, and the ultra-Orthodox wouldn't be driving on Shabbat, so every quarter-mile I spotted a few men walking long, empty roads while the snow and wind were whipping. (At first glance I thought they were Amish; forgive me, but I live thirty minutes from Lancaster, where a beard and a big hat mean you're a sought-after carpenter with a horse that pulls your buggy.)

When the bungalow colonies closed, the Haredim moved in and purchased parcels for their communities—good land at a good price, and a nicer place to spend your summer than Brooklyn. But relations between local residents and the ultra-Orthodox had been tepid, tinged with a wary eye about too many new neighbors. The Hasidic villages are considered by some to be an eyesore (visit Sullivan County and you'll see them by the dozen; most could use a coat of paint, and their tall wire fences don't inspire the cheeriest welcome), while others view them as a community that doesn't contribute to the county (some of the communes are tax exempt as religious institutions). The Haredim certainly contribute when they shop and build and pay for municipal services, and it isn't as if there's a line of buyers waiting to scoop up derelict properties. Others resent them for not assimilating and participating in Sullivan County at large, which isn't entirely unfair—they're an insular group, with their own language and customs. But so are the Amish. So are country clubs. There's a hint of nativism to the debate that frames their presence as a problem, but if you were looking to sell 180 acres and stop losing $50,000 every year, their affinity for Sullivan County looked much more like a solution.

So the land would sell the moment it was listed. For two guys who didn't want to see a town that had lost so much lose its golf course as well, it made for a complicated decision, and a willingness to try something I'd never heard of when it came to golf course transactions.

We agreed to a kick-the-tires year. I would handle payroll, taxes, insurance—the whole kit. If I could promise them that they'd have to do and spend nothing this year, I was welcome to take over as the golf course operator. And if all went well, I'd have the option to purchase the course at a pre-negotiated price (on the long shot that I could make the place profitable, I didn't want to make it more valuable should I somehow want to buy it). We decided to let our lawyers iron out the details (I'd need to get one of those) and settled on a concept—that Sullivan County Golf & Country Club would open this spring, and I would be running it.

Golf course operator. I felt like stopping for business cards before I got home. Maybe putting it on a hat or getting a tattoo. What a weird and wonderful game we play—the people it places into our path, the places it drops us, and the unexpected titles it can add to our signature line. I went to the Catskills and instead of getting a T-shirt, I got a golf course. Granted, that golf course lost money and had almost no functioning facilities and was only nine holes and would require funds I did not possess, but I sort of owned a golf course, a golf dream I had never even bothered dreaming.

And Allyson sort of owned one, too.

I've written before about the careful forging and confident gauging of low spousal expectations, and how attempting absurd golf boondoggles sans the safety net of a well-seasoned partner was a recipe for marital angst. (Put simply: Don't try this at home.) Allyson had tolerated my wandering most of the golf world, so when she heard about the golf course I was taking over, she agreed—it was the best idea I'd ever had. She was thrilled, and for good reason: I had not given anyone any money (that would come later, but why spoil her enthusiasm), we might actually *make* some money, and compared to my Ireland and Scotland and America cross-country jaunts, I'd be in one place, just three hours from home. And what if there was a *second* home? I had not begun thinking about where I might live as a golf course operator, but Allyson was already planning our family's summer in the mountains.

It was new territory for us in every way. I had finally proposed a project that wasn't entirely self-centered; I'd even suggested something my family might enjoy. A solo golf life was now a shared golf life. I wasn't sure how it was all going to work; aside from a few four-person trips to Scotland, I'd maintained a church-and-state line between family and golf, but golf had now made my wife happy—not just amused, but genuinely excited—and that was long overdue.

I showed her pictures of the clubhouse, and she saw nothing but country charm and potential. She made plans for the flower beds and imagined summer jobs at the course for our girls. She was already living in a new chapter of our lives, far out ahead of me, as my mind was stuck on golf carts and mowers and whether you could order scorecards on Etsy.

"Do you think we could actually make any money?" she asked.

I don't know how often other wives pose this question to their husbands about their line of work, and raise it with a tone of zero expectation, but I know Allyson had asked it more than most, and with good reason.

I told her the place was currently a financial loser, but that I had ideas for turning that around. And I did. If a lifetime spent around golf gives you anything, it does give you friends to whom you can come pleading. The current owners didn't really know the golf business, I explained, and I'd be doing things differently.

I failed to add that I didn't really know the golf business, either, at least not from the side of the counter responsible for taking the money instead of offering it. But I loved a challenge and considered myself a quick learner, and after being a golf consumer for so long who had taken so much from the game, it felt like a timely chance to try my hand at providing tee times rather than chasing them.

Besides, I wasn't a total industry novice. During my teenage summers, I caddied and worked the shop at the club where my dad played his golf, and as Allyson went off to look for rental homes on the internet, I recalled those summers and remembered the acute misery from which my co-workers suffered. The members who asked the most agonizing questions (*Pro: The course is closed, sir. Member: For everyone?*); the lady who tongue-lashed us for the filthy state of her clubs; the complaints about the caddies, the price of range balls, the backup on the first tee. I'd forgotten that working at a golf club meant you had to do shit, fix shit, and take some shit, too. I remembered the assistant pro who'd grown so jaded that his *good morning* to the members was punctuated by a behind-their-backs middle finger, and the other who drank himself into a numb oblivion. Providing golf might be hard, tedious work. You had to serve and please and impress, and I'd never learned how to do any of those things. I'd spent my life writing alone in quiet rooms, and now I would have real responsibilities, not just to our golfers, but to employees and to vendors, to the state of New York and whoever collected payroll tax, whatever payroll tax might be. There is a thin line between our dreams and our nightmares, I was realizing, and I wasn't sure which I'd be having that night.

SULLIVAN COUNTY DEMOCRAT, DECEMBER 26, 2019

WESTERN SULLIVAN PROPERTIES PRESENTS PLANS FOR GOLF AND COUNTRY CLUB

By Matt Shortall, co-editor

LIBERTY—Plans to transform the Sullivan County Golf and Country Club are progressing after Western Sullivan Properties acquired the site from Darbee District Hospitality, Inc. earlier this year.

During the Town of Liberty's final board meeting of the year, Sims Foster of Western Sullivan Properties and Foster Supply Hospitality, along with Managing Partner Christopher Monello, presented an overview of their proposal and asked the board to consider two zoning amendments.

Foster said they'd like to enhance the country club by expanding the clubhouse, adding a swimming pool, tennis courts and a health club.

The proposed plan also calls for 21 single-family condominium units, a resort hotel and tent sites for those who want to camp outdoors.

"We're excited about Liberty," said Foster. "Liberty needs to continue to progress and have momentum, not just for the sake of Liberty but for the sake of the county."

Foster said the nine-hole golf course would remain, although they might have to shorten fairways nine and eight to accommodate other development.

Monello said they would like to keep the golf course open for the 2020 season and while other phases of the project are developed.

"One goal is to keep the golf course and all the natural beauty of it and develop around it, where it looks right," Monello said.

Outgoing Councilman Russell Reeves commented that the Fosters' reputation precedes them. "You've done amazing things with properties in the county and it's nice to see you in Liberty."

APRIL 2023

SULLIVAN COUNTY GOLF COMPANY
CHECKING ACCOUNT

Beginning balance: $0

Additions: $10,000

Subtractions: $0

Ending balance: $10,000

I quickly got to begging.

I brushed aside visions of the locker room, blocked out memories of the clubhouse roof, and tried to stop wondering about the Barbies. I was biased toward urgency and impatience—see something, fix something, or at least call someone who could. But Sullivan County Golf & Country Club was an unchecked font of dilemma, and approaching its woes required a psychological rearrangement. I'd have to get stoic about our goals and accept our limitations. First things first: We'd baby-step our way to a better golf course.

I withdrew ten grand Allyson and I had been saving for something other than operating a golf course and opened a checking account at a bank with a branch in Liberty. (I had no idea whether $10,000 was enough to start this new business and get payroll moving, but a larger debit might send up flags for Allyson about this golf course we were getting for free.) Then I pinged a superintendent buddy for contacts in the mower world. He called a friend who had a name, and that name had some good deals on refurbished equipment. Sadly, I wasn't in the market for discounts— our budget was more inclined toward come-take-this-off-our-hands deals, and I naively assumed there were superintendents out there with overcrowded sheds, waiting for a mooch like me to come lighten their load. This wasn't how the agronomy world worked, I would learn. The clubs owned the machinery, and when it reached the end of its useful life, it went on the secondary market that had essentially become a primary market since Covid. Supply chains had yet to recover since the pandemic, and with off-the-charts golf demand—more courses, more players—it seemed that every reel and mower was being utilized or bid on somewhere. If I wanted brand new equipment (I didn't), I was told it could take years. So I recalibrated. Maybe we should try making some money first.

A few locals eventually signed up for memberships—less than a dozen—so we had a handful of dollars in the new bank account for a new LLC that had just finished a new contract with Foster Supply/Western Sullivan Properties, drawn up by my new lawyer who would be getting most of that new money. But with New York City just two hours away, and plenty of subscribers to *The Golfer's Journal* (the magazine where I was editor) who liked to visit golf curiosities, I wondered if we could sign nonresidents up for golf-inclusive memberships without waiting for them to come pay our modest daily fee (I'd raised the visitor price to $30 with a cart, $20 to walk, and Shaun did a good job of shielding me from the local backlash).

I went on the website of which I'd recently been given control, and I added a nonresident member category for anyone outside Liberty's zip code. For $400, you'd get a nice bag tag plus USGA handicapping service, if you forked over another $40. But that would require that we order bag tags, and to offer handicaps to our members, resident or nonresident, we'd need to be a member of a USGA golf section and get the course rated for handicapping. Bag tags seemed an easier lift, but to get those, now we needed a logo.

I paused my work on the website and called a friend.

Lee Wybranski had grown up a few towns over from me, and after college I'd become a pal and regular bar mate of his cousin, through whom I eventually met Lee. Today he paints the official posters for the US Open, the PGA, the Open Championship, and the Ryder Cup, and his work is collected by golf fans around the world, but when I first met him, he wasn't even thinking about golf. He was doing portraits out of a studio in Center City, Philadelphia—homes and buildings, mostly, and he was damn good at both. A friend eventually asked him if he'd draw the clubhouse at Winged Foot, and soon Lee was firmly planted in the golf world, where, aside from those posters, he designed club logos, scorecards, and yardage books for the likes of the Old Course in Scotland and Merion in our hometown. His stuff was gorgeous, and though I couldn't afford him, I told him I was now running a golf course and asked whether he might take a shot at sketching us a logo. Once he accepted that I wasn't kidding about operating a golf club—*Do you know how to do that?*—in two weeks he had researched our club history and turned around a portfolio of samples for Allyson and me to choose from. Flipping through a real artist's renderings of images we might attach to our little golf dream, each logo more exciting than the last, made our commitment feel more genuine than any contract or handshake. There it was, our place, our club, an abstract idea brought to life in a way that only an artist can.

In the end, choosing from Lee's options was an easy deliberation. Shaun, Allyson, and I agreed: the St. Andrew's cross (called that because of the crooked cross on which Scotland's patron saint asked to be crucified, considering himself unfit to be executed by the same means as his savior) with a golf club and Otto Hillig's propeller.

Lee produced scorecards, too, and we would need some of those. But since all we had were hole numbers and vague yardages—no hole handicap indexes or ratings from which to derive those handicaps—I called another friend who knew folks in the Metropolitan Golf Section that encompassed all the golf clubs in and around New York City, including the Hudson Valley (which I'd learn is where our golf course was). I eventually reached the person who could sign us up for membership in the Met (they noted that Sullivan County's account had been defunct for some time) and connected with the handler of handicaps and course ratings.

A golf course receives a numerical slope and course rating meant to gauge its difficulty (or lack thereof) so that scores from said course can be used in calculating a player's handicap (a number that quantifies a player's scoring potential, or lack thereof, thus allowing matches to be played between players of varying skill). If your course doesn't have a rating, players can't enter their scores toward their handicap, and if we were going to be a real golf club, we needed golfers to be able to do so. Without that, all we had to offer was a walk with your clubs—fine for some, but selfishly, I didn't want to spend my summer going around a course where score was just a mood instead of an indelible index of my golfing worth.

Besides, authentic handicaps were a service we could provide that might attract new members, and if we wanted more revenue from league play, those players needed handicaps. Shaun explained that the die-hard Monday Men's League had been using homemade handicaps calculated by their chairman, and I assured him we could offer them something better. Shaun seemed unconvinced. "You haven't met the Men's League yet."

The Met took pity on our endeavor and sent up a rater within two weeks of my first email. We soon had a course slope and rating and our name popped up in GHIN (the Golf Handicap Information Network) where you could post scores from Sullivan County, now a dues-compliant member of a golf section. We had a logo and proper bag tags on which members' names would be laser engraved. This didn't stop local members from asking when they were getting their seasonal golf cards in the mail, the pieces of paper that had heretofore entitled them to their greens fees. I explained that their engraved bag tags that read MEMBER now served that purpose—in my battle to push forward the golf culture at Sullivan County, the front lines moved one hard yard at a time, but genuine club badges seemed a small victory. As were proper scorecards with a proper logo and an indulgent touch: Billy Collins, a two-time US poet laureate, had somehow become a golf buddy of mine, and he lent some words for the back of the card where a course's local rules were usually printed. They might confuse some of our guests and members, but if I ever had the chance to make my own scorecard, I wanted it to be a cool one, and what's cooler than a little poetry where you don't expect it:

The Rules
say you cannot touch your ball
unless on the green
where you must mark it

though between holes
it's perfectly fine
to carry it in your pocket

which is unheard of
in football,
hockey, or soccer.

—Billy Collins

Scorecards, handicaps, some art, and some verse—we had not opened for the season yet but we were on our way. I went back to our website, covered it with our new logo and our new nonresident offering, and I announced Sullivan County to the world of social media and shouted it to an email list of every person to ever write me about my books (not a vast database, but a reasonable collection of die-hard golfers and perturbed grammarians). And wouldn't you know, the golfers were listening.

Everyone appreciates an underdog, but golfers—certain golfers—have a sweet spot for ambitions that buck the norm. Maybe it grows from a frustration with golf's slow-moving status quo, or a resentment of golf's steep costs, or guilt about enjoying the golf (and private golf courses) that others can't, but something about our efforts to bring new life to a rural, forgotten, accessible, and affordable golf club struck a chord. Nonresident memberships flew in from all over—New Jersey, Pennsylvania, Florida, Texas, California, even Ireland and London. I knew most had likely joined for the novelty, that they wouldn't actually come play the course they'd just joined, and that was fine (preferable, really—I'd rather they imagine their handsome clubhouse in New York than experience its grim realism). They could have spent that $400 on a new putter, but instead they wanted to help keep golf going for people they'd never met. When the golf community gets behind something, the results are quite impressive, and for a vital moment, they decided to get behind us, buying up some $50,000 worth of memberships.

Not everyone was moved by our intentions. Beneath our Facebook post about the course being under new management, some locals voiced their outrage: *They're charging less for people from the city and more for people from Sullivan County! How is that fair?*

Every yard, a battle. I responded with a gently worded post, explaining that our nonresident members from outside the area will use the golf course far less frequently than our resident members, thus the difference in price. I also noted that we had received payments from golfers in California and the UK, people who will never visit Sullivan County, and if they did, might pop in once. These nonresident members were essentially underwriting local golf and keeping our prices low. Without them, the course had no prospects for financial survival.

And it didn't. Our regular Liberty playing population was less than a hundred—probably closer to fifty—which, as previous owners could attest, was some dire golf math. The nonresident concept started making sense to those regulars and the complaints ceased. Plus, the new bag tags were popular, and I sensed a bit of pride among the neighbors who quickly affixed theirs to their bags. But that initial brush with local opinion opened my eyes to a few things: First, I wasn't from here, and that mattered. Second, I shouldn't assume that my Sullivan County players shared the same golf culture to which I was accustomed. I had taken over a course where golfers wanted nine cups sunk in the grass, two-dollar domestic cans, and carts that could make it up the mountain. Perhaps the decades of decline had eroded expectations, but I wondered if any locals even cared that their course was now rated and they could keep a USGA handicap. Judging by the tiny number who signed up for it, not even a half-dozen, they didn't. Were they going to care if we had hats and shirts to sell? Did they want new golf balls, or just that red basket of used ones? Was I running a golf club, or just a place to play what sort of felt like golf?

I was going to have to serve two masters in my role as operator: the denizens who weren't looking to be impressed, and the out-of-towners we needed to impress. The financials Chris shared proved that the club's future depended on dollars from outside the county. I wasn't sure what that kind of golf club looked like, but if I could give them a better golf course, I might win over both factions. And I needed to give Shaun a chance to make something of which he could be proud. From the look of our inbox, a lot of people were going to see Sullivan County for the first time this year, and if we had any hopes of keeping our momentum going beyond an initial rush of goodwill, we had to give them golf that wasn't just quaint, but quality. I got to work chasing down the things quality might require.

The responsibility of operating a golf course had quickly proven to be more than the moonlighting I hoped it might be, and I already did plenty of that. One of my side hustles was speaking about my adventures in golf, at country club events and member-guest tournaments where the enthusiasm for my presentation hinged on whether I was speaking at the start of the evening or at its conclusion. Put me onstage before the open bar was plundered, I had a chance of winning a sincere ovation; put me up there afterward, and I was ready to dodge half-eaten desserts. I've been cheered in St. Louis and shouted down in Boston where the audience felt compelled to inform me, often and at full throat, that Philadelphia was a shithole. I've been invited back in Buffalo, and I've stood at many a urinal while the gentlemen behind me announced that no, they weren't sticking around for some damn golf writer. Sometimes I book corporate gigs where hopefully half the audience cares whether Scottish or Irish golf is better (it's a tie) while the other half makes mental lists of keynotes they might have preferred (athletes, tycoons, their kid's second-grade teacher). Such speaking tours are a way to sample new courses or meet golfers with access to tee times on my wish list, but I never expected that addressing a roomful of turf scientists in New Jersey would be handy beyond a paycheck. Then I got some turf, and it was.

Before I knew where Sullivan County was, I had been hired to speak by a company called Aquatrols, which I suspected might be in the fire-fighting or water park business. Turns out they manufactured surfactants (the stuff that manages water intake on your golf course) along with a variety of plant foods to green up your course. Inputs, as they say in the agronomy business, and a product that doesn't come cheap. I'm glad Aquatrols liked my talk because a year later I was rummaging through a drawer overflowing with business cards—found it—and was soon on the phone with their director of North American sales, telling him about a nine-hole golf course in the Catskills.

Alas, I'd never spoken at a convention for mower manufacturers. After striking out on used equipment—everything Shaun and I found was out of our price range, even with memberships flowing in (payroll would gobble up those funds quickly enough)—I took a shot with Toro, whose red machines sat atop the greenskeeping food chain. I found an address for one of their executives and sent a long-winded email pitching the story of our golf course. We didn't need much, I said, but we needed some help with a mission that I framed as the noblest of golf pursuits. I beat the drum for affordable mom-and-pop courses, and I beseeched with woebegone paragraphs about our imminent demise should we not secure spinning reels for our superintendent. Sullivan County deserved a shot, I pleaded, and said we'd take their castoffs and their half-builts—absolutely anything was an upgrade. For some reason, he replied, connecting us with Grassland, the local Toro distributor, who knew our course and agreed that it should stick around a little while longer.

Three weeks later, Shaun sent me a video with a text that read, *THE CAVALRY HAS ARRIVED*. At home in Philadelphia, I watched as two flatbeds pulled into the Sullivan County parking lot, their backs loaded with beautiful red riding machines, Shaun's voice in the background shouting, "Yeah, baby! Here they come!" I played the video over and over again and felt like a kid watching a circus train stop at his front door. If everything else went to pot, at least Shaun had this day of pure greens-keeping joy. Pallets from Aquatrols soon followed, with enough grass juice to drench a hundred greens.

The work cart and the fairway mower and the sprayer and the greens unit from Toro were not new—they'd logged an interstate's worth of miles—but they ran well and we had them on loan for the year, and they would change everything about Shaun's working days. He'd be able to schedule tasks like a real greenskeeper rather than wonder which machine would start today, and he would no longer have to stand by and watch our fairways turn gold with dandelions. I told him I couldn't wait to see the new fleet, and I'd see it soon—I was driving up to Liberty tomorrow. It had been fun and games until now, but Shaun said it was finally time for my sit-down.

I wondered if they wore hats like in *The Flintstones*—something tall and furry with bones affixed to the front—or shared tribal handshakes by which they would identify me as an outsider. I'd never entered a fraternal lodge of any sort, and as I sat in my car and waited for Shaun to arrive and walk me into the Elks Lodge, I felt the nerves of an undercover informant.

I wore no mic but I would be taking mental notes with eyes peeled for robes and paddles, listening for low murmurs in indiscernible tongues.

The building, a white block at the end of a street in downtown Liberty, didn't suggest grandeur, but the lack of pomp seemed to add to its impenetrability. This was no temple or grand hall accustomed to visitors; no signage to welcome or direct a first-timer. This was a place for people who belonged, and in short time, the bartender would make it clear that I did not carry that distinction.

Shaun led me through a side door into a white meeting room with folding chairs and a small stage. I could hear the voices of men coming through a wall, but couldn't tell from which direction, the sound echoing around us. I'd traveled up from Philadelphia for one night to meet a crowd of Liberty locals, to pay homage to and seek the support of the golf club's elders. I felt very much like an explorer whose ship had arrived on unknown shores, ready to do business via wampum, but I was bearing no beads, no gold, no guns to trade as Shaun led me through another door and into a hidden and dimly lit space where the lights were tinted red and, at the sight of a newcomer, the conversation died. The room's soundtrack went silent as if someone had yanked the cord.

"Evening, guys. This is Tom, the guy I told you about, from the course."

I responded to Shaun's introduction with the meekly raised hand of an anxious freshman, saluting a bar full of men whose faces I couldn't quite make out but whose eyes I could feel fixed on me. I was met with a low-toned "Hey" in welcome.

A U-shaped bar was surrounded by red leather-topped stools, and every inch of the room was covered in Liberty history: union badges and Polaroids stuck to the walls, bar mirrors flecked with age, some hunting trophies—one must have been an elk—staring down at us as Shaun and I took seats at the far end near the door through which we had just entered, careful not to take up too much space.

This wasn't Shaun's scene, either—he'd given up on the bar scene and wasn't a Liberty native, and I was happy to have a partner here who matched me on those two counts. But when I asked the bartender for a club soda and then watched him pour vodka into a short cocktail glass, I was sure I was about to break with some rite of initiation roughly two minutes into my pledge for support.

"Sorry. I asked for a club soda?" I said, stating it as a question so that I might absorb some of the blame.

"You said vodka and club," the bartender spoke through his voluminous beard. He was large and his voice was the sort that came from a part of one's chest I was pretty sure I lacked—deep and uncompromising—and I wondered if I was about to dump twelve years of sobriety for the chance to not offend a stranger. I had long ago become uninterested in peer pressure, unmoved by the temptation of a buzz, but none of my recovery literature had discussed a scenario where a large mountain man slides forward a glass and stares down upon you in a way that affirms you are neither mountain nor man. I summoned all the swagger that a soft suburban golf upbringing could muster and squeaked, "I'm pretty sure I said club soda."

I knew I was right—even in my drinking days as a dedicated wino, an ask for vodka never left my mumbling lips—but he didn't move. He glared at me as if to render my point moot; I'd received vodka, I was to drink vodka. When I called his bluff by not reaching for my drink or my wallet, he conceded by swiping away my glass and filling a plastic cup with bubbles from his beverage gun, and I sipped it like a toddler through a thin red straw. I didn't dare ask for a lime.

As my eyes adjusted to the low lighting, I made out faces and the din of conversation resumed. There was hockey on the television and the men all seemed to be of varying yet similar ages; even the young ones had a look like they'd been sitting here for decades, the weight of work and of winter spread evenly across their shoulders. They wore hoodies and sweatshirts of a durability you don't find at Lululemon, their pants adorned with hammer loops and extra pockets that, in this room, looked useful instead of decorative. Their toe-darkened boots were the kind we'd all like to own but rather not earn. This was a room for people who didn't moan when it snowed, from a world where it snowed in feet instead of inches. And as Shaun had explained it to me, and why I'd driven up here on a Tuesday evening—these were now my members.

Sullivan County Golf & Country Club had been member-owned for most of its life, and until recently, these men (and their fathers and mothers, grandfathers and grandmothers) would have been its proprietors. When the club ran out of money ten years ago, there was something of a schism within the membership over whether to sell or pony up and stick it out. They eventually leased the operation to restaurateurs who gave it their best shot, before Chris and Sims stepped in as a benevolent backstop. So while I was already up against a course that bled money, it became clear as I sipped my soda water that I might also be pitted against a membership who likely felt as if they owned the place, because once upon a time, they did.

I'd come prepared to make a presentation, armed with photocopied paperwork that announced my plans and the new fee structure for members and visitors (the website had been updated with the same information, but this seemed more like a see-it-in-writing clientele). I'd envisioned a sort of champion's welcome where I'd pass around sheets of promise to a roomful of eager listeners, their eyes wide with hope, a rally for a bright future with arms raised in golfing solidarity. But this course and these men had been here long before my arrival and knew the place better than I ever would. This was a novel adventure to me, but I could tell by their indifference that my talk of a new day at Sullivan County was going to be old news to them.

Shaun had warned me about the reception that change received up here. Persistence was the Catskills' charm as well as its tragic flaw. People traveled here from the places where things changed all the time because these hills and rooms and streets were reliable, consistent, fixed in time. But that inclination had allowed the resorts to flounder and the downtown to deteriorate. Such was the futile retort of every struggling region—fix it, but don't change it.

The customers here were accustomed to cut-rate greens fees and discount memberships, and had grown to stomach the conditions those two things could afford. They were used to coming and going as they pleased—no pro shop check-in, just grab your cart and play. I liked the idea of that arrangement, but if it had worked, I wouldn't be sitting here. The balance sheets proved the course had two options—change or close. As I waited for Shaun to cue me to say something, I wasn't sure which possibility this room was going to prefer.

A woman in the corner had made a tray full of beef and cheese sandwiches for the room to share tonight, the season's first meeting of the Sullivan County Men's League. If I could win these guys over, Shaun told me, we'd be in much better shape than if I didn't. They were the club's most regular visitors and most active participants, even if that meant most of them only showed up on Monday nights and paid $20 for nine holes with a cart. Given the condition of our carts, one could argue they were being overcharged. Once we each had a sandwich on a napkin in front of us, a man named Mike stood up and asked for everyone's attention. Heads slowly turned toward his corner of the bar, opposite ours, and he thanked everyone for coming and announced there was good news. "I know we all heard the course was closing this year and going up for sale, but it's not. It's going to be open. We've got Tom here from Philadelphia to tell us about it."

I'd once given a book reading to a crowd of three people, all three of whom I'd gone to college with, at a Barnes & Noble in Chicago, and to this point in my life, that had been my most humbling crowd. Mike was clearly on my side; he'd asked Shaun to invite me and had been the only person to introduce himself to me so far, but as I stood up and looked at a room of hard eyes and set jaws, I felt myself longing for that store above Michigan Avenue where I could at least bury my face in a book and read until it was over.

I'd rather Mike had not mentioned my home city—I already felt like a carpetbagging golf Music Man, and my yonder zip code now confirmed it—but I thanked him and quickly got to the happy news. Indeed, Sullivan County Golf & Country Club was open for business this year. I had taken over as the golf course operator, I was looking forward to a busy season, and I was grateful to everyone for supporting the club, in the past and in its new future. "As you know, the club has been losing money for a number of years," I said, quickly regretting pointing out a fact these former operators might take as an accusation, "so we are going to have to make some changes to the prices and fee structure this year." The first "Here it comes" issued from the back of the bar, but I soldiered forth, passing around a stack of papers with the updated numbers.

"Memberships are going up a little bit this year, and same for greens fees," I explained. "We'll go up to $550 for regular memberships, and $450 for seniors."

If you belong to a golf club elsewhere, you might think those are absurdly low monthly dues. But these weren't monthly dues I was proposing—these were dues for the season and entitled one to free golf for a year. What I thought was the greatest deal in golf was met with mostly quiet indifference, and a few shaking heads.

"Will there be a discount for veterans?" one of the men asked. Another asked, "What about firefighters and cops?" These initial inquiries caught me unprepared. I'd loitered around golf clubs my entire life, but not the kind where you took service into account. I'd arrived from a golf world where it was assumed and accepted that golf club membership was the worst investment one could make. Between dues and initiation, you never truly got your money out of a country club, and the correlation between expenditure and return was fuzzy math lost in the shuffle of member-guest tournaments and wine dinners and logos of particular prestige. You joined to belong, but there was another golf world out there where you only belonged if it made sense to your checking account at month's end, and I wondered if maybe the latter golf world was even bigger than the former one from which I was visiting. I knew in which one I was now standing, and said we'd definitely be looking into those discounts.

I tried to lift the room's spirits with more good news—they could expect improved course conditions this year. Shaun had some new (used) equipment and new inputs for which the grass at Sullivan County was surely starving, so they could expect a greener, tidier course come June. A few gentle nods—conditions seemed secondary to pricing. Nobody here was going to complain about scruffy mow lines or unrepaired divots, but courting golfers from outside the county, I explained, was the only path to prosperity. To recruit more visitors, I'd have to inch Sullivan County Golf & Country Club closer to that second part of its name.

"Will the greens be better?" someone asked. "Used to have the best greens in the county."

Shaun assured them that they would be better this year—he could now spray to control the dollar-spot (those light rings you often see on putting surfaces) and had a greens mower that would let him mow almost daily.

My spiel finished, I returned to my sandwich. Shaun patted me on the back. "Nobody threw anything," he said. "That's good."

A man in a heavy flannel jacket took the seat next to us and introduced himself.

"Dan Yaun," he said, extending a hand. "We're really glad you're here."

I could tell from Shaun's happy hello that Dan was an ally, and I recognized his surname from the club champion board. He was tall with a settled look in his eyes and a strength in his voice that revealed him as a leader, a gentle but firm sort of man who watched his crew growing louder and chasing shots with beers while he silently sipped from a glass he wouldn't quite empty.

"The course means a lot to me, and to my family. It would break our hearts to have it close, so what you're doing means a lot."

"You'll get to know the Yauns," Shaun said. "They're Sullivan County legends."

Dan demurred. "I don't know about that."

Shaun explained that Dan's nephew was playing on tour, and his cousin's son was the pro at the Century Country Club in Westchester. The Yauns had grown up on Sullivan County's fairways and their family's business had been a centerpiece of the town, a plumbing supply and contracting company that put the pipes in all the golden-age resorts. His was a name that mattered around Liberty, and proof of that was just down the street from our golf course, where you could turn left onto Yaun Avenue.

He'd just returned from a trip following his nephew at a Korn Ferry event down south, and I'd never been so excited to make small talk about the Korn Ferry Tour. What a relief—a golf I recognized. A respite from dead carts and golf by Groupon (Shaun had warned me that some of those were still floating around out there, along with a Catskills calendar with a free golf coupon that a previous boss thought was a good idea).

Once Dan had deemed me approachable, other members of the Men's League followed suit. I met a guy in his twenties who said he sucked at golf but liked the guys and wished me well in what we were doing. Another man with a bald head and muscles asked me if there was still going to be a hotel. I told him that certainly wasn't in my plans, and he seemed pleased by that news. A man with a mustache that covered his mouth was glad the course wasn't going on the market—they didn't need another Hasidic colony in their backyard, then qualified his take with, "I mean, I'm Jewish, but enough already."

Then a very large man—heavyset, but in an offensive tackle kind of way—threw one of his tattooed arms around my shoulder and asked if I was a Flyers fan. Of course I was, I said, and feeling at ease admitting that in New York was a sign the night was moving in the right direction. When Mike, the league chairman, wandered over to tell me he loved what we were doing, I noticed that the barman had taken my cup and refilled it with soda water and added a lime.

Shaun and I didn't stay very long—we'd accomplished our goal of showing our faces and sharing our plans. He said the night had gone better than he expected. There were some egos in that room we'd have to look out for, he said, but with his new rigs from Toro and the boxes from Aquatrols, he was champing at the bit to give them nothing to complain about.

As we returned to our cars, I remembered: "I forgot to tell them we're changing the name."

Shaun shrugged. "I doubt they'll care. You're the owner now. Call it whatever you want."

I had been tempted to try a full rebrand. Sullivan County Golf & Country Club didn't quite roll off the tongue and made the course sound as if it were owned by a municipality—fine if it was, but it wasn't, which masked some of the desperation of our plight. We weren't backed by tax dollars or sustained by a township's budget. Friends had texted me some bad ideas—*Coyne Links*, *Ginger Mountain*, *The Catskiller*—and while dreaming up a name was part of any run-your-own-golf-course dream, it seemed important to keep history in place and show pride in where our holes were planted.

Still, it had bothered me since I first saw that sagging sign.

There was nothing country club about our golf course. No pool, no tennis, not even a poker room anymore. We had a horseshoe pit at the end of the parking lot, but I doubted whether that counted as a country club amenity. And if it was good enough for Shinnecock, Pine Valley, and Augusta National, calling it just a golf club was plenty. I'd already ordered a flag with our new name to hang in our breezeway, and had it printed on the scorecards that were currently en route to Sullivan County Golf Club.

A small change, but those were the only kind we could make right now, and if we made enough of them, who knew what they might tally come October.

THE TIMES HERALD-RECORD, JANUARY 11, 1961

HELP WANTED MALE OR FEMALE

WANTED: Couple to operate semi-private and success-ful, seasonal golf club, including concession. Good op-portunity for those with initiative and imagination. For details and terms, write George A. Yaeger, Secretary, Sul-livan County Golf and Country Club, Liberty, N.Y., de-tailing experience or qualifications and giving references.

It seemed everyone was getting themselves a golf course.

I'd recently joined Old Barnwell, which, despite its name, was brand new, and I had done so at a reasonable price (operator's disclosure: No golf carts went unrepaired at Sullivan County so that I could pay membership dues elsewhere). Located in the sandy outskirts of Aiken, South Carolina, it had been imagined and built by an individual owner, Nick Schreiber, who wanted to use it as a mission-based club, focused on caddie scholarships and youth mentoring and charitable golf causes.

It wasn't far from another new course imagined by the PGA Tour's Zac Blair, a place called The Tree Farm, and every month there was word of a new course coming to South or North Carolina, to Georgia or West Palm Beach or the California desert. These were high times for golf course construction. The world had fallen back in love with golf following Covid; we'd taken fresh air and long walks and good company for granted, until they were all we had left. Add new golf demand to a strong stock market, and it seemed that every hedge fund manager in America was looking for three hundred acres of sandy soil on which to build their own golf playground. Big-name architects were scheduled out with five years of work waiting on their books, shaping holes as quickly as their dozers would allow.

It was a different sort of golf party than the one Tiger threw in the early 2000s. That boom saw an expanse of golf communities and country clubs and high-end public facilities, plenty of which went belly-up or stalled after the bust that was 2008. This new wave of golf was driven by individuals, not corporations and developers, and to me, it began in 2018 with the opening of a course near Vidalia, Georgia, a town from which the course took its onion logo.

The Ohoopee Match Club wasn't the first exclusive retreat built according to the vision of a lone proprietor (Warren Stephens had his mighty and reclusive Alotian Club, and even Augusta National was born of a singular vision), but Ohoopee had been dreamed up by its owner, Michael Walrath, and his friends over post-golf cocktails, where they wondered what their own version of an ideal golf getaway would look like: great food, no crowds, no carts, plain but comfortable sleeping quarters, plus the freedom to play an extra nine or eighteen if daylight allowed, and a focus on mano-a-mano golf where sandbaggers found no refuge. Gil Hanse and Jim Wagner designed them a course for match play where, as the Ohoopee motto goes, no one cares what you shot (no course rating means no score posting, as does the lack of set tees—the previous hole's winner selects the next teeing ground) with an alternate routing of bonus holes that offered options after a sleepover. This new a-place-for-us approach caught the imaginations of every golfer who had cashed out on crypto or sold their company to Google. It broke the country club mold not just with its tiny membership (its initiates are said to be a small collection of Walrath's friends), but with a bold new concept for a golf club: fun.

Some call it the hang or the vibe. For too long golf clubs had been de-prioritizing fun for the sake of size and scale, for rankings and resort amenities, when all golf's next generation wanted was a good time. A place to play and feel comfortable. Stuffy country club rules and crowded tee sheets sent millionaires searching for their own Ohoopee, utilizing its fun-without-frills blueprint: a getaway but not a resort; cozy but not luxurious; exclusive but not snobby.

As I drove north in late April for my first visit to Liberty since my pitch at the Elks, I wondered what chance our little nine-holer had in this shifting golf landscape. Did golfers want what we could offer? And what did we have to offer them? Affordability, charm, great views, and a breathless walk up to our third tee. Was that enough? We didn't have the firehose capital from which all the hot new projects were drinking, but perhaps that could be to our benefit. Maybe we could be a small zig to the golf world's zag. Something simple and intimate, where you felt like the whole place belonged to you. Maybe we wouldn't be all that unlike a visit to Ohoopee in this regard. We had to nail the vibe—I'd already decreed that dogs would be welcome on our course, and we had no tee sheet on which you needed to reserve a time. If nobody was there when you showed up to play, we had an honor box stuck by the door—just slide in some cash. And I'd ordered a dozen Adirondack chairs with cup holders, and had sourced local beers from the Catskill Brewery that guests might place in them.

Our beverage selection was indeed a window into our identity crisis: I was told we needed to stock Bud, Miller Lite, Twisted Tea, and Mike's Hard Lemonade for our regulars, while the golfers I was courting from Brooklyn and Hoboken, the kind who'd started following us on Instagram and who would drive two hours rather than fight the crowds at the city courses, wanted pale ales and wheat beers brewed down the street. So they sat there on the shelf in the pro shop, side by side—two-dollar domestics (I'd raise the price to three) next to tall cans with artsy labels that would cost you seven bucks. It seemed the battle for Sullivan County would boil down to Bud vs. Grass Wagon IPA.

I wasn't sure what we had in the golf course yet. Aside from pictures on our website, all I'd seen was a snow-covered hillside, but on this visit, I was determined to play my golf course.

As I approached our parking lot, my clubs rattling around the back of my car, I felt the anxiety and excitement I would come to know well over the course of the next year, a pause of breathless anticipation known to any business owner as you brace yourself for the counting of the cars. More savvy MBAs might have studied P&Ls and point-of-sale metrics, but all I cared about was whether anybody had shown up. And on this morning, the tally was two—or eight wheels, which sounded better—and I feared they all belonged to people who were now on my payroll.

Shaun was mowing the first tee when I pulled up, and he hopped off his new ride to introduce me to our most recent hire in the pro shop. With Keith out for this season, he had been searching for someone else to help inside, and last week he'd found a candidate—or caught one—sneaking onto the golf course.

Shaun had been out inspecting the state of the spring fairways—winter held on tightly up here, and it would be a few more weeks before they'd dried—when he spotted an unfamiliar truck in the lot. He'd cut holes and put out the flags (we needed more of those, too—the old cotton flags were classics, but they were torn and frayed and, in the breeze, looked like the last gasp of a sinking ship), and he was curious whether we had our season's first golfer. We might not; apparently people came up to raid our dumpster for cans, or maybe it was someone questing for Otto's gold, but he eventually found a man swinging away on the seventh fairway, and thought he'd ask a few questions of a face he didn't recognize—rare for Sullivan County in April.

The man had raised his hands in surrender as Shaun's cart approached. He tried to pay, he explained, and was going to try again when he finished, hoping the shop might be open. He apologized; he didn't have cash for the honor box, and Shaun told him not to worry. He was glad to see someone out here and there was always time to settle up, today or tomorrow or next week. Better to enjoy the course, he said, and figure out how to pay for it later, a policy I wholeheartedly endorsed. Two sets of tires were better than one, whether they'd had money for the box or not.

The two men talked for longer than either of them expected. The winters here left you eager for conversation and new faces, and Shaun learned that the newcomer's name was Jimmy, a recent transplant from Staten Island who had been running a plow truck since December, riding shotgun and working the blade for the driver. Jimmy didn't miss the city much, aside from the friends and the food. He said he'd be up here a lot more if the place was going to open this year, and Shaun explained that it was, and that he might be looking for a guy to help in the shop. Jimmy was a retired diesel mechanic who'd done two stints in the Army—he'd never worked in the golf business and hadn't played much since being the fifth man on his high school golf team, but Shaun assured him there were no prerequisites for the job, other than a willingness to babysit the register for a modest wage. They shook on it and Shaun said he'd let the new owner know he'd found a shop guy. Now the time had come to meet my life's first official hire.

Jimmy had a thick build and an olive complexion and he introduced himself with an energy that seemed more teenage than retired. He wore an Army baseball cap and jeans and boots—we weren't going to be picky about our dress code up here. If it was good enough to plow in, it was good enough for putting cash in the drawer.

"I ain't quite figured out this system here yet," he said in a speedy Staten Island accent, and he showed me the iPad screen he'd been poking at all morning. "I ain't real good with computers. I don't got email or, whattaya call them, smartphone things. Still got the old flip phone," he said, pulling it out of his pocket to show me, a point of genuine Luddite pride. I told him not to worry about it, that I'd put in the new prices, and thanked him for taking the job.

"Are you kidding me? Working at a golf course? Man, this is like a dream come true for me."

I was glad to hear it. I liked Jimmy instantly. He talked fast and talked a lot, which is what we wanted in a front man. He was authentically New York, and such authenticity would be our primary commodity.

He lived about twenty minutes away on the top of a mountain. No cell service, he confessed, but his landline worked fine. Without this job it would just be him and his wife and his garden—he grew eggplants and cucumbers and peppers and tomatoes, and said he'd bring me some this season. I ate none of those things but thanked him anyway. "You can't get no good produce up here," he explained. "That stuff they sell at the ShopRite? Garbage. Forget about it."

While I plugged numbers into the register, Jimmy told me he might not golf all that well, but I'd never have to worry about him calling out or being late. "I don't get sick, and I don't need no alarm clock. Ever since I left the Army, my feet hit the floor every morning at five a.m. like clockwork."

His two stretches in the service came a shocking thirty years apart. He'd worked as an Army mechanic out of high school, then moved on to a job with the city for most of his life. Then he recalled for me his reaction to watching the towers fall on 9/11. "Man, I'll tell you, I felt like I had to do something. I was fifty years old but I marched right down to the recruiter's office and told them to sign me back up."

I was sure he was embellishing. The Army, at last check, didn't sign up guys in their fifties, and he explained that, at first, they weren't going to take him, but when he agreed to forgo a pension (his previous service would qualify him for one if he added more years), Jimmy was off to boot camp where he put the younger recruits to shame.

"We'd be out on a run, humping full rucksacks, and here comes this old guy blowing past all the kids. I tell ya, I was in the best shape of my life."

He'd expected mechanical work as his assignment but somehow found himself operating a gun on the back of a Humvee. "I saw some shit," he said. "You wouldn't believe the shit I seen."

I could have spent the afternoon listening to him, and it sounded like Jimmy could have filled those hours without taking a breath, but there was a golf course to see. Shaun grabbed his small quiver of a walking bag—the telltale sign of someone who listens to golf architecture podcasts—and met me on the first tee, not twenty steps from the pro shop door.

I was already glad to see Shaun liked my suggestion of using just one tee marker. He'd found enough of the old plastic 1970s golf ball markers in his shed, the kind that looked more appropriate on a mini-golf course than a proper one, but we both liked them as kitschy throwbacks. He'd painted them blue and white for the back tees, red and yellow for the forwards (he'd also made the most of that spray paint by buying some square paving stones at the hardware store and marking them with 100, 150, 200 and using them as distance plates in the fairways—to whom little is given, little is required). The course had nine greens but eighteen tees, and though most tees were directly opposite one another, some made for entirely new angles and yardages, allowing you to play a different nine holes on your second loop. I didn't love the idea—I was more in-clined to identify the nine best holes and play them as many times as you wished—but it was Sullivan County custom, and it at least allowed us to pretend, if people called and asked (and they did), that yes, we were an eighteen-hole golf course.

Breaking with the custom of having two parallel tee markers was something I had insisted upon, having discovered it in Ireland just a few weeks earlier. I was south of Dublin working on a story for *The Golfer's Journal* when I noticed that each of the tee boxes at the European Club contained one solitary stone. It was the owner's inspiration—it meant you could never blame the tee markers for aiming you crooked, and it saved your crew time, not having to reset tees as they mowed. Anything Pat Ruddy thought was a good idea, I tended to agree with, and I'd been thinking about my Irish friend a lot of late.

The European Club wasn't part of the magazine story I was writing, but I made a detour south to Brittas Bay to check in with Pat and tell him about Sullivan County, since I was now loosely following a career path that mirrored his own. He was an Irish golf writer who got involved in course design, eventually becoming one of Ireland's most prolific archi-tects and then a golf course owner when he raised the money to purchase some of the last available linksland on the island and carved himself a golf course. I had not built Sullivan County, but I could use any advice from someone who'd gone from writing about courses to running one.

I had not bothered to call ahead—few folks in Ireland were as ac-commodating as Pat—and I found him holding court in the pro shop with a few visitors from America. Always in a tweed fedora and, in recent years, his cane by his side. He was pushing eighty but still had a glint of mischief in his eyes, and what he'd built at the European Club indulged a mischievous bent. It was difficult, but it was beautifully unique, too, the clear product of an uncommon perspective. Plaques around the course told stories about the hole ahead; tiled works of playful art were plastered into the clubhouse walls; each visitor was welcomed with a card that outlined Pat's golf philosophies, my favorite being STAY AWAKE—GET AROUND IN 4 HOURS—YOU ARE AN ATHLETE! He'd built twenty holes instead of eighteen, so that he'd always be able to close one on either nine and tinker, and he'd shaped the longest green in Europe, 127 yards back to front, because it was his course and he could.

He welcomed me back and offered me beef stew and apple pie and chocolate, as was his custom—I declined and we sat down in the restaurant and out came my stew and apple pie. As I ate a lunch too large for my stomach, I told Pat about my endeavor in the Catskills, and he warned me: Don't ever stop playing. Stay in love with golf. It was an easy love to lose, he said, when you're too busy worrying about money and conditions and the tee sheet.

"I'd always wanted to own my own golf course," he said. "To have my own golf course all to myself, wouldn't that be something. But then we built it and people started showing up! How about that. And I didn't have my own golf course anymore, not until the Covid came. And when it happened, I was standing in the middle of the eighteenth one day, and I was the only person on the property. We hadn't seen a golfer in months and I finally had my own golf course, and I thought, well now, this isn't very good at all!"

I would soon be able to relate. It was a strange business, because golfers make owning a golf course possible, but kind of spoil it, too. You nurture and tend to the place as best you can, prepping and perfecting, and then the people come and you hide in the shop or leave. It's like readying your house for a party to which you aren't invited. A rowdy party, too, that rips around in carts and leaves divots in your carpet. Your host gift is a list of complaints you'll hear about tomorrow, and I only hoped we would be so lucky at Sullivan County, to have enough golfers to make us want to quit.

Pat told me to remember—don't dare forget—that this course I was telling him about probably needed less of what I was trying to give it, not more.

"All you need for a golf course," he explained, "is space, grass short enough to find a ball, and people with which to play." He told me how, as a boy, he'd ride on the back of a friend's tractor and find an overgrown field where they'd offer to cut the grass for the farmer who'd get hay for his cattle while they'd get a place to make a golf hole. They'd use the field as their course until the grass got too high, then get back on the tractor in search of their next layout.

As I listened, I wondered if I loved golf that much, if I could be that kind of golfer, just happy to have a field where I might find my ball. I'd spent decades hiking mighty courses, trying to summon words that might convey their quality; how was I meant to appreciate Sullivan County when my brain had been washed by places with million-dollar maintenance budgets and crews the size of NFL teams? How could our course ever compare to places like the European Club, where guests were happy to pay $400 if they were fortunate enough to get a tee time at all?

But Pat was right. Every pristine course is pristine in the same way; a course like ours was a chance to experience something unique, to forget golf's trappings and recall that our game, at its core, is about traversing a field with a flag at its end. And nine holes was plenty—I'd learned that in Ireland as well. Back in 2007, I'd fallen hard for Irish nine-holers like Spanish Point and Cruit Island and Mulranny, and felt a golf epiphany wash over me. Nine-hole golf in America had long been relegated to the realm of pitch-and-putts and kid courses; nine holes were for practice or a quick fix after work. But plenty of proper Irish and Scottish golf clubs thrived with only nine holes attached to them. And it seemed a solution to many of golf's ills, the three primary of which were: too expensive, too hard, takes too long. Nine holes weren't necessarily any easier (though they could shorten one's suffering), but it enabled cheaper golf via lower maintenance and overhead, and in two hours you could feel like you'd had a full golf day and covered the entire property, with no tenth tee to tempt you or make you feel like a quitter. It was a case I'd made in a *Sports Illustrated* column nearly twenty years ago after returning from my Irish trek, a story I'd completely forgotten writing until I set foot on Sullivan County and recalled that I'd championed places just like this. It seemed the universe was now calling to see if I meant it.

I decided that if people wanted country club golf, they should probably play at their country club. Who didn't like a little pampering and fine grooming? But if their golf souls ever tired of perfection, if they wanted the chance to feel like a kid riding on the back of a tractor unsure what kind of hole he might discover next, I was pretty sure we could give them that. And I was about to discover our first one for myself.

It was a small oval of short grass through which the roots of a cluster of pines were poking. We'd need to chop those down, I noted, if we wanted sun to shine and grass to grow on this tee box.

I would never have noticed them if I wasn't running the place; would not have seen where the mower scalped their wooden bumps. But now that I was, I prepared myself to notice everything, like the sagging state of the skinny green box affixed to a rusty pole. It reached thirty feet into the air, and I had not seen one of these since I was a kid—a golf course periscope through which you could see the hidden bottom of a fairway, making sure you were clear to hit.

"Now this is awesome," I said, and with nostalgia I approached the box, grabbed its iron handles, and stared into a vision of black nothing.

"Yeah, that doesn't work anymore. I need to take it down and adjust the mirrors. Needs a coat of paint, too," Shaun said. "Don't forget to check out the rock."

Beside the post was a boulder with an iron plaque:

This tablet is dedicated
by the citizens of the town of Liberty, New York
to one of its honored townsmen
OTTO HILLIG
and his able pilot, Holger Hoiriis
to commemorate their successful
airplane flight June 26–27 1931
to Copenhagen, Denmark
in the airplane "Liberty"

Holger really got second billing, I thought. Sort of unfair to some-one whose life was in just as much danger as Otto's. I appreciated how the rock left out the part about their pit stop in Germany—they were going to Denmark, and they got to Denmark—and as I sank my tee into the ground (Shaun insisted I take the honor), I felt a quiet kinship with Otto and Holger, another hopeful soul taking off from this golf course and heading toward the unknown, over-invested in the outcome, with a landing spot uncertain and very far away.

I eyed a black-and-white-striped marker post in the fairway, slid back the head of my three-wood, and cracked a solid baby-cut off that post, my ball falling just beyond our horizon.

"Yeah, that's probably gone," Shaun said.

Gone?

"What? It's just right of the post."

"Yeah, you sort of run out of room down there," he explained. "You'll see."

He grabbed a five-iron from his bag, thus divulging the course knowledge I lacked, and pumped one far left of the marker.

"That's kind of where you want to be," he said. "It's a better angle to the green."

After he fixed the periscope, he might get to moving the aiming post as well, I thought, but I wasn't out here to score. I was out here to see whether I was a fool, and that had nothing to do with how I played.

HOLE 1/10 - 300 YARDS - PAR 4

Shaun was right. Gone. I tromped around the right side of number one and found that, after about two hundred yards, you met a drop-off that ran into tall grass that ran into a stream. Far better to have laid back or gone left as he did. I did get a sneak peek of the alternate blue tee for number two, but there was no Sullivan County Titleist to be found (at least I'd remembered to order logo balls, and someone with waders might someday have mine).

The first was a fickle par-four where the aiming post wasn't exactly wrong; it was planted dead center of the fairway, but left was the safer play (there were miles of grass over there). The green was blind from the tee and the fairway sloped out of view and then ended at 240, where you met a stone retaining wall in front of Shaun's trout stream that snaked its way around the green. The card would tempt guests to pull driver, but less than perfect contact was going to end up in that shallow creek that needed cleaning out; its waters were clogged by sticks and overgrowth. Far better, it seemed, to knock something two hundred yards that would leave you with a nervy wedge into the green. It sat forty yards below you in the damp belly of the property, with tree limbs guarding its right flank (more incentive to play left).

I dropped one in the fairway and misjudged my altitude, flying the green, then chipping back and holing out after three vigorous putts. It was early days and Shaun wasn't about to cut the greens very close; plus, they weren't designed to run quickly. The slopes were too severe for slick putting surfaces, and this green was pitched steeply from back to front. It seemed to roll smoothly enough, and I had an affection for slow greens. They required solid putter contact, and striking the dead center of your putter face was a skill that technology had rendered moot. Just get your ball started on a speedy green, and it's going to get to the hole. I missed the pop-putting strokes of yesteryear, when Palmer and Player seemed to blast their flatsticks, their balls racing but stopping dead beside the cup. Modern green speed had turned putting and ball-striking into two distinct skill sets, but on hairier surfaces, they both required good timing, good balance, good hand-eye coordination, on greens where a good chip and a good putt didn't feel all that different.

Number one checked my boxes—handsome, and harder than it looked—and after Shaun finished up his par, we moved on to number two, but not before pointing out, beside the green, a tire hub with a green garden hose wrapped around it and nailed to a post.

"There it is," Shaun said. "Our irrigation system. Pray we don't need it this year."

HOLE 2/11 - 305 YARDS - PAR 4

Another invitation to drive the green, but this one mixed eagle-putt potential with acres of lost ball. Turning right from the first, number two started our climb up the mountain, and Shaun explained that when the fairways went firm, drives slotted up the left side could bound their way onto the green.

The fairway was a good thirty feet higher on its left edge than its right, and I noted the bushy Christmas tree planted on its lower side and wondered if I could take it out with an axe or if we'd have to invest in a chainsaw. I don't hate all trees, just conifers, the dandelions of the tree world: Cheap to buy, easy to grow, they'd been overplanted through the middle of the last century to toughen up golf courses, turning wide vistas and expansive fairways into dark, foreboding tunnels.

Shaun said we could take it down, but that this tree served a practical purpose, as anything landing in its proximity would kick hard right and exit the mountain. It was a different sort of guidepost—one to play away from—and to prove his point, I watched a drive I expected to land right center take two hops and disappear. Shaun aimed left of the fairway, and his ball came to rest in its middle.

The approach on two was no holiday, either. "If your ball lands on the green, it's going to go long," Shaun said, and my second ball followed his orders—one bounce and over. The greens were already a puzzle; they felt spongy underfoot, but they refused to accept even a hint of spin—springy, almost. "That's the thatch," he said. "The greens haven't been top-dressed or aerated in, who knows how long. We don't have the machines. The thatch layer is thick."

Thatch, I would learn, is the buildup of organic matter between the soil and the putting surface. It's the thing your greenskeeper is trying to avoid when he closes your course for two days to either punch holes or rip lines in your greens. That thing most golfers bemoan and gripe about—aerated greens—was something I would come to covet. Or I could just learn to play different shots around Sullivan County. The approaches were shaped to allow you to run the ball into the green, which seemed a more likely solution than acquiring the hardware for punching holes. And the need to play short of the green and let the ball work back to the pin—it was retro and natural, an accidentally Scottish links touch that guests might enjoy.

HOLE 3/12 - 384/470 YARDS - PAR 4/5

Most courses have at least one, that walk they call Heart Attack Hill, and as a young caddie, I still recall that walk up the eighth at Rolling Green that made all of us wish, for a moment, that carts would go ahead and put us out of business. But Sullivan County's needed no hyperbole—there was cardiac liability here, and as the operator, I had to take such matters into account. From the second green it was a half-mile up the mountain and into the woods, made worse by a blue tee halfway into your climb, tempting you to stop. But that tee was for your second nine—on the front, number three played as a par-four; on the back, a par-five. I was in reasonable shape, but when we finally reached the forward tee, I tossed down my clubs like a sack of rocks and grabbed my knees for breath.

Shaun laughed and told me a guy used to sit at the bottom of the hill in his Jeep and offer golfers rides for a quarter. He must have made a mint, I thought, and understood why all the locals took carts and had been clamoring for better ones.

"That hill . . . ," I huffed. "It almost makes the course unwalkable."

"It's all downhill from here, I promise," he said. "I always thought it would be cool to build a kind of connector hole par-three in the woods here. Break up the walk. I've hiked every inch of the property and there's a natural punch bowl right in the middle of all that."

I looked where he was pointing; all I could make out was midnight. Acres of dense, towering pines. It would be cheaper to buy another Jeep than try to clear that, I thought, and turned my attention to a golf hole that seemed to ask a half-dozen questions, none of which hinted at an answer.

From the back tee, the drive seemed straightforward: hit out to the corner and hope for the best. That corner, however, was closer than it appeared. You might call it a dogleg, if your dog had endured some sort of trauma where its leg now bent at the ankle instead of the knee.

The hole had multiple turns to it, and the first one came early, and if you went through it, there was nothing but forest to save you. And if you wanted to get home in two, you had to turn your drive left around the corner, but I recalled that this was the chicken wire hole, and who could guess if a hooking ball would hold. It didn't get any easier from the forward par-four tee, where you most certainly had to bend your ball, but in both directions—the fairway kinked hard left, yet only a fade had any real chance at survival. Overgrown sycamores had eliminated much of the hole's safer right side, turning the hole into a game of roulette where you were the gambler and the course was the house.

But the view . . . it was the worst best-looking hole I'd ever played. Survive your first two shots, and you were left with a wedge you needed to cut (the green pitched left, same as the mountain) off a dead-hook lie, your ball perched higher than your knees. Shot after shot, I launched balls into the woods like paratroopers filing out the back of a plane, while Shaun made it look kind of easy. I loved some quirk, but the quirk here was emptying my bag. It was clear the overgrowth had sucked the strategy out of its initial design, and Shaun said that if we had any money to spare, he wanted to take out these overhanging trees and open up the green.

If I'd had checks in my bag, I would have stroked one right there. I told him to do it, no matter the cost. We had one of the best views in golf up here, and nobody was going to see it if they were too busy looking down at their bag and digging for another ball.

TIMES HERALD-RECORD, JUNE 29, 1964

SILVERS GETS HOLE-IN-ONE AT SULLIVAN COUNTY CLUB

LIBERTY—Joseph Silvers on Sunday aced the Sullivan County Golf and Country Club's par three, 187-yard No. 4 hole, for the 13th hole-in-one in the Club's almost 40-year history.

In a fourball match with Bernard Newman, Robert R. Rothblatt and Ernest Tanous, Silvers hit a No. 5 iron to the green, 12 feet from the cup, and the ball rolled in.

The ace was a sort of compensation for a tee shot which Silvers hit into the hole earlier this year but which could not be scored as a hole-in-one. That time, he flubbed a first shot and it rolled into deep underbrush. Believing it might be lost, he played a provisional ball and that went into the cup.

Finding the first ball, he called it unplayable and picked it up. But as that action is contrary to the rules, it technically nullified the ball which had holed out.

The fourth hole previously was aced by Gardner Le Roy, Tom Mangan, the late Teddy Labouseur, George Yaeger, Robert Keller, Ralph Griffin (twice), Louis Fox, Abraham Kleinman, Rudolf Moehs and Harold Borish, of the Club membership, and two visitors whose names were not recorded.

HOLE 4/13 - 163 YARDS - PAR 3

Now this was a proper golf hole. Backed by a sentinel of pines and divided by a hillside that obscured your view of the left half of the green, this downhill par-three was both angelic and angry. Shaun warned me that it played two clubs downhill and that the ideal approach landed left and short—I was sensing a theme—where the right kick gave you the best chance of holding the green. The green sat on something of a plateau, horseshoed by a bunker that wasn't three feet wide, and balls that landed on the middle of the green were likely headed there, if they were lucky. Skip through the bunker, and off the mountain you went.

I hit what I thought was the ideal shot—left and short—and Shaun lifted my expectations.

"Wait for it, wait for it," he said, as we anticipated my ball rolling rightward across the green. I'm still waiting. No ball.

His tee shot landed shorter and more left, and again, "Wait for it, wait for it," but this time, "Here it comes." We watched as his ball rolled into view and snuggled up to the pin.

When we got to the green, we found my ball had stopped short in the rough, and Shaun explained there was a flaw in the kicker here. "It's a great hole. You get the reveal of whether your ball took the hill or not. But I'd like to iron out this slope a little bit. The way it is now, the closer you land to the green, the less chance you get the right kick."

Since I'd just paid to take down a dozen trees, I figured we'd hold off on regrading the mountain. I took my four while Shaun tapped in for two. Good thing we weren't playing a match or Shaun would be on his way to winning himself a golf course.

HOLE 5/14 - 269 YARDS - PAR 4

As golf found itself embroiled in a debate over technology and whether the modern ball flew too far, the fifth hole at Sullivan County was prime evidence for distance being an overrated asset. Every hole I'd played so far could be added to that argument. I was at least a club longer than Shaun and had not even sniffed any of his scores. The fifth begged you to drive it—there it is, right in front of you, a straight par-four of modest distance here in the lowest, flattest part of the course. But being low on this property meant water, and a stream guarded its left side, a swamp protected its back, and its right side was the bottom slope of the mountain. The fairway was like Alice's Wonderland hallway, shrinking and pinching as you moved closer to the green. The farther you ventured, the smaller your hope.

The approach was pitted with linksy humps and hollows, and having acquired some semblance of local knowledge, I opted for six-iron, which rolled to safety between hillocks of short grass. I tossed my next shot onto the green, and two-putted for my first par as a golf course operator. I even bested Shaun when he three-putted, and it seemed the key to my playing well on this mountain golf course was carrying enough balls to last me until the holes left the mountain.

HOLE 6/15 - 258 YARDS - PAR 4

It was a fun place to perch a tee—back up the hillside, hitting off the mountain and across a stream—if only it offered some grass on which to plant your ball. Choked by a nest of trees, this teeing pad was mostly dirt with patches of vegetation, and a whole lot of stone.

"It's impossible to grow grass in here. We didn't have sand to top dress it so we tried some gravel blend we had," Shaun explained. "It actually kind of worked. This is much better than it was."

At our first obvious driver hole, we were using long tees that didn't care if they were stuck in dirt or grass, but it seemed a shame that such a fun piece of the course had been overtaken by forest and rock. The remainder of six was simple—over the creek, up to a green atop a gentle slope, and here in the thin mountain air, 260 was more than gettable.

"You can pretty much haul off from here in," Shaun said. "It's driver the rest of the way."

I hauled off and hit something we guessed was around the green. The best part of the hole was the walk around the stream and back up to the fairway, where we passed a large and glassy pond over which a heron was flying low, its wings spread full, its long, lax neck nearly touching the water.

"I think she lives back in that corner there," Shaun said, pointing to the far edge of the pond. It looked like a good spot for the bird to grab fish, though not for Shaun, who was a dedicated creek dog—no bait and cast for him, a fly fisherman to his core. We stopped at the old pump house, a tired green shed with a wide PVC pipe busting out of its side. The pipe connected to a smaller pipe, that connected to one more, that was taped and tied to a downspout that barely touched the water.

Shaun opened the door. "There he is. My nemesis." It looked like someone had dropped an old motorcycle engine on the floor. It ran okay, he said, but it lacked the power to get water to each of the greenside hoses. And when it broke down, which it did often, he'd have to run back and forth from the hoses to the pump—this relay would take him all day during the dry spells. "This thing eats up all my mow time. All depends on the weather. If we get enough rain we can get by without it. This month looks decent so we'll hope for the best."

I liked how he talked about the weather in terms of months, and I imagined him in the shed poring through the pages of the Superinten- dent's Almanac. All we needed was a gentle shower each night, followed by days of uninterrupted sun, plus a thermometer that held steady be- tween 64 and 74 degrees for three months, and this course might yet see year one hundred.

I found my ball a few yards left of the green in a nest of weeds and rye. I'd avoided a bunker of dark red clay, and while the greens to this point had all been classically sloped for one-way drainage, six got spicy with a nasty hog's back in its heart. My heavy wedge failed to reach the top where today's pin was planted, and three putts later Shaun had again proven that going for the green wasn't the way to play this golf course.

He had sort of a homemade swing that might have looked out of place in fancier environs, but out here, fit in as naturally as the deer that were nibbling down the rough. In his bag he carried ten clubs, and he played blades because he liked the look of them, old Hogans mixed with Titleists with sweet spots the size of pinheads. It was a bag built for fun with a handful of clubs he'd pulled from the dungeon's lost-and-found and was taking out for a spin.

Shaun played with a narrow stance and a ten-finger grip; it was a move that said, "I know how to golf my ball, now leave me alone." It was far more Sullivan County than my own swing, born of studio lessons and too many YouTube videos, and I felt somewhat self-conscious about it, a golfer who admittedly prized pretty over score. But this wasn't a place for fine-tuned sweeps. There was no range where you might groove positions for the camera, and you didn't need to play handsome here; you just needed your ball to last to the next hole. It reminded its guests that golf was essentially about moving your ball forward with clear intention; chasing speed and distance and angles and lag . . . that whole conversation sounded sort of silly up here, especially when that's what you'd been all about and you were getting boat-raced by a dude with woods and wedges from a bucket in the basement.

HOLE 7/16 - 410 YARDS - PAR 4

I had not visited all our holes yet, but I'd already picked the seventh as a favorite. From the tee, the Catskills opened their arms to us, a wide view of clouds and distant mountain ridges that begged us to pick one and swing away, painting a golf ball onto this backdrop.

The target was out there, somewhere, and when we crested the hill to see where our drives settled, a long, wrinkled runway slid down toward a deep and hopeful green. A stream ran around its far edge, and Shaun spoke his siren's song—play short, or you'll roll over into the creek—but the pin spoke louder and I went hunting. Then I went bobbing for golf balls, poking a wedge at my Titleist as it ping-ponged its way through river rocks on a gentle creek current.

Emptying my bag of balls was a small price for finding the Sullivan County Swilcan. An arched stone bridge about one-third the size of the St. Andrews version traversed a stream of no name, and I waited for

Shaun to putt out before I dared crossing it. There was a wooden alternative two feet to its right, and I stood there wondering what sort of gamble I was making.

"It's still good, you can cross it," he said. "They must have put in the other one when it cracked."

Indeed, there was a large seam through the center of the Sullican Bridge, but the sagging stones seemed safely jammed against one another. It safely carried both our weight, leaving us steps from the next tee.

HOLE 8/17 - 375/498 YARDS - PAR 4/5

The top of the clubhouse came into view on this closing stretch that wrapped us around a corner of trees, a hard dogleg right that tempted one to cut the corner when played as a par-five, then surrendered that corner when played from the par-four tee. After a short climb, we arrived on the same flat land on which the clubhouse sat, and aside from being the longest hole on the course, there wasn't much to the eighth hole, aside from standing water. This wasn't the course's low point, but Shaun explained that the soil up here was different—lots of clay—and was always the last to drain. The green had some character; a sideways double plateau with a backdrop that made you wonder if it belonged on the same course as number seven. Where seven had offered a long glimpse of nature's abundance, number eight showcased a gas station where I read that thirty-packs of Natural Light were on sale as I replaced the pin.

"You like our halfway house?" Shaun asked and said the sandwiches over there were pretty good. He was right—I'd eventually get my lunch there every day, at the cleanest gas station in the Mid-Atlantic. We'd steer visitors there or to the diner for lunch and we tried to discourage locals from hopping the broken rail in the picket fence and buying their beers there instead of the cans we were selling in the shop (a losing battle as our trash cans remained full of Rolling Rock and Busch Light, two brands we didn't offer).

There had been talk of us serving hot dogs from a roller machine Sims had found in the depths of the kitchen, but after three expensive phone calls with my lawyer as we drew up my operating arrangement, hot dogs were ruled off-limits. Preparing food, even wieners spun on hot aluminum, introduced all sorts of paperwork and liability for which I was unprepared. Rather than have him research hot dog case law, I said we'd just sell Snickers and beef jerky and be done with it.

SALAMANCA CATTARAUGUS REPUBLICAN, MAY 29, 1935

A golf ball was "sliced" off the course of the Sullivan County Golf and Country Club at Liberty, N. Y., and shattered the windshield of an automobile driven by August Sachs, a Bronx salesman, on the main highway. He sued the golf club for $100,000, and also brought suit against E. R. Fletcher, principal of the Middleville high school, driver of the ball. The golf club carried liability to the extent of $10,000. With this and an additional $5,000 raised by putting a mortgage on the club's property, the club has effected a settlement out of court. The plaintiff reserved the right to continue suit against Mr. Fletcher. Golf clubs whose courses run close to public highways have more than academic interest in this case.

HOLE 9/18 - 370 YARDS - PAR 4

After so many peaks and valleys, a flat finisher seemed a disappointment, but the green was viciously tilted, a reminder of the mountain from which you thought you'd escaped. Where Rayner and McCarthy found tamer terrain, they'd added intrigue via wild greens, and number nine's was split with a deep chasm that added a full shot of difficulty on a hole with a tough enough drive already. A pocket of trees to the right had to either be carried or avoided entirely, though going left meant soggy rough and a longer approach. Shaun said those woods were stuffed with golf balls, and people trying to fly the corner often found the road and the church parking lot across the street. Every few weeks, he said, a woman from the church would come into the shop with a dozen or so balls they'd found, never complaining, just graciously returning them as if Keith in the shop had been wondering where they'd run off to.

We finished up and shook hands, and I could tell Shaun was waiting for a verdict.

It was a good golf course. A fun golf course. A very natural golf course, and a hard golf course. Our course rating had come back two strokes below par (meaning a scratch golfer would, when playing well, expect to shoot two-under) and I found that tally preposterous. In fairness to our raters, rating numbers mostly have to do with length—they didn't play the course, Shaun said, but they measured it meticulously. If they had teed it up and learned the havoc that hill could wreak on your scorecard, I expected we'd have been rated in the ballpark of Oakmont and Bethpage. Maybe not, but I'd scored better at both than I did today.

Once I learned the bounces and the angles and the must-avoid corners, I might play closer to our rating, and who cared—that we had a rating at all was a victory. This was a very real golf course; not a pitch-and-putt, not a lazy walk through the woods, but a place one could grind, with holes that demanded you study and plot your path. I was worried about the tees—patchy at best—and the composition of our turf—some spots were pure bent grass, others were tightly packed clusters of weed—but Shaun liked the blend with which he was working.

He spoke about it as if it were a reliable old workhorse, grass that hadn't been overfed or spoiled with fertilizer, that showed up every spring and did its job. While other courses burned out their fairways to reseed them with perfection, that seemed anathema to his sensibilities. He was a horticulturalist, after all, and turf that had been finding its own composition for a hundred years was stuff to be cherished, not plowed under.

"We have to remember what we are," he said. "That's the tricky part. Everything here can get better, no doubt about that. But there's something special here we have to be careful with." He talked about the bunkering and how it had been designed not to penalize but to assist, placed to keep your ball in play. I thought back to the bunkers I'd just seen, and though they could use a few tons of new sand, he was right. He spoke about the spirit of the place and what we needed to maintain. "You can feel it when you're here, it's just a nice place to be. It's golf for everybody and we don't want to ruin that."

I'd be wary of my intentions, too, if I were Shaun. My bag tags and headcovers from places that weren't golf for everybody would have given me pause as well. I assured him that I understood. We weren't going to ruin it, not on my watch. But how long that watch would last, neither of us could guess.

Whatever happened to this course and this club this year, we were in it together. We were an unlikely pair of foxhole buddies; Shaun a musician and a skateboarder who'd go bare-chested before wearing a collared polo from some stuffy club in the 'burbs, now joined to a partner who had so many of those that I'd had to initiate a nightclub policy for my closet: no new golf shirts in until another exited. In his spare time, Shaun drew and practiced photography and listened to underground punk bands, and in mine, I plotted my way onto more of those stuffy courses. I knew golf trends; Shaun eschewed them. I embraced golf technology;

Shaun rejected it. Sullivan County felt like something of a golf culmination for me, while for Shaun, it felt like a beginning.

But I used to skateboard, too. If Shaun could get past the crisp collars and the logos, he'd find a kid who used to jostle in the pit in front of obscure indie bands, who wrote poetry and smoked cigarettes with bohemians in coffeehouses and had an earring in college (I can't believe I had an earring in college). I was not very cool anymore—not a Shaun kind of cool—but I still wanted to be, and I envied the courage of nonconformity. While my thirteen-year-old's friends were listening to Taylor Swift, she was buying Frank Sinatra and The Cure on vinyl, and I wanted to believe she got some of that from her old man. I may have been fully consumed by the tucked-shirt world, but I was now tied to a man whose shirttails could not be confined, and I wanted him to see we had more things in common than we didn't, whether that was true or not. I wondered if I was here to save a golf course, or to win the acceptance of someone whose comfort in his own skin I coveted. As a recovering people-pleaser, I was leaning toward the latter.

And when Shaun found himself driving Bill Murray to Tractor Supply the following week, I felt like I'd made some strides in that direction.

MAY 2023

SULLIVAN COUNTY GOLF COMPANY

CHECKING ACCOUNT

Beginning balance: $10,000

Additions: $51,326.76

Subtractions: $37,920.41

Ending balance: $23,406.35

It was rare for Bill to text me out of the blue. Our typical cadence of communication was for me to ask him a question, follow up on that question a week later, then receive a reply the following week that was pithy but vague, and difficult to connect back to the initial inquiry. But this one came out of the blue: *Did you buy a golf course?* Borrowed, I told him, with an option to buy.

I'd known his brother Brian first, the actor from movies and *SNL* and the co-writer of *Caddyshack* whose distinctively scratchy voice inhabited many a popular kids' cartoon. Brian had played a caddie in the film adaptation of my first book, *A Gentleman's Game*, and if you haven't seen it, count yourself among a vast majority of movie watchers. Brian and I kept in touch over the years, and through Brian I'd meet his brother Joel and then Bill, and after taking the Murray brothers and their kin on a golf tour of Ireland, we shared a bond known only to those who have spent ten days together on a bus. I say none of this to name drop, but to get out ahead of the question I get asked more than most others: *How the hell do you know Bill Murray?*

I knew him because of golf, the same way I knew most of the people in my life. Play enough in enough places, a few unexpected faces are bound to wander into your life, and that Bill had remained in mine somehow wasn't that shocking. I wasn't a Hollywood type, which probably made me palatable as a golf partner. I didn't want anything from him. And I was good for a trip or two to Charleston every year, where Bill spent a lot of his time and where I'd gotten to know his guest room (the accidental décor included a framed Cat in the Hat sketch from Dr. Seuss himself, plus a shelf of yarn dolls depicting his roles in Wes Anderson movies, sitting beside a short trophy that happened to be the Mark Twain Prize for American Humor).

We weren't best friends, but we were good friends, and it was an ordinary kind of connection between guys with golf and travel in common. The question that typically followed my ties to Bill was an ask about how he behaved on the golf course—was he hilarious? Wacky? Just an absolute riot? Sometimes, but no more than any golf buddy with a sharp and dry sense of humor. What surprised me most about Bill, and still does, is that the carefree, boyish persona whereby he seemed to walk the world without aim or concern—it belied a man who was keenly aware of everything. A day with Bill could feel accidental in the best way, but if you mistook accidental for absentminded, you didn't know him yet. He noted every detail, every ask, every gesture with the sort of intellectual poise that didn't require him to announce he was doing so. His life might have looked like a series of random interactions, but I never saw him treat a conversation that way. Always present, always invested, and I'd find myself forgetting—not everything was a joke. Misread his sincerity as sarcasm, and you were missing out on a lesson on how to live with curiosity and intent.

And as a golfer, he was sort of a grinder. His golf mattered to him. He didn't take it too seriously—definitely not a club-tosser—but he cared and was there to play well and was usually working a new swing thought. When we traveled, he'd be in the gym early or late, stretching on a foam roller to loosen up for the golf ahead. His wit was quicker than your average partner's, no doubt, but aside from the reactions his presence elicited from staff and other players, hanging out with Bill was typical fun. Then, sometimes, it was less typical.

I wasn't staying in his guest room when I visited Charleston for a speaking engagement in December (my hosts put me up in a hotel) but Bill called me after we'd played that afternoon and said, "Chevy's in town. We should have breakfast with him tomorrow."

I agreed.

He wasn't sure whether it would happen or not—he didn't know Chevy's schedule, who was in town doing a *Christmas Vacation* tour, where they'd screen the movie and do a Q&A—but Chevy had experienced some health issues of late and Bill wanted to catch up with him. As with most things we tried to schedule, he wanted to keep the commitment vague (agenda ambiguity seemed to save him from disappointing folks when conflicts intervened), so he set forth a clear protocol: He'd call me at 7 a.m. if breakfast was on, then head over to pick me up. If I had not heard from him by 7:30, go back to bed. I had a flight home at ten o'clock, so either alternative had an upside, though I was certainly hoping to have to rebook.

My phone rang at 6:30. I hopped out of bed and answered it.

"Where are you?" Bill asked.

"I'm in bed. Where are you?"

"I'm in the lobby. Let's go."

I packed in thirty seconds and piled my golf bag and suitcase into the back of his car, and off we headed to Yeamans Hall where a member had put Chevy up in one of the guesthouses. My head still heavy with sleep, it all felt very unreal. I was on my way to perhaps the rarest of Lowcountry retreats (Yeamans was a hidden golf elite, founded for and by families with familiar American dynasty names) to have breakfast with Bill Murray and Chevy Chase. And I didn't even like breakfast. I don't think I believed it until I was standing at the door of Chevy's cottage, shaking hands with Ty Webb, then walking with him over to a patio table where he asked how I knew Bill and explained that he really didn't play golf but enjoyed watching it.

He sat down and ordered the fruit plate. I'm sure I ordered something but can't recall what; I doubt I touched it as I listened to them trade stories of old friends, some whose names I knew, others I didn't. Chevy was on the mend from a heart scare, feeling better every day, he said, and Bill was glad to hear it. This meal was two old friends showing up for one another, guys who didn't see each other often but, today, were making sure they did. If Bill Murray and Chevy Chase could make time to check in on a friend, I thought, I had no excuse for being so thoughtless about checking in on mine.

How a guy who wrote stories about courses where he didn't belong, and about golf at which he most often failed, had found himself at this table—I sat there, a morning lump, paralyzed by my present circumstance but vaguely aware that my debt to golf was deep.

When they'd finished their breakfasts, Bill looked at his watch. "What time's your flight?"

"Boards in forty minutes. Don't worry, I'll catch the next one."

"No, we can make it." I'd brought nothing to the conversation that morning, but as I knew Bill had a full day ahead of him, I at least offered a reason to conclude our breakfast.

As we cruised for the Charleston airport at a speed that only felt reasonable for it being pursued by the foot of Bill Murray, I was sure our efforts were for naught, and that was fine. But when his tire hit the curb of the no-loading zone, we had a few minutes to spare. The traffic cop noticed the driver and approved our unattended parking with a nod, and Bill left the engine running, grabbed my golf travel bag out of the back of the car, dragged it inside, and tossed it up against the check-in desk with the vigor of the last man in a bucket brigade.

"Would you mind helping my friend here?" he said, flashing a smile. "He's running late and needs to get home to his family."

The agent grinned and said of course, and within a couple hours I was back in Philadelphia with a story for Allyson about her husband who usually skipped breakfast but didn't skip this one.

It was lucky timing, but tragic weather. Bill was staying at his home in Westchester for a few days, checking out his son's new restaurant in the city; my course wasn't far away, and he said he'd like to come see it.

I had not yet begun to compile a list of investors should we arrive at a point where we wanted to buy Sullivan County at year's end (I had barely figured out the cash register), not until Bill visited, at least. When he asked if the course was in an economic opportunity zone, I didn't push him on his intentions, even if they did hint at hope for a second century of Liberty golf. I just confirmed that it was and invited him to visit us. Then I started making that list. It was a short list, with one name on it.

So on the coldest, dampest, foggiest of May mornings, he arrived in Liberty with two of his sons, and since my own Sullivan County adventure had started at the New Munson Diner, I took him and the boys there first. I'd gotten to know Jackson and Cooper, both in their twenties, during our Ireland trip, and they were rare young men. Modest, polite, and smart, they didn't own an ounce of the entitlement one might expect from the scions of a movie star. Bill arrived in shorts and a T-shirt, and I wished I'd warned him that it was always at least ten degrees cooler up here. Then I wished I'd taken him somewhere else for breakfast. In a glass case by the hostess stand, an Ernie McCracken rose-encased bowling ball was on display, a nod to the Munson name that tied the diner to Bill's movie *Kingpin*. I'd made a rule never to ask him about his movies—I didn't want to be that guy doing lines from *Caddyshack* because I'd spotted Bill Murray—and I feared he'd think I was being clever by bringing him here. He saw the ball and just nodded. It was early and everybody needed coffee, so the ball went unmentioned, and we moved to a table in the back, turning heads at each booth we passed.

I was pretty sure our waitress wasn't expecting to serve egg whites to Bill Murray that morning, but she played it cool, calling us "hon" as she did everybody else and not bothering him for an autograph, though he'd have certainly obliged. Bill didn't always enjoy being interrupted by fans who wanted him to be funny, take a picture, give us a line from *Groundhog Day*, but he was excessively deferential to staff—servers, cooks, caddies. He tipped with abandon and wouldn't hesitate to jump behind the counter and lend a hand.

Liberty was a small town, and by the time we got to the course, Jimmy told me he'd already gotten three calls that Bill had been spotted in our vicinity. I'd asked Shaun to caddie for Bill as we didn't have caddies and I didn't want to subject the Murrays to our carts. Bill was something of a movie hero to Shaun (to whom wasn't he?), and he was thrilled at this new gig. But Bill and his boys arrived at a golf course that looked like it had been sucked into the outset of Armageddon. The wind was whipping, and the sky was an unnatural shade of orange, casting an ominous neon haze across the property. Forest fires in Canada had covered us with strange clouds for a week, and today's were the strangest yet.

Bill stepped out of the car and shivered. He had a winter vest in the trunk, but there was no way he was going to enjoy anything about our golf if he attempted it in drawstring shorts, and I needed him to enjoy himself. I asked Shaun where the closest place was to buy a pair of pants. Liberty had no mall, no TJ Maxx, no purveyor of men's finery. "Honestly," he said, "probably Tractor Supply."

Bill was usually up for a detour. I'd come to know him as a wide-eyed traveler, looking out for curiosities and ready to pull over if he spotted the unexpected (on one of our golf trips down south, we'd spent two off-itinerary hours in a fruitcake factory). I expected a visit to a place called Tractor Supply would pique his interest, and I was right. He gave Shaun the keys—Bill certainly didn't know the way—and off they both went in Bill's Volkswagen Jetta circa 1993. (He was kind of a car guy, so I guessed it was the only ride his boys had left him in New York.)

I lit the logs in our modest firepit by the first tee, where Jackson, Cooper, and I tried to keep our hands warm while we waited for them to return. When they did, Bill emerged from the passenger seat not in a pair of golf-ready slacks, but in baggy brown overalls with the tag still stuck to the back. Shaun reported, "I was trying to show him around the jeans and pants but he saw those and fell in love. He put them on in the store and started walking around. The salesgirl had to chase him with the scanner to get the price tag."

I gave Bill and the boys a quick tour inside—we'd cleaned up the dining room, and I figured he'd appreciate the authenticity and age of the place. He did, but the golf course itself wasn't love at first sight. He couldn't have been comfortable in overalls and a puffer vest, and just as my golf ball had, his suffered the inexorable fate of a first time around Sullivan County. He liked the view from up on three and took pictures of one of the stumps our recent tree spend had left behind. The tree removal crew's machines had left heavy tracks through the fairway, but for ten grand they ripped out a dozen dying sycamores in two days, improving the hole immeasurably. We couldn't afford stump removal, however, so their bottoms littered our edges like old cigarette butts jammed into an ashtray. The one Bill admired wasn't so much cut as ripped from the ground, leaving a shredded chunk of wood that, with time, would look like some sort of natural art installation.

Shaun filled Bill's ears with course history and angles of attack, but I feared he wasn't hearing it. I knew the look of a golfer who was playing for the parking lot, and soon enough we were there. He did stop for a picture with his boys on the Sullican Bridge, and posting it on social media scored us a few dozen more members. He also handed Shaun a handful of bills, you know, for the effort. It would be poor taste to say how many, but suffice it to say, I told Shaun he should retire his caddie bib now. Nine holes for that money and a round with Bill Murray—he'd summited the caddie mountaintop on his first loop. Overall, a good day for Sullivan County, and a memory Shaun wouldn't forget. But as Bill graciously declined lunch at the gas station and made a quick exit, I feared he'd forget about our muddy, smoky golf course soon enough. And as I headed for my own car to crank up the heat and warm my hands (forget the pro shop; it was colder than the course), I would not have blamed him one bit.

The girls didn't care for it, but as far as I was concerned, these digs would do.

It was tough finding a rental for the season, which was good news for the Catskills but bad news if your wife and daughters were expecting a restored mountain chateau with shiplap and tall windows with long mountain views.

Sims was kind enough to settle me into one of his rentals that was going to be vacant for the summer. The house had been in his family for decades; his father had grown up there and his grandfather had built the place by hand, a nice midcentury modern on a street corner in Livingston Manor, twelve minutes from the course and close to a downtown I wished for Liberty. Manor (as the locals called it) had a gourmet food shop and breakfast spots and an ice cream parlor, and directly behind our home was the brewery from which I'd ordered the club's new beers. Forget the gas station: it boasted a good barbecue place with outdoor seating, and more picnic benches down the street at a crowded pizza restaurant called the Kaatskeller where, if you didn't grab a table by seven, they were going to be sold out of dough. But our rental house had only one air conditioner (in the master, thankfully) and the second half of May had been hot for Sullivan County, so when they visited for Memorial Day weekend, thirteen-year-old Maggie and ten-year-old Caroline were stuck sleeping on foreign beds in a sweatbox where, for some reason, the word FEAR was painted on the closet door in red. I'm not sure they slept at all, actually, and I made a note to ask Sims about the guest bedroom décor.

I'd been living in Manor for three weeks when they traveled north to join me for the holiday, and much had changed in a short time. A flag displaying our new logo waved large beside the porch opposite the pro shop, and in that shop we had things to sell: those new beers and some local beef jerky, a supply of Snickers and energy bars that I'd deftly sourced from an exclusive purveyor called Amazon. Our logo was stamped onto Yeti bottles and coffee mugs, and we even had proper Sullivan County hats that visitors collected by the stack. We were shipping dozens of hats to golfing pilots (there are plenty, apparently) who appreciated the propeller theme, and thanks to a revamped website with an online checkout where one could purchase our logo on forged ballmakers and a bespoke headcover featuring Otto's flight and the flag of Denmark, we opened an unexpected stream of revenue. The time and cost of processing and packing and mailing the orders (I was learning the cruel minus of credit card fees) probably drank too much from that stream, but I wasn't fretting over margins. We were just happy that people cared, and the more Sullivan County logos out in the world, the better.

I'd been posting pictures of our golf course on social media, careful to trim out our bumper crop of dandelions that had consumed the closing holes. If you liked yellow fairways, ours shone bright in the afternoon sun. Our dull bed knives were powerless against their stems, merely pushing them over so they could stand tall again the next morning.

With images of our course popping up on golfers' phones, our story was trickling out and people wanted to help. Holderness & Bourne was an apparel brand accustomed to high-end pro shops, but they liked our rural golf mission and offered a deal where we could sell their products without carrying inventory we couldn't afford. I bought a small display where we hung some sample tops and hoodies and attached a QR code where visitors could order that hoodie and have it shipped to their home, each piece embroidered one at a time.

In a small effort to signal lifted standards, I printed that QR code on a sheet of SCGC logo paper and placed it in a picture frame from Target. I did the same with all our notices to golfers: *Please, no outside beverages* and *Please be prepared to repair divots and pitch marks and rake bunkers* (such notes would have previously been written in pencil and taped to the bar where they'd serve as coasters for the Men's League). Little attention was given to either notice, but the effort at least signaled improvement. I felt like a golf culture missionary knocking on doors; few doors opened, but I was happy enough to be doing golf's work.

There was little I could do about our golf carts, but I sent our rental sets (leather sacks stuffed with twenty unmatched clubs of unspecific purpose) to the grave they'd long been seeking. I replaced them with a half-dozen of my own used sets, bags and clubs I'd been saving out of sentimentality. It was a tough parting—I'd been a hoarder of former clubs, even if they'd only seen a few months' worth of use—but sacrificing them to the hands of tourists was proof that my golf priorities had realigned. I didn't let my own kids touch my sticks, and here I was, now prostituting them on the rental market and watching them go out the door on the shoulders of first-timers who weren't ready for Mizuno blades and a Scotty Cameron putter and last season's driver from Titleist with an extra stiff shaft that was worth more than the golf cart in which it was now riding.

The clubs came back dirty and bludgeoned and protruding from the wrong slots—they looked forsaken and weary, their headcovers disappearing over the course of their ordeal (the putter covers never stood a chance). My beloved 917 three-wood returned from its very first outing in two pieces, a guilty-looking man in cut-off jeans apologizing for having hit a root in the woods. Why he was swinging a three-wood in the forest, I didn't ask, but at a course for vacationers and nongolfers who saw a sign and a chance to kill a few hours, the rental sets moved. At $10 a pop, they were a revenue leader with a price worth the pain.

Our counter had been crowded with free tourism booklets and old golf magazines. With one impatient sweep I dumped them all in the trash, replacing them with copies of The Golfer's Journal. I put out a bowl of free tees. I bought golf pencils with our name on them, and I put out a sign that told golfers they needed to check in at the pro shop before playing (seems obvious, but for the longtime denizens, it was a novel detour). I banned the sale of used balls and started selling Titleists and Pinnacles. I wasn't trying to install country club practices or revel in rule-making, but the old ways were failed ways and we needed to prove to our golfers that this was a place about which they should care. Small changes, but by the end of May we looked like we cared. And my guys did.

So far Jimmy was right about not needing an alarm clock. He showed up for his morning shift early and had the carts lined up before 8 a.m. I coached him on their presentation—hose them off, park them straight, add a scorecard and pencil to each one—and he liked every new idea I offered, as if I were importing insights from golf's major leagues.

With no golf pro on staff, Shaun worked out a weekly shop schedule that would rotate between three staff, with Sunday afternoons our only blank spot that Shaun and I would take turns covering. Gary had been working the shop the last few seasons alongside Keith, who had apparently taken a turn for the worse, confirming he would not be returning to the course anytime soon. The Irishman who had lived upstairs remained a mystery to me, and I hoped for his health and the chance to meet him someday and hear what he thought of our small but earnest improvements.

None of us working at Sullivan County were Sullivan County natives, which wasn't unusual for the Catskills, where city couples came to retire or buy their summer getaway, but Gary came from farther afield than most. He'd grown up in Washington State, where his dad worked the shipyard and loved golf so much, he helped talk the mayor of Bremerton into building Gold Mountain, now one of the finest municipal golf facilities in the country. Gary caddied and played music in Seattle funk bands, then in 1976 bought a bus ticket and landed in New York City with few prospects and a saxophone. He caught on as a chauffeur and learned to program computers, which landed him jobs on various data desks at Wall Street firms. He played piano and sax in city troupes in the evenings, then retired up to nearby White Lake where his wife had fond memories of visiting as a child.

They still kept a co-op apartment in Manhattan but Gary spent his summers here. He wore glasses and dressed in tucked polos and a baseball cap—no fancy logos, but he looked the part of a Catskills course employee, and he played golf as well. (It was useful when your staff could take advantage of free golf; only being able to offer a $16/hour wage necessitated some perks.) Gary was mild-mannered and organized with a relaxed nature that hinted at a life spent making smooth notes in jazz clubs. He managed the mail and swept out the shop and kept a written list of daily questions for me: *How much are we charging for the logo balls? What do you want to do about the broken toilet paper roll? Are we honoring these Groupons?* He seemed handy with the point-of-sale system and knew how to input our prices (something Jimmy and I avoided), and when he wasn't busy tidying up, could be found pushing his fingers into the tablet's screen, studying the data and mastering its checkout minutiae.

At least that's what John said he was doing. "Gary's in there staring at the machine again," he'd tell me when he arrived for his afternoon shift. John was a buddy of Keith's and a Sullivan County regular who lived in the neighborhood across from the clubhouse, where the street names— Par Road, Eagle Drive, Fairway Avenue—gave credence to the legend that the club once owned that land and had planned a second nine. He'd taken over some shifts to help Keith out around the club last year and would now be the third full-time member of our three-man shop squad. They weren't PGA certified or qualified to give lessons; they'd never run an outing or bought shirts from a vendor or sat down with a golf committee, and that was fine. We didn't have any of those, and their job would entail taking money, moving carts, and pointing golfers in the right direction. A little Catskills hospitality wouldn't hurt, and they all seemed capable of making sure our visitors would consider coming back. More importantly, Gary, Jimmy, and John all seemed to be invested in our success. They weren't here for the paycheck, certainly. They played golf and loved our little place and wanted us to keep opening its doors each morning.

John was just shy of six feet, heavyset with a pronounced limp. He dressed in long gym shorts and baggy T-shirts, and what he lacked in agility he made up for in old Brooklyn authenticity. He was thoroughly Italian and had detoured to the Catskills as a young man, distancing himself from the lure of a Cosa Nostra future. The branches of his bloodline mingled with those of the Genovese family, and while some of his relatives pursued that path, John sought gentler careers elsewhere. And he seemed to seek them all—stockbroker, real estate agent, counselor, truck driver (he'd somehow learned to drive a tractor trailer on the streets of Brooklyn, a training ground that saw him pass his driver test on the first shot), and now pro shop assistant. He knew where the bodies were buried up here—literally—since quiet Catskills winter had made these mountains a notorious Mafia dumping ground. He knew everyone in town, too. He was well tied in with the Liberty locals and the Monday Night regulars and would be a valuable ear for local opinion. Along with Staten Island Jimmy, he was a welcome touch of authentic New York for visitors from afar, with a ball-busting sense of humor that would hopefully put guests at ease. And he wasn't a bad cook, either. Hot dog ban be damned; he was embarrassed that all we could offer hungry golfers was a Snickers bar, so we procured a cheap grill from the hardware store on which he would whip up sausages and peppers on the weekends, free with your greens fee. While I wondered how well he would mesh with loquacious Jimmy and cerebral Gary, he showed up early for his shifts and hung around late. He treated our place like his home—they all did—which was more than I could have hoped for when I started worrying about how we were going to staff our shop.

Three shop guys, plus Shaun and his assistant and a few seasonal hands on the grounds, some of whom would trade hours for free golf—payroll restraint had been achieved, with too few names to bother setting up direct deposits. These guys wanted Friday checks anyway, so the entirety of our business affairs at Sullivan County Golf Club was contained in one unorganized red folder that the bank had given me when I opened our account. I'd pull it out of my backpack at the end of the week, check the spelling of last names, and write out a handful of sums. No spreadsheets consulted, no file cabinet opened, no software applied; I feared for my accountant and the mess I'd send him when someone had to figure out payroll and unemployment and disability taxes, but those were headaches for another day. More important was getting to know the guys I was paying, and there remained a lone figure out there who I knew only by the clippings he left in his wake.

When Shaun described his assistant to me ("He doesn't say a lot; he rocks out to Korn and pounds Monster energy drinks while he mows"), I envisioned a headbanger mowing crooked lines across the course, a bearded man in black bouncing atop his Toro, hopped up on caffeine and death metal as golfers kept a wide berth and played through.

Chris did have a beard, but he wore headphones on his Ventrac and I couldn't confirm whether or not Korn was his taste. Energy drinks certainly were, and he was rarely without a can and a cloud from his vape stick. I noted our shared interest in nicotine alternatives, but that wasn't all I had in common with a man who, if not for a place like Sullivan County Golf Club, I would never have been lucky enough to call a colleague.

Shaun had told me his assistant was sober, too, and though that didn't make us three sober musketeers come to save a golf course, it did seem a positive omen. Since *Caddyshack*'s Carl Spackler wasn't an imprecise depiction of some of the assistant greenskeepers I'd known, having one who showed up on time and put his energy into the job instead of a load only buoyed our chances. And Chris did more than that. He was quiet and reserved and didn't interact with the golfers; he didn't play golf, either. He just showed up and did every job you could throw his way, at a golf course that offered myriad opportunities for a fixer.

Roof leaking? Call Chris. Replace a tire on the triplex? Ask Chris. Chop down that sign by the entrance, put up the new one, empty the trash cans out on the course? He did the stuff Shaun and I weren't even thinking about, and his mom got in on the act as well.

For the first month, I had no idea who she was. A woman seemed to appear out of nowhere, planting greenery around the pro shop and hanging flowerpots in the breezeway and returning at odd hours with a watering can to ensure they were blooming. A fairy gardening godmother, I figured, and I didn't ask any questions. When I watched Chris get in her car one afternoon I put the pieces together—she was his mom and they lived together here in Liberty where he'd gone to the high school down the street. He grew up without a dad around but his wasn't a sob story childhood. His mom had a good job managing properties, and he'd ridden horses most of his life and briefly pursued a career in the equestrian medical world. Of course I didn't get any of this backstory from Chris, at least not initially. It was mostly one-word conversations during the first months: *Need anything? Nope. Everything good? Yup.* But when I kept showing up early to mow fairways, Chris seemed to accept this blow-in from Philadelphia. At least he accepted that I wasn't going anywhere and perhaps appreciated that I was willing to get my hands dirty, if not as dirty as his.

Chris wore tank tops and baggy shorts on cold mornings; his beard touched the top of his chest, and he was thin, as if he might be subsisting entirely on those energy drinks (he might have; Shaun and I enjoyed raiding the Snickers stash, but I don't think I ever saw Chris actually eat). He had no connection to golf, and I couldn't tell if he enjoyed the job, but he never stopped working. He seemed a bit wounded in some inscrutable way, but if you could get him to talk or laugh or even complain about something, it was a good feeling, at least for an interloper from Philadelphia.

He eventually started coming up to the pro shop after his shift to listen to me and John or Jimmy or Shaun shoot the afternoon shit. These were my favorite hours at Sullivan, when we were a team bonded by aching muscles and shared grievances and course gossip: carts driving in all the wrong places, the neighbor kid with the four-wheeler, the guy who didn't understand why *both* golfers had to pay a cart fee if they were riding in the same cart ("The guy thought he was leasing the fucking thing").

I'd spent most of my working life at a desk, alone, unable to write with even a radio playing; I'd missed out on the reward of looking a co-worker in the eye and knowing you'd each put in the time. My friend-ships were mostly built upon shared rounds of golf, and if my time up here gave me nothing else, it gave me the quiet joy of shared effort, a few simple minutes of us, not them. We the useful and permanent pieces. It was like I'd been provided a backstage pass to a world of sincerity and kinship known only to those who punched the clock beside you, and even if I sometimes felt like a pretender in that setting, there were plenty of times—the sore, sunburnt times—when I didn't.

Over the course of those early afternoons, I learned how Chris had done a few semesters at a SUNY before giving up on veterinary medicine, and how some old injuries got him hooked on pills that landed him on probation. He'd hustled jobs in construction and roofing before being asked to come out and mow fairways a few years prior to Shaun's arrival. I think he liked the solitary nature of the job; nobody to bother him, and at that time, almost no golfers to get in his way. He'd been off the pain pills for six years by the time I showed up, and he was the youngest-looking addict I'd ever met. Guys who'd been hooked seemed to age five years for every year they used, so I was floored when Chris told me he was thirty-seven—I'd had him pegged for twenty-eight, even with a much older man's beard (so as not to confuse him with the Chris from whom I was borrowing the course, we'll call him Bearded Chris from here). Maybe it was his dressing for the beach that made him look younger (even in July, Catskills morn-ings started in the 50s). I should have known from his skills with a wrench and hammer that he'd lived more life than I was guessing. Whenever my tractor stalled or the reels stopped turning, give Bearded Chris ten minutes on Google and he'd have it broken down and put back together, slicing rough for another week until he'd need to find an assembly manual on the internet again.

Since we couldn't afford a mechanic (I didn't even know that was a full-time golf club position, not until Shaun told me we couldn't afford a mechanic), we were lucky that neither Shaun nor Bearded Chris was afraid to take apart an engine. Or maybe necessity emboldened such endeavors. Either way, I had the hardest-working greens crew in golf—the smallest, too (the latter reality required the former). I knew what Shaun got out of it; this was his home course, where he played and hoped his daughter would play, and we were partners in the promises we'd made to Sullivan County's members and owners. Now that I was signing paychecks, I felt the pressure of making sure those checks cleared, and I imagined Shaun was feeling that same heat, plus more. Some guy had moved from Philadelphia to New York because Shaun believed this place could work. I'd come of my own volition and would never blame him should we fall on our faces, but as someone who was in the whim business, I knew the weight that came with wrestling your best and worst ideas to life.

When it came to Bearded Chris, I wasn't sure what inspired him to work as hard as he did, or what drove him to show up at all. Even in Sullivan County's quiet job market, a smart guy with good hands was valuable, and that thing that pushed me and Shaun—the possibility of a special place to play golf—had no purchase for someone who didn't swing a club.

And then I put in more hours on the fairways. I learned how to cut cups and handle the greens mower. I figured out how to hotwire the fairway unit, and I got used to arriving before sunrise. And soon I understood the things Chris got from a golf course that even the most well-seasoned golfer might never understand.

For sunrise golfers, it spoils shoes and turns socks to sponges, but for a greenskeeper, the dew is a gift.

First car in the parking lot—even before those players, the ones who make you wonder whether they sleep at all—and it's still midnight dark. July with a chill coming off the mountain, and you need a hoodie and boots and heavy pants. Today you're wearing gloves and plant your tall cup of gas station coffee into the drink holder on your mower, then climb up into the seat and feel the springs give under your weight. Turn the key—it clicks and coughs until the engine kicks out some clouds, the smell of burnt oil that says you're on the clock. You pull around the corner to the pump and fill up with fresh gas, making sure you've parked on a level spot. Nothing worse than your tank tilted sideways to give you a bad reading, meaning you won't get through two holes without having to haul back in for more.

Plug in your earbuds, or don't. The other guys like to listen to podcasts or music while they cut, but you don't mind the noise of the engine, and you don't want to get too lost in the work. Cutting fairways comes with options and a bit of artistry, so you give it your full attention.

Your favorite part of the work is the drive out—today you're mowing six through nine, and with the mower kicked into cruising gear, there's a feeling that the place belongs to you, that you're cutting your own yard, the baddest ass on the block with fifty acres to tend and a machine that could shred your neighbor's electric-push-thing into shrapnel. And since you don't really hear the engine anymore, it all feels calm and quiet. Deer are nibbling the rough and barely lift their heads to notice you. The woodchuck scrambles for cover under a bridge. This was their place for the last several hours, but as you bounce across hills and hollows, you're announcing that the caretakers are back to take their turn.

Start with seven and work your way back—it's long and you're tempted to cut back-and-forth parallel lines (easier to see your last pass that way), but you did that last week and you've been told to keep the grass guessing. Better cut if you switch up your approach. Today you go for a middle stripe and a figure eight; got to nail that center stripe, though, or you'll end up looping back with your blades up—wasted gas, wasted time. You hold steady, but not too steady. It's like painting, you think, if you were a painter—hold on too hard, you'll get shaky and your wheels will wander.

Eyes ahead, soft hands, you look back and see a straight dark strip down the length of the fairway, and you know this hole is going to go well.

Some mowers drop foam from the end of their reels to show where they've already cut, but on your course's budget, you're grateful for the dew. It shows your lines clear as day—just keep cutting the wet stuff until it's gone. You want to go quickly; not because the golfers are coming, not yet, anyway, but because when the dew burns off, you'll be guessing at your mow lines and you'll cut yards of what you've already hit, circling back to touch your misses. Fairways that shine with water make for great mornings, and that's what you had to remember when your alarm went off at 4 a.m. Get out early or the work gets harder.

You leave seven looking tight—not a single line of dew left—and six goes the same. The sun has reached the treetops and now you're racing to finish up. You'll have to turn the course over to the golfers soon, and though you do this work to make the course look good for them, to make them feel happy about spending their money here, you don't think about them at all while you're on your machine. It's just you and your lines, your blades spitting grass so fine it looks like green dust, golf the farthest thing from your thoughts. You're here to take care of this space because it's yours, at least for a little while, and you want to pull your mower off to the side and take a look and feel like you could not have done it any better.

Funny, you think—do golfers ever feel that way out here? That they couldn't have done it any better? Probably not, and you glimpse some back on the tee box, and it's time to finish up and go, and though it feels a shame to turn over this grass to their carts and their divots, this field where you're attuned to every blade and bump and wet patch, you're fine to loan it to them for a little while, until the dew and the deer return.

Our pro shop was a general store meets a haberdashery crossed with a curiosities boutique. Nearly a century of golf and hospitality miscellanea had piled up behind our counter and in our closets, and you never knew what you'd find sitting on the bar when you arrived each morning. No pro in our pro shop, but if you were looking for a stuffed black crow or a towering pile of old chafing dishes, we had you covered.

On Memorial Day, I was greeted by three cucumbers on the counter, beside the new basket of free tees (John wanted to sell them in Ziploc bags; I emptied them out and decreed we could afford some country club touches). Jimmy's garden was popping, and he'd brought some of his bounty to share. I sifted through the mail—most of it for Keith, which went in a pile we expected someone would someday collect, plus some notes from advertisers looking to sell us space. Those would go in the trash can, which I couldn't find, so they went back on the bar. What I could find was a half-empty bottle of chocolate milk, two left-behind range finders, a book of golf quotes, a tool for stamping your initials into a golf ball circa the mid-1980s, a walking cane, and a lost-and-found bin from which no sweater or headcover had ever escaped.

The things we did need—pens, trash cans, scissors, paper towels, tape—had a brief shelf life before they disappeared, swept away on the Catskills breeze. My pro shop trio had three different systems for putting things away, plus distinct methods for leaving me notes with updates and questions. Gary wrote his on a legal pad that John could never find, so John wrote his on leftover pads of restaurant tickets, which Jimmy would put in the register beneath the cash tray. When I did find my messages, they weren't always actionable. John's handwriting had a hieroglyphic quality (after three days, not even he could decipher what he meant to ask), and they typically conveyed something that had already been answered via daily briefings that began with, "Hey, Tom . . ."

Hey, Tom . . . I heard it in my sleep, on my mower, in the cold clubhouse bathroom where I sat for ten minutes at a time, pants still up around my waist, my Sullivan County sanctuary, until I noticed the toilet paper roll sitting on the floor and recalled our most regular *Hey, Tom,* the one about what to do regarding the busted toilet paper holder. It had become a point of steady contention and pro shop debate. Who's going to go buy one? Where? What kind? And where to install it in a bathroom stall that was barely shoulder width? I considered assembling a committee to study the toilet paper holder predicament and return with a short list of recommendations, but it seemed easier to just leave it on the ground until somebody complained.

I had arrived in April on my white steed, armed with Windex and paper towels and a long checklist of ways to improve our golf club. It was only May and I wasn't beaten yet, but I recalled a saying my friend Gramma Billy liked to share: It isn't the mountain that wears you down, but the pebble in your shoe (when she heard I had a golf course, she sent me a plunger and toilet bowl brush as a congratulatory joke, but they were a godsend and put into immediate and regular use). From a macro perspective, we were making it—memberships were up, and carts were lurching their way across the course at a regular clip. It was the small details that broke my heart. The windows that wouldn't close. The crumbling cart paths. The fat mountain flies that filled every corner of the shop. Dandelions hardier than jungle vines. The door that needed a new lock because three generations of Liberty residents had keys that could open it. *Hey, Tom, what about the broken benches? The trash in the carts? The moat of weeds around the clubhouse?* Thanks to Shaun and Bearded Chris, the course was improving by the day, and maybe that's why I enjoyed the mowing so much. Out on the course, it was easy to remember what business we were in—the trimmed grass business. I had to learn to divide my attention between two different causes: things to chase, and things to shrug, and if the grass was looking good, the crooked state of the windows had to be met with the latter. For now.

I did find Gary's legal pad and there were three new member

signups listed, which was happy news, and I added the names to a spreadsheet that would remind me to order engraved bag tags for our latest joiners, labels that had done little to curb the locals' curiosity about when they would be receiving their annual golf cards in the mail. *Hey, Tom, are there going to be passes this year?* I explained that no, you no longer needed to show a card every time you wanted to play. My shop guys weren't bouncers. There was consternation over this change in protocol; why pay a joining fee if you weren't going to get a pass? I assured them that we had a list of their names inside, and we would know our members by sight when they arrived. Such an arrangement seemed a little far-fetched in their minds, while a club where the staff didn't recognize its members seemed a little far-fetched in mine. The tug-of-war tugged on.

Gary was busy running more carts out of the shed. We were almost crowded with holiday visitors, and the parking lot was good and full (*Hey, Tom, are we going to paint lines in the parking lot? Nobody knows where to park*). When I saw the green carts chugging their way toward the first tee, I knew we were doing a steady business in $20 greens fees, plus $15 for those carts. We kept the old green ones in the back, machines abandoned by deceased or relocated members. *Hey, Tom, are you going to get any new golf carts? We sure could use them.* Carts wasn't quite a shrug—I'd made some calls—but given prices in the post-Covid golf market, a pair of used buggies would empty our new bank account with one swipe.

I checked in a few more players and thanked them for coming up to visit while Gary managed the traffic outside. There were two black cases behind the counter that could have been holding anything—sales samples? Explosives? More cucumbers? I didn't give them a second thought as I watched Allyson's car pull up outside, and as my two redheaded daughters piled out, for a moment I felt like I was running the damn

Augusta National. It was rough and rural and frayed around the edges, but my family had a golf course, and for a moment that felt like the coolest thing in the world.

They had visited earlier that weekend when we took the girls for a spin on golf carts at sunset (*Hey, Tom, these carts are terrible*—even Allyson had taken to Sullivan County parlance), climbing up to the third fairway so we could take in our small and temporary kingdom together. Allyson was nearly moved to tears.

"I can't believe how beautiful it is," she said as she looked over a valley ribboned with fairways, the clubhouse a small yellow block in the distance. On this first family weekend in the Catskills, I felt her falling in love with life up here. Quiet, green, unspoiled, and, for us, at least, a world where the distracting hustle of home—calendars, drop-offs, pickups, dishes, and dinners—seemed very far away.

She hadn't fallen for my rental. Modern art mixed with a collection of wobbly cobalt bottles didn't fit her pastoral vision, but the area certainly did. She and the girls would go down to a pastry shop in Livingston Manor for breakfast, walking home along a wide river into which men with tall waders were stepping. They passed the outdoor BBQ whose ribs had become my evening staple, not far from the Dette Flies shop that was a pilgrimage site for fly fishermen and, along with our golf course, was one of the two longest operating businesses in the county. Then they came up to the course where Allyson got to see her husband riding a tall mower, and I imagined that she found something appealing about her soft-handed spouse engaged in manual labor. When I hopped off in my boots and greasy work pants, she eyed me like a stranger, but one she would like to know. Funny, we paid someone to mow our lawn at home, and here I was leaving the house while she slept to go cut grass. She was accustomed to golf making me do strange things, but conspicuous work was probably not one of them.

I showed them around our one-room shop and gave the girls candy bars and water bottles from the fridge—you don't really feel like an owner until you just take something without paying for it—and we chipped balls together over on the little wedge range Shaun had built in front of the maintenance shed, an eighty-yard space with short flags that offered visitors a miniature warmup. It seemed a good idea until one group of kids didn't understand what "wedge range" meant so they pulled out drivers and launched every one of the balls I'd brought from my shag bag into the woods and down to the eighth tee, clear across the first fairway. We'd recovered enough to fill a small basket, but the girls were more interested in the horseshoe pit we'd just cleared off, and the swing Shaun had hung from the tree beside the cart barn. With a few small touches, our place had become thoroughly charming.

The clubhouse was getting touched up as well. Men on ladders were scraping off decades of peeling paint, after Sims and Chris found a guy on their crew who would paint the whole place white for six grand, a spend that Allyson agreed was worth it. Old yellow wasn't working, and fresh paint, even if it couldn't hide every lump and crack, was the clearest signal we could send that somebody here cared. Our course sat on busy Route 52, and better than any billboard, a change in color would tell folks there was something new in a town where new had been keeping its distance.

Allyson had been studying the clubhouse weeds and flowerbeds with a close eye. She'd entertained a career change that would take her from the world of M&A to the world of selling plants (briefly entertained, praise be, or we'd likely be moving the four of us into Keith's old apartment), and she was a master of populating housefront planters. She appreciated what Bearded Chris's mom had already done—planted some flowers and hung baskets in the breezeway, added American flags to both in the spirit of the holiday—but two green thumbs is one too many for any clubhouse. I saw plans spinning in her eyes, and she arrived the morning of Memorial Day with an SUV loaded for work: gloves, pronged tools, barrel planters, and a host of potted plants none of us could name. Shaun chopped down our dead old shrubs and whacked down the weeds for her, and by afternoon, our walkways were guarded by wide wooden buckets that looked like they'd come from a competition. They blended nicely with Chris's mom's work, and a horticultural peace reigned over a clubhouse that had not looked so welcoming in years.

Caroline, our ten-year-old, had spent the day down by the creek, spotting turtles and fish and hopping from rock to rock. Maggie was thirteen, and I'd worried about what she might find interesting at a golf course. She wasn't the rock-hopping type, and having just reached her teens, wasn't doing much these days without headphones covering her ears. But she had found something she liked—the tree over by the cart shed, its branches casting long shade and its base the perfect angle for resting one's back.

She'd asked me a few months ago about what she should pick for her summer reading (along with a prescribed list, they got to choose one novel), and I told her that at her age I loved reading S. E. Hinton. I tore through all of her books when I was twelve, and I recommended she begin with *The Outsiders,* which I considered the perfect teenage novel and would be more fun than highlighting motifs in *Lord of the Flies.* I'd even given her my old paperback copy from the 1980s; I still kept it on the bookshelf in my office, a reminder of a first love and the young joys of reading. Maggie took it with a maybe look in her eyes and put it on a pile somewhere in her room. I didn't see it again until I looked over and saw her sitting beneath the tree, turning its pages in the shade. For all the places and shots and people golf had shown me, none had or would ever match the beauty of watching my daughter get lost in a book I loved, seated quietly along the edge of Sullivan County Golf Club.

•　　•　　•

Later that afternoon, I spotted Phil making his way across the first fair-way. He was in his eighties and visited almost every afternoon, not to play, but to chip and putt. He walked with a wedge in one hand, a put-ter in the other, holding both by the clubhead, using them as two canes while he moved slowly across the property. (Watching him, I recalled the Sunday sticks I'd seen in Scotland, where golf on the sabbath was once banned so gentlemen strolled with hickory golf clubs masquerading as canes, sneaking in a few blasphemous swings on the seventh day.) Phil had paid for a membership, but I don't think he played the course very much, if ever. Instead, he got out of his car and moved around the grass near the clubhouse, dropping balls and putting on our shaggy saucer of a putting green, then wandering over to nine for some chipping. We usu-ally waved hello to each other but today I met him in the middle of the first as he followed one of his pitches.

Phil's family had played here for two generations, and his last name showed up on the club championship board several times. He wasn't the ace in his family, he said—that was his brother, though Phil had been a fine player in his day. He was retired from his work as a guard at the nearby prison, and these days his legs wouldn't let him do much more than chip and putt. He wore a flannel jacket and baseball cap and walked with a bend in his back. He told me he was glad the course hadn't closed.

"I like what you're doing here," he said. "It's good for me because I just need two hours. Somewhere to go for two hours, to get me out of the house. I keep a pretty good schedule and coming here fits right into my day. Get some walking in, and that's all I need. I go home and have dinner and I'm all set."

I thanked him for being here and told him he was always welcome at our course. He nodded and kept shuffling his way toward the ninth, where he'd putt around an empty green for another thirty minutes, then probably be on his way.

Two hours. So much time and money spent on improving and elevating; so much worry lent to whether the carts were clean or the pro shop stocked, when some people just wanted a place to be. In fretting over what real golfers—or what I once thought were real golfers—would think of the patchy state of our tee boxes, I'd forgotten the primary purpose of a spot like Sullivan County: a place to spend some in-between, where you left believing that time had been well spent. Being a decent place to kill a couple hours wasn't going to keep our doors open or the cash drawer full, but for every golfer who'd complain about the greens there was probably one like Phil who was just happy to be somewhere, and I needed to remember that even on our bad days, we were still a very good somewhere.

We soon learned what those cases in the shop were carrying. A foursome of local members finished up around three o'clock, came inside and retrieved trumpets from those black boxes, and walked back out toward the first tee where our flagpole waved the Stars and Stripes. It was a flag with particular significance for our crew—it had been presented to Shaun's wife, Marisol, originally from a small town in central Mexico, when she became a US citizen just last year. She was immensely proud of having passed her tests and earning her oath to the United States, and we all felt that pride and that gratitude as two men in golf shirts stood before it and played taps promptly at 3 p.m., just as it was being played all around the country that Memorial Day at precisely the same time.

About a dozen of us stood there and listened. I held Caroline around her shoulders, and Maggie came over from where she had been reading and joined us. Shaun looked on quietly. We didn't applaud, but we all thanked our musician friends for doing that, and for doing it here.

I can easily recall my best Christmases and Thanksgivings, but I can't remember how I've spent most of my Memorial Days, other than calling my dad to check in and thank him for serving. I did that, and then I looked around and watched my wife admire her plantings while my daughter leaned back into a tree and read, and guys who had just played our golf course sat in a circle of Adirondacks, the chairs Jimmy had put together with only a handful of leftover screws. The men laughed and smiled and drank Budweiser on this sunny start to summer, and while I wasn't sure what it was meant to look like, I recognized it instantly as it appeared before my eyes in Liberty, New York: a real-life American dream.

PART 2

SAND IN THE BOXES

MIDDLETOWN ORANGE COUNTY INDEPENDENT,

THURSDAY, AUGUST 1, 1929

TRACTOR SETS LIBERTY GOLF CLUB ON FIRE

Backfire in Basement Starts Blaze Which Causes
Loss of More Than $10,000
EMPLOYEE IN HOSPITAL WITH BURNS
ABOUT FACE
Clubs and Playing Equipment of Nearly Every
Member Destroyed by Flames

LIBERTY—The temporary clubhouse of the Sullivan County Golf club was wrecked by fire which started shortly after eight o'clock Tuesday morning. Frank Hyzer, twenty-five, a club employee was burned about the face and arms. Loss is estimated at $10,000.

Fellow employees who were just outside the building took Hyzer to the Liberty hospital, where he was given first aid treatment. It was reported at noon that his injuries were not serious, though he was still at the hospital.

According to Fire Chief Walter Travis, who directed the fighting of the fire for nearly two hours, a gasoline tractor owned by the club and housed in the basement, exploded while Hyzer was trying to start it. J. R. Gerow, president of the club, said that according to information he had been able to gain, the blaze originated in a backfire.

The building was a mile west of the village. It was used as a temporary clubhouse, pending erection of a modern building, Mr. Gerow said. It had been converted from a large barn and an addition had been added for club-rooms.

The loss includes clubs and other playing equipment of nearly every member of the club. The membership was made up largely of Liberty residents.

JUNE 2023

SULLIVAN COUNTY GOLF COMPANY

CHECKING ACCOUNT

Beginning balance: $23,406.35

Additions: $56,737.26

Subtractions: $42,576.82

Ending balance: $37,566.79

There's a world when you're there and a world when you're away; the place you see as a golf course operator, and the one you hear about later.

When your feet are on the property, you watch the cars pulling in, the golfers unloading their clubs and changing their shoes, ready to tap a credit card in the pro shop. You hear the mowers humming in the distance and can guess by how many carts are left in the barn whether you'll make enough that day to cover payroll. But when I was back home in Philadelphia or tromping around Ireland on assignment for *The Golfer's Journal*, I ran a golf course through a gossamer blindfold, checking our daily sales via website and guessing at why the register was or wasn't ringing. The point-of-sale site was better than any weather app for Liberty—I knew whether it had rained by how much or little we'd banked (on a good day, we'd see over $1,000 in cart and greens fees, plus more in memberships and merchandise; on a rainy day, often less than $100). And since nobody ever reached out to report happy news, each time my phone buzzed, the cold veil of complaint descended like a quick, dark night. Grievance, it seemed, was a dish best served by text.

The Monday Men's League was upset that we weren't offering dollar hot dogs anymore; a woman was irate about her expired Groupon not being honored (just honor it, I replied); Bearded Chris's mower was busted again and would need new parts, which would require my credit card, which I turned over while begging restraint (cashflow was surprisingly positive, but we had three months to make money; summer visitor golf would cease but payroll would push well into the fall). The members—well, one member—was moaning to other members about the one-tee-marker system and the lack of ball washers on the course. "They're amenities people pay for," I was told, and I had never considered that perspective, and wondered if the golfers at Oakmont and Shinnecock thought they were being cheated by not having a green post where they could plunge their Maxflis (washers had gone out of fashion elsewhere so Shaun and I had left them in the shed, but maybe tastes were different here).

And Teddy was driving John nuts. A local who played alone, Teddy returned his cart in the dark every night (which kept John on the clock until past 8 p.m.) without so much as a thank-you, after John had watched him cruise past our NO CARTS signs and park on the collars of the greens. Other members still refused to stop parking their trucks on the grass beside number one, even though the pavement held plenty of space and I'd purchased a sign asking them to keep their tires off the turf we were trying to grow. We needed new flags for our pins. The roof was leaking, and a kid was driving his four-wheeler through the woods at night and doing donuts on our second fairway. At least Shaun had a solution for that.

He was in line getting a bagel at the halfway house/corner gas station, waiting behind two Liberty policemen. "Excuse me," he interrupted, and inquired as to whether the police still did those scared-straight house calls for kids who were causing trouble. Turns out they did and were happy to help. Shaun knew in which driveway the kid parked his four-wheeler, and within a week, the tire tracks in the bunkers were gone.

Not every crisis arrived via message. Some needed to be witnessed to be believed. After a week spent scouring Ireland for a handful of obscure links I had missed while writing my Ireland book (there were five, and I played them in four days at the cost of one new tire and a dozen Titleists), I drove straight from the airport up to Sullivan County where my jet lag met the worry on Jimmy's face. I could count on Jimmy for bright energy and a regular refrain about this being the best job he ever had: "Are you kidding me? Getting paid to be at a golf course? I should be paying you." I always told him I'd accept those terms and he'd laugh it off. But not today.

"Hey, Tom, there's a problem in the ladies' room," he explained. "It rained all week and I came in this morning and the roof caved in."

I felt my hand reach for my phone—rote instinct—to see if Ireland had called and might take me back. "The roof caved in?"

"Yeah. It's gone. Here, I'll show you."

I had noticed that the ceiling panels in the women's were stained with brown circles, but whatever created them was far down our to-fix list. Perhaps we should have bumped it up, because in a moment Jimmy and I were looking at a small, tiled room that looked as if someone had lit a stick of dynamite, tossed it in the toilet, and sealed the door. Piles of cracked foam ceiling filled the stalls, and the floors were sopping wet. We peered up into the rafters through which we could see cracks of sunlight.

"That's not good," I said.

"No. This ain't good at all."

We only had one functional women's room that was serving double duty as the ladies' locker room when guests asked where they might change. The plumbing still seemed to be in working order, so if we could clean it up and if it didn't rain this week, we might buy ourselves a few days to get it fixed. In the meantime, we could offer an open-top rest-room facility to our female visitors, which at five-star golf clubs in Hawaii were a popular amenity that people took pictures of and shared on Instagram. Maybe a breeze in our bathroom would bring the crowds.

A quick call to Sims and Chris had a two-man crew on the way; our contract required them to address any clubhouse failures during my tenure, and this collapse certainly qualified. Two Mexican laborers showed up and made quick work of the mess, and the next day they were back to add some drywall. I spoke just enough Spanish to slow them down and confuse their progress; they seemed to think the studs were too rotted to hold sheetrock and that the entire roof needed replacing. I nodded along, then I either told them to try to do their best, or that they should eat more cheese. Chris sent over a roofing guy the following day who patched the shingles as well as he could, and we crossed our fingers for a dry forecast in the ladies' room.

We had a sunny week—good for mowing, good for golf, good for dandelion propagation—and I'd gotten into a steady rhythm with my Toro. I rarely forgot to engage the reels anymore (which meant I'd be cruising up and down the fairway without clipping a single blade) and I was learning the wet spots to avoid. Numbers eight and nine by the clubhouse were a minefield of muddy pits, even on the driest days. The holes up on the hill shed their water easily, and the other holes tilted toward the creek did the same, but the fairways on eight and nine leaned toward nothing, so not only were they a massive mow, but their clay base grew a patchwork of turf that befuddled my blades, from stretches of lush bent grass to soggy runs of weed and rot. I spent a full morning working both of them, double-cutting in opposite directions. It took a full tank of gas, but once you'd lifted the grass upright on your first run, watching your reels spit clean clippings on your second pass was immensely satisfying.

I parked by the shop and dragged stiff legs off my machine and limped inside for our noontime huddle. We didn't have set meetings, but midday was a good time to find Shaun and Bearded Chris wrapping up their morning work and discussing plans for the afternoon. And this afternoon we'd have a decision to make for which no amount of golf or greenskeeping could have prepared any of us to play arbiter.

The mood was contentious when I walked through the door. Shaun was shaking his head and John was holding out his hands with a look of stubborn dissent.

"What else are we going to do?" John asked. "We've got to close the hole."

"There is no way we are losing a hole because a turtle decided to climb into a bunker and lay eggs," Shaun said.

I felt my feet doing an about-face—surely there was a fairway some-where that needed cutting—but I'd been spotted, and today's crisis was rendered in full detail. John was out playing last evening and had watched a mother snapping turtle lay and bury her eggs in the bunker on number five—the only bunker on that hole, which happened to front the green and saw plenty of action.

"We can't close the hole," Shaun explained.

"Well, what are we going to do about it? We can't have people in there smashing up her eggs," John replied.

"A fox is going to get the eggs before any golfers," Shaun said. "I've got two men and eighty acres of golf course. I can't be spending my time nursing turtle eggs." To which John replied, "I'm not asking you to sit on them and read them bedtime stories."

"Hold on, let me look at something," I said, and consulted Google for a solution. It turned out that the common snapping turtle was the only unprotected native turtle species in New York.

"That's good," Shaun said. "Then we let nature take its course." Shaun was as devoted an outdoorsman as one could find in the Catskills, but the prospect of adding zoologist to an unwieldy workload could turn anyone into a turtle cynic.

"It says here they could take ninety days to hatch," I said, suddenly an expert on reptilian incubation.

"Three months. That's the whole season," said Shaun.

"Well, we have to do something," John said.

To this point, I had been a reluctant authoritarian. I was the de facto boss—I signed the checks every Friday—but rules made me uneasy, at least when it came to staff and their responsibilities. I deferred to Shaun on all things grass-related (even if I did nudge him a few times a week about spraying the dandelions, which he was reluctant to do until he was sure he wasn't going to kill most of our weed-dense fairways in the process), and the pro shop guys had their own methods in place that didn't need my nitpicking. I'd put up signs, but they were anonymous commands, hardly confrontational and rarely obeyed. More than someone to mow fairways and order hats, Sullivan County needed a strong golf leader, and I was going to have to put myself in the uncomfortable position of not just hoping everyone would read my mind and catch on. I'd have to be a boss and take some shit. I'd carefully arranged my life to take as little shit as possible, but when I'd signed that contract to take control of a failing golf course that required a complete overhaul in standards and practices, all those pages could have been summed up in one line above my signature, an oath known to club pros and managers the golf world over: *I hereby agree to be the asshole.*

Decreeing that the fifth hole would remain open but that the bunker would be roped off and deemed ground-under-repair until we could celebrate the birth of our baby snappers was easy enough. I put John in charge of the egg-monitoring committee and told him I'd pay for a cake when the shells showed up empty. Then I decided to hang around for the afternoon, so that I might have a talk with Teddy.

He showed up at 5 p.m. on the dot. "Like clockwork," John said under his breath as we watched through the pro shop windows. He had long hair and played in a saggy T-shirt; John said he was a musician or artist or something, retired up here from the city. He didn't talk much or interact with the local members, just played alone seven nights a week and made a strong case for nixing the $250 seasonal cart pass—he'd crushed us on that deal. He loaded his bag on a cart and headed directly to the first tee, driving straight past the sign that asked golfers to leave their carts in the lot while teeing off one, rather than driving over the lawn in front of the clubhouse.

"Son of a bitch. Every time," John said as we logged his malfeasance. "You want me to say something?"

"Let him go," I said. "I want to watch him a little bit. Before I talk to him."

John grinned and nodded in silent approval.

I hopped in a cart and tailed Teddy from a distance. I watched him pull off the path beside the first green and find himself a nice damp spot to leave his cart. I watched his wheels try the walking path up the hill on two instead of taking the tiny detour back to the asphalt, then waited for him to circle back down the hill to five where, as I expected, he'd eschew the path and splash his way down our dampest fairway. When he squeezed his cart between the turtle bunker and the green and parked it nearly in the fringe, I'd seen enough and swooped in like Sullivan County SWAT.

I slammed my brakes as he putted out, setting the tone for our conversation with some skidding gravel. He looked up, unbothered, walked to his cart, and dropped his putter in his bag.

"How you doing, Teddy?" I said.

"Fine. Greens are a little slow."

"Yeah, well, you know we're trying to improve the course, right?"

"I can see that," he said.

"So we need you to follow the cart rules and go where the signs point you. There's no reason for you to park your cart there. The signs in the shop ask you to stay thirty yards away from the greens."

He didn't look at me, just sat in his cart, thinking for a moment. Then he turned to me and with a flat tone of condescension, he said, "I didn't know cart parking was such a concern." The subtext was blaring—*Why don't you fix up the tees and greens and cart paths and leave me the hell alone?*

"Everything here is my concern," I said. "We're trying to grow grass and improve the course. For everyone. You're driving your cart all over the place and that isn't helping."

He sat there quietly, waiting for me to say something else. I eventually did.

"If you can't follow the cart rules, you're not going to have riding privileges anymore."

He tilted his head, still not looking at me. "Well, I already paid for a cart pass."

"And I'll prorate it for the carts you've taken and give you a refund," I said, both of us knowing that tally would be zero.

No response. He scratched some numbers onto his scorecard, waiting for me to leave him alone.

"So are we good?" I said.

He put his pencil back in its holder and looked my way. "Yeah."

"Great," I said. "Enjoy your round." My wheels went in one direction, and his went in the other.

I arrived back at the shop like a general returned from the front lines, my troops (or troop) eyeing me with new battleground respect. "I talked to him," I said to John, and for a moment we shared a quiet understanding that didn't feel too unlike how he might have once handled things back in Brooklyn, where problems were settled with a consenting nod.

A few days later, I felt a bossman's righteous indignation bubbling again, but it came void of satisfaction this time. Self-sure resentment was an emotional favorite of mine, but not when it was directed toward a couple of teenagers; their fear was too real and too easily summoned.

When the high school golf coach asked Shaun if the team could use our course, it was an easy yes—there were few better perks to having your own course than to lend it out to the local team. Anyone on the team could play the course for free, as long as they behaved and respected the property. And they had to walk. When I heard that one of the seniors was renting a cart at practice, I asked John to ban the team from taking carts, no matter that one had a driver's license or that we could use the cart fees. It felt like a sin against golf to see a seventeen-year-old tooling around the fairways while his teammates schlepped their bags up and down our hills.

I was standing outside our freshly painted pro shop, reviewing a series of *Hey, Tom*s with John, when I spotted something strange through the pines, over on the ninth green about thirty paces away. Two high school boys and a girl without clubs, which wasn't particularly unusual up here—maybe the social menu was shorter in Liberty, but it was common for nongolfing girlfriends to spectate while their beaus showed off, launching prodigious drives deep into our woods. But one of these kids was taking full practice swings on the green with a wedge. Showing off for his lady, he reached back and fired his ball back down the fairway, ripping a pelt of turf that I watched flutter across the green. I heard some laughter and an *oh shit*, and he turned around with a guilty glance to see if anyone had been watching, and clocked that I had.

I imagine that someday my children will do something that will send my feet marching toward them without thought, fueled solely by rageful disapproval, but they hadn't yet, so this was my first time feeling as if my body were being piloted by instinctual parental fury. Before I reached the young man, he was already apologizing and chasing the divot. *Sorry,*

sorry, didn't mean to do that, but I felt myself raise one summoning finger and intone my deepest bass, "Come over here. Now."

The young man studied his shoes while I explained to him that playing here was a privilege, that we were giving him and his friends free golf to which they were not entitled, and that if I ever witnessed anything like that again, that arrangement would end not just for him, but for the entire team. I felt myself aging as I spoke the words. I was quoting from the bible of half-bald disciplinarians and posing as a person who enjoyed scribbling out detentions. I wasn't, and as I watched his lower lip quiver, I hated making a kid feel afraid. Legions of old golf men had singed fear into me at his age—*don't step in my line, don't rattle my clubs, don't speak unless spoken to*—and though I'd never wanted to mimic them, their admonishments had taught me golf's unwritten rules, one tongue-lashing at a time.

The offender just nodded, but his friend had looked me in the eye the entire time and apologized for both of them. He wore glasses and had a tan complexion and sported the shadow of a teenage mustache. They knew better, he said, and it would never happen again. I headed back to the shop and they made their way to their car, but in a few minutes, the friend was standing in our doorway looking like he had something to say.

John and I looked in his direction. "What's up?" I said in a new, friendlier tone, trying to prove I wasn't the course ogre.

"I just wanted to apologize again," he said. "I really appreciate you letting us play here. And we're really glad you opened the course this year."

"Thank you," I said. "Things happen. I know it won't happen again."

"It won't," he said, and he approached and stuck out his hand. "My name's Henry. Thanks again."

"Good to meet you, Henry," I said, shaking his hand. "I'm Tom."

"I know. The course is in really good shape. It's cool what you're doing up here."

If he was just buttering me up, it was a wise and well-executed decision. "How old are you?"

"Sixteen. Going into my junior year," he said.

"How's the team looking?" I asked.

"Not bad. I'm playing a lot now. I'm pretty hooked."

"He's here every day," John said. "Probably the best player they got."

"That's what this place is here for," I said. "Keep grinding, Henry. Just replace those divots."

"I will," he said. "Good to meet you. Thanks again," and he turned and walked toward his friend and girlfriend waiting by their car.

We watched them leave, and I turned to John. "We should hire that kid."

"Way ahead of you," he said. "I've been talking to him about it already."

The following week, we had a new member of our staff responsible for cleaning and running carts, and for hustling after whatever John needed. John's back was a mess; he had no feeling in his right leg and walked with an uncomfortable lurch. Some help shuttling carts back to the barn at close would be welcome, and we needed some young blood on our crew. If I could put some money in the pocket of a Liberty kid who was falling in love with golf, it would be the best money I'd spend all year.

Henry worked three days a week after school and Saturdays as well. Sundays were off-limits as he spent the whole day in church with his family. When school ended, he played eighteen every day before his afternoon shift, and I laughed when I caught him heading out to play in a too-tight tank top. He probably didn't weigh 150 pounds but with his girlfriend joining him in a cart, why not show off his tan.

I approached and exchanged a high-five. "Now tell me you've got another shirt."

He sheepishly confessed that he didn't. "Not your fault," I said. "But for future reference, tank tops on a golf course aren't a great look. Not even here."

He apologized and I told him not to worry about it. "Do me a favor and go into the shop and get a shirt."

"That's okay, I can run home and get one," he said.

"No, you're staff, you get a shirt," I told him. "Pick whatever you want. Take one of the samples and tell Gary it's on my account." I didn't have an account—or maybe everything in the shop was on my account since I'd purchased our stock. Either way, it sounded more official than telling him to go take something.

"That's awesome," he said, surprised. "I love this job." And a few minutes later he was driving off in a new Holderness & Bourne polo, inviting his girlfriend to feel the material of its sleeve.

The next week he showed up at the shop looking for me. Unusual, as he was John's right-hand man, but when I came out from the back, he was holding a new wedge in his hands as if presenting me with rare treasure.

"I bought this with my first paycheck," he said as I held its grip and waggled it at the air.

"She's a beauty," I said.

"It's a Vokey. It wasn't cheap!" he said. "But I needed it. My short game has been terrible. I'm pretty psyched to try it."

I handed it back to him and he studied the clubhead, eyeing its every curve and groove with genuine pride. He'd been a good hire. He hustled and met visitors at their cars and asked if they needed any help. He arrived early and stayed late. And he was learning something, it seemed, because he was spending his money on the right things.

I recalled the first club I ever bought with my caddie money—a Ping Zing putter—and I envied Henry, because I knew there would be few purchases in his life that he would love more than that golf club, that it would forever stick in the bright, romantic corners of his mind.

I can still see the bronze shine of that old putter. I can still feel its weight in my hands.

•   •   •

Cart day was a good day.

I hadn't told anyone that I'd been working back channels with friends at a cart company and that I'd found six used specimens for a reasonable one-season lease. I was still cash-cautious as I knew that one rainy week could sap our reserves, but the weekly take had been promising, and after writing out Friday checks for the guys, there was money left in the register to deposit at the bank in town (I'd forget that cash was still king up here, and would leave piles of $20 bills sitting in the drawer all week, in a room where a gust of wind could unlock the door). New hole signage had run me about $8,000, but clean metal plates advertising our new logo and yardages were a well-received investment (only half the old signs were still standing, and as a course that catered to first-timers, we needed obvious directionals). Another six grand for six carts for the rest of the season was a deal I couldn't pass up, and when they showed up one morning in our parking lot, they were oohed and aahed by members and staff alike. If there was any doubt as to whether our efforts had won over the locals, this small batch of smooth-running conveyances had us expecting a downtown parade in our honor.

I found Jimmy and Gary walking slow circles around them, admiring them like hot rods at an auction.

"These are really nice, Tom," Jimmy said. "The members are going to go nuts."

By modern cart standards, they weren't really nice—the pedals were worn and the seats cracked from years of bouncing backsides—but contrasted with the convoy they'd be parked beside, they were a sight to behold. And best of all, each came with two buckets on either side for holding sand to repair divots. Some of the boxes were even topped up with fresh dirt. We'd had no divot-fixers to give our golfers, and a now-busy course was showing the wear. I was ready to order sand and spend my evenings driving the fairways with a bucket and shovel, repairing our most conspicuous rips, but it now looked like I might not need to.

Shaun whistled his approval at the carts, seeming to have forgotten that yesterday he'd been attacked by a swarm of hornets while unstacking a pile of sawhorses behind his shed (he tore off his shirt and ran into the pro shop, and to give you a sense of our dress code, Gary's first guess was that he was a golfer showing up to play). The same day the carts appeared, so did the first-aid kit that John had been asking for, newly procured from the drugstore down the street.

Hats were selling in the shop, and people were snapping the QR code that led them to an online shop for Sullivan County shirts. We had Titleists to sell and even two custom golf bags with our propeller logo that both went in a week. Headcovers and ball markers were now in stock, and I couldn't order Snickers and Clif bars fast enough. And after a dozen years of striking out at halfway houses with thirty-seven varieties of booze-in-a-can, I indulged myself by stocking the pro shop refrigerator with Hal's New York Seltzer and Heineken Zero, treats you'll only find at a golf course run by a recovering alcoholic.

Even the Orthodox Jewish community was showing up at Sullivan County Golf Club—sometimes to play, and sometimes to inquire about the price of a cart. Earlier that week I'd answered the shop phone, always enjoying the chance to attempt a sincere *Sullivan County Golf Club, Tom speaking* (I couldn't do it without the dumb grin of someone imitating a legitimate businessperson), when the voice on the end of the line spoke with a heavy Slavic accent, inquiring, "How much to rent the cart?"

Turned shy with confusion, I tossed the phone at Gary. He spoke to the caller with practiced confidence.

"No, the carts aren't for rent. They're for paying golfers only," he said.

"Uh-huh . . . yeah, you have to be playing golf to take a cart . . . Okay, bye." He hung up and explained that he got the same question every week from different voices; they were calling from the Hasidic communities who saw carts riding around the hills and thought we were a sort of amusement park. The golf part always ended the conversation; they either didn't play or didn't know what golf was. I'd felt sympathy for many of them, walking the hot summer roads in heavy black dress, but never having heard of golf elicited a grief for such insulated lives.

"What if we just rent them a cart for fifty bucks for an hour or something?" I suggested.

"I wish, but we can't. They don't know what a golf course is. They'll be driving over greens and into bunkers. They'll get killed out there."

He had a point, and he explained how a few years ago Keith had grown tired of sending home a threesome of ultra-Orthodox who showed up every week, looking to purchase a cart ride. He told them again and again—no clubs, no cart, until they called his bluff one morning. "We have golf clubs! We are here to play!" they told him, and even though he was confident they didn't know how to use them, a deal was a deal. He took their money and handed them keys and off they went.

An hour later, a member of the pre-Shaun greens crew showed up in the shop, asking who let out that Hasidic threesome.

"I did," Keith said. "They said they had clubs, so I let them play."

"They're playing with toy golf clubs," the greenskeeper explained. "The little plastic ones from the dollar store."

There were moments when Sullivan County Golf Club felt like any good golf place out there, when the fairways were running and the greens were smooth and you crested a ridge with clubs on your back and found a bright flag waving at the bottom of a hill. Imagining three men in scriptural garb playing said course with tiny purple golf clubs was not one of those moments.

Not all the Orthodox were golf novices. Some older men would show up and rent clubs and leave their long coats in the car, roll up their sleeves, and swing away with yarmulkes pinned in place. I'd been born into a golf world where clubs were organized by religion—my dad had joined a Quaker club because they welcomed Catholics, unlike the Protestant outposts around Philadelphia that did not. Jewish clubs had a proud legacy in our section where Jay Sigel grew up playing at Bala Golf Club and would become one of the most celebrated amateurs in golf history. Such divides softened in the 1990s, and soon Jay Sigel was playing out of mighty Aronimink. Jewish clubs all along the East Coast struggled to maintain their identity and membership—much like the resorts of the Catskills, when the next generation was presented with the chance to go anywhere, why limit their options because of their faith? Most of the historically Jewish Philly clubs were sold or forced to rebrand, and some wouldn't have survived if not for a Covid refresh. It was good news–bad news; good that anti-Semitism wasn't dictating member rolls, but sad to see formerly thriving clubs that had been centerpieces of a community become businesses on the brink.

At Sullivan County, the club champions board hiding in the dark side of the clubhouse listed names of all backgrounds; it was an ecumenical heritage worth celebrating and broadening, so I made sure to thank the Orthodox players for their business, asking them to come back soon and bring their friends. It was particularly encouraging when boys from the villages showed up looking to play. The new golfer was always the most important golfer, and if they'd never played before, John would take them down to the wedge range and show them some basics. Then he'd take them into the shop and, seasoned salesman that he was, he'd shepherd along teenagers who were eager to spend. I'd heard other courses in the area weren't as welcoming to the ultra-Orthodox, so they must have appreciated John's hospitality and attention, and they'd leave the shop with not just rental clubs but at least one of every item we stocked—T-shirts, hats, gloves, a dozen Pro V1s each—almost giddy at the loot they had scored. One foursome of Hasidic kids would be our biggest ring of the day, and it did my heart good to see smiling young men with Sullivan County hats propped high on their brows, not quite covering their kippahs. I wouldn't want to be playing behind them, but I doubt any golfers had more fun out there than they did. A break from studying the Torah to go golf and shop must have felt like a stolen summer escape.

I knew the brothers would love the new carts, and even though they no longer possessed the legal documentation required to drive one, they were among our most reliable customers, and I was happy to look the other way. They paid their cart fees, didn't complain, and we always knew when they were arriving and leaving. The taxicab pulling into the parking lot was our clue.

The four Murphys had been playing at Sullivan for decades. Each of them was north of fifty years old—mid-sixties, I'd guess, but mountain life made ages hard to estimate up here. All four of them had lost their driver's licenses from DUIs, and though enough years had passed to get them back, they told me they weren't interested. Not worth the trouble and cost of having a car. Instead, they piled into Liberty's lone taxi minivan each afternoon and headed for the course. They played so often that I ignored it when their carts beelined from the first tee to the fallen fence line beside the gas station, where they'd stock up on thirty-packs of cheaper beer than we were selling inside (at $3 a can, I thought our prices were rather competitive, but I wasn't ready to argue with golfers who had already paid for a cab to get here). After their golf, they were usually good for a few cans of Miller High Life in the shop, unless the taxi was already waiting in the parking lot as they came down nine. We didn't have a ranger, but that minivan was a reliable indicator of precisely where the Murphys were on the golf course.

The morning after cart day, I was pleased to find that half the new carts were already out by the time I'd finished mowing the sixth fairway. I was less pleased to see that their divot repair boxes were gone. They'd been in our possession for less than a day, and we'd already either been robbed or vandalized. I marched toward the shop to find out who had forgotten to lock the barn. I had no idea what anyone would want with boxes of dirt and sand, but this theft cut deep—it seemed confirmation that no, we could not have nice things at Sullivan County, and since it meant we were once again defenseless against divots, the course would suffer, too.

I found Jimmy inside behind the counter, where a fresh row of eggplants was proudly displayed.

"Hey, Tom, you like eggplant? Look at these beauties, fresh from the garden."

I did not like eggplant, not a little bit. "Jimmy," I said, "what the hell happened to the boxes on the new carts?"

"Oh, them things?" he said. "I took them off and put 'em in the barn. They were all just full of dirt."

He wasn't wrong. They were, indeed, all just full of dirt.

If something looked like a small cooler but was full of soil, how would Jimmy or our guests know what to do with it? How would they heed our sign to fix pitch marks if they didn't know what one was? Why would they not park their carts beside a green if grass was grass—drive here, not there—but why? I was ready to blame malicious intent when most of our golf breaches boiled down to the game's customs being just as inscrutable as the swing itself.

I'd cringe when someone dropped their bag on one of our greens instead of the fringe, but had anybody ever told them why that was sinful?

And was it? I weighed plenty more than a sack of clubs and nobody was forcing me to stay on the collar. Statistics proved that of the 25 million golfers in America, occasional public players vastly outnumbered the country club set. We shouldn't assume that people know golf's secret handshakes and unwritten codes. We should only assume that they don't. And we should probably spend less time fretting over them. I should, anyway.

I smiled and shook my head at Jimmy, who had done the absolute right thing. I explained to him that the buckets weren't coolers but were meant to carry dirt for filling divots, and that he should bolt the buckets back on when he had a chance. He was a hard worker who had taken it upon himself to make our new carts look nicer, and I was happy to have an employee who had sought out a job that morning rather than staring at the TV.

A friend who had married a Swedish golfer told me how courses in Scandinavia required players to have a golf license they needed to produce when checking in to play. It proved they'd been instructed on golf practices and etiquette and possessed enough skill to navigate the course in reasonable time. It seemed a handy idea and I understood why it worked in a more bureaucratically inclined Europe, but in the land of liberty—give me golf or give me death—I'd rather see a greens fee than a greens license. I was learning that golf didn't have to always look or play the same way; what a shame it would be if it did. I'd played sand greens in Missouri and mud greens in the Navajo Nation and been entirely satisfied. Golf was larger than sharp-cornered tee boxes and members in Peter Millar, and just because I was running the place didn't mean I had to make it resemble my stock brand of golf. Sullivan County was proving, time and time again, that golf could feel biggest in its smallest places.

The sand buckets were soon back on the carts, and I left that day without touching Jimmy's eggplants (I'm not a vegetable lover, and after once being duped into a big bite of eggplant parmesan that was supposed to be chicken parmesan, I've never forgiven it), but John was happy to take one when he came in for his afternoon shift. He liked talking about his recipes and next month he'd be harvesting mushrooms from the bases of our trees, adding chicken of the woods to his at-home menu. Jimmy gave him the prized eggplant of the bunch, a flawless purple beauty, and in doing so, ignited a controversy and mystery that would hang over Sullivan County Golf Club for the indiscernible entirety of its existence.

After locking up the carts that evening, John hustled home and forgot his eggplant, leaving it on the counter for Jimmy to find the next morning. When John arrived that afternoon, the eggplant he found waiting for him appeared to be different from the one he'd left the previous evening. It seemed slightly smaller, with a few subtle blemishes that had been absent from the pristine vegetable he had picked from Jimmy's lineup. Had there been an eggplant switch? Was Jimmy an eggplant recanter? Had John's callous disregard for Jimmy's gift whereby he abandoned said aubergine overnight inspired a planter's resentment, and caused Jimmy to switch out the choice garden egg for a lesser imitation?

John relayed all this potential eggplant subterfuge to me in a long, conspiratorial text message and hit send—unfortunately for him, he'd placed Jimmy's name in the send field next to mine. As I sat in bed in Livingston Manor trying to piece together the pieces of a mystery, I informed John that, one, I didn't believe Jimmy would do that and, two, his finger fumble meant we would find out soon enough. His return text— OH SHIT!!!—confirmed that an eggplant showdown was coming.

The following morning, Jimmy was chipper as ever. The carts were clean and parked with scorecards in place. The shop was swept out. He asked if I wanted him to refold the T-shirts, and I told him that sounded like a good idea. No mention of any vegetables, purple or otherwise. I messaged John to tell him that I didn't think Jimmy saw the message, but he still approached the shop slowly that afternoon, creeping up to the door and offering Jimmy a cautious hello. Jimmy replied with his customary upbeat welcome, "There he is!" and ran down the list of carts and golfers out on the course.

Truth-seeker that I was and seeking the chance to make John a little more uncomfortable, I asked Jimmy whether he ever received any texts on his phone. It would be good to know, I explained, in case I needed to get in touch with him.

"Never gotten a text in my life," he said, removing his flip phone from his pocket with pride. "No texts on this baby. Works just fine. Don't think they even sell these anymore."

John looked down and shook his head, small wags that suggested I'd be facing swift retribution.

After Jimmy left that day, we convened to break down John's accusations. It seemed far-fetched to me that Jimmy would pull an eggplant swap, but John knew his vegetables; he couldn't be fooled by a counterfeit. Maybe the eggplant's condition had deteriorated over the course of the evening, I suggested, but John stood by his case. I assured him they both probably tasted the same, but John was more interested in knowing whether he was working alongside a colleague who was playing loose and fast with his garden gifts.

The eggplant mystery remains unsolved and perhaps forever will. Jimmy was spared any public accusations (until now, I suppose) and to counter John's unflinching confidence that he'd been bamboozled, I took Jimmy's side in the dispute, assuring John that he'd overestimated either his eyesight or the quality of his pick. But the eggplant seeds of distrust had been planted among my staff, and if we were going to soldier forth and function as one unit, we'd have to pull together, put our heads down, and fall in line behind the boss and agree that eggplant was disgusting anyway.

KINGSTON DAILY FREEMAN, OCTOBER 1, 1926

BIG GOLF TOURNEY ON LIBERTY LINKS

The Sullivan County Golf and Country Club at Liberty is shortly to become the golf mecca of central and eastern New York state for a professional tournament to be held Columbus Day, October 12.

Since early spring, when the course was first reopened, visitors have been flocking to it to try their hand at the place where the crack pros will compete for cash prizes next month.

The Sullivan County Golf and Country Club is located practically in the center of the "Playground of the Metropolis." This course is located on the highest point in Sullivan county and is incidentally the highest course in New York state.

The course, in the belief of those who have played it, will tax the skill of all the contestants. It is a nine hole course laid out amid rolling hills affording abundant natural hazards and calls for accurate tee shots and super-fine second shots, in order that one may keep out of trouble. This fine course has never been played in par and it is hoped that this contest will see someone make it in par.

This course was laid out by McCarthy & Rayner, well known golf experts, and it is a fitting monument to their ability. Mr. Rayner expects to be present and the Yahnundasis Golf Club of Utica, N.Y., will also be represented as well as Cooperstown, N.Y.

Pros from any club in New York state are eligible and also anyone playing professional golf. All entries must be sent to the Sullivan County Chamber of Commerce, Monticello, N.Y. before October 4. The cash prizes are: First prize, $100; second prize $50; third prize, $25.

JULY 2023

SULLIVAN COUNTY GOLF COMPANY

CHECKING ACCOUNT

Beginning balance: $37,566.79

Additions: $77,292.14

Subtractions: $61,345.25

Ending balance: $53,513.68

Of all my life's matches, it's the one that didn't happen that I remember the most. I was heading into my third year of college, and though I'd had success in the junior championship at my dad's club, I'd failed to qualify for the men's club championship since leaving the under-eighteen ranks. But that year I was playing well and passed through qualifying. I'd won my first two matches by the sixteenth hole, landing myself in the club champs final four with a name in my next bracket I believed I could beat.

After the opening weekend when the top-sixteen scorers were inked onto a tournament bracket, the championship format was somewhat malleable. You scheduled your matches on your own time and had to complete them by a certain date, but with July vacations and weekends at the shore, those deadlines were soft, and the championship dragged on for most of the summer. But I was eager to set a date and scratch Bob

Bellingham off the board; good golf was fleeting, and I hurried to get another tee in the ground before it ran away and hid.

I knew Bob was punching above his weight by landing in the semifinals. Maybe he'd caught better players on an off day. He was a slow, methodical golfer with a mechanical move; he was thirty years my senior and last year had won the B flight championship. Bob was now stepping up in class, a golf aspirant whose handicap had plummeted over the last few seasons through daily play and weekly lessons, the sort of player who wanted his spot in the finals so badly that he'd hand you a few holes just from the nerves. I was twenty-one and hitting drives that could upend his gameplan, so I got busy trying to schedule our match for the following week.

With nothing but morning loops on my calendar, I told him I was free any weekday afternoon to play. He offered one excuse after another—appointments and meetings and more appointments—until we were up against that vague Saturday deadline by which we were meant to have anointed a winner. I told Bob I was away that weekend for a wedding and that we'd have to find another time to play, and he said that was too bad and he hoped the pro shop would accept my excuse. Having been the more available member of our twosome, I didn't give it a second thought, and expected our match would take place soon after I returned.

It never did. As was explained to me by my friends in the pro shop (as a caddie working extra hours as a range picker and club cleaner, I had more friends and allies among the staff than the membership), Bob had shown up that Saturday morning asking the pro where I was. He said I wasn't here, of course, and Bob feigned bewilderment that I was missing our match. It was our last day to play, he protested, so he should win by default. The pro told him that it was between me and Bob to report the winner but agreed that our match was meant to be completed by the end of the day. Everybody in the shop saw through his ruse, but when it's a matter for members to decide, any golf pro who's lasted more than two weeks knows to stay out of it.

"Well, I'm here and he's not," Bob said before adding his name to the next line in the bracket, Bob Bellingham now a club championship finalist.

He got waxed in the finals by a friend of mine who I'd beaten in the junior championship a few years prior, and our final would have been a fun rematch, but that was the last time I'd reach the semis of the club championship, and within a couple years I was no longer a member. I never spoke to Bob about his amnesia regarding my whereabouts that day, but the grudge sticks with me (obviously), and I nurture it annually when I come up short in another club championship. A decade after losing without hitting a shot, I'd qualify as a medalist in a club championship elsewhere, then get bounced in the first round by a guy playing in high-tops and a tie-dye hat. A few more years passed before I missed qualifying for a top-eight field by one shot, when on the eighteenth I struck my ball with a practice putting stroke (this was a few months before the rule change that would have saved me a penalty stroke, which only gave the sting a more lasting bite). I'd qualify the next year and lose in extra holes; another season I'd go from two-up to losing on seventeen, and on another I'd drop five of the first six as my focus shifted to concluding the misery on a green close to the clubhouse. I accepted the fact that a club championship lingered beyond my reach, unless I someday joined a club void of scratch golfers. Alas, I was sure such golf clubs didn't exist, until I found myself operating one.

I grappled with misgivings about entering a club championship at a course I was running. Sullivan County hadn't held a championship in three years, and they'd stopped updating the championship board in 2014, where beneath the gold-lettered names a handwritten Post-it note was stuck to the board with a pushpin, listing five years' worth of winners who got pencil instead of paint. If Sullivan County was going to return to its status as a real golf club, it needed real competitions. I was determined to hold a few tournaments this season, at minimum a championship and a member-guest. We were excelling at a relaxed vibe and friendly welcome—bring your dog, no tee sheet, go ahead and go around again—but our golf club needed some grind.

I hung signs for a club championship to be held in early July, and both local and visiting members added their name to the list. I waffled about whether to add mine. My reluctance wasn't born of arrogance—we had some players up here with decades more course knowledge than I possessed, even if I knew none of their handicaps because they hadn't signed up for our GHIN service. It had more to do with resurrecting a tournament and then entering it myself. If I did win, it would be like throwing myself a birthday party, and a championship should be played to celebrate and reward our paying members. I didn't see a lot of upside to throwing my hat in the ring, other than a chance to cast off my decades-long championship curse.

Then I wrote a check for $20,000 that went from our personal savings into the Sullivan County business account, and I decided I was the paying-est member of all.

Don't let the account statements fool you—much of our July take wasn't from tee times and hat sales, but from a bulwark deposit against our spend outpacing our flattening revenue. We'd already made more money than the course had in its previous two years combined, but we'd reached a time in the season when new memberships were going to stall, and we'd hired two part-time helpers for our greens crew—Charlie home for the summer from Virginia Tech, and Mike a high school science teacher on vacation. I'd also continued to make small purchases—a chainsaw for Shaun, a popcorn machine for the shop—and I'd rented a movie screen for an outdoor showing of *Happy Gilmore* that I hoped would lure more locals and families to the course.

I didn't anticipate a popcorn machine from Amazon to occupy most of our collective time over the ensuing weeks, but its arrival was met with work-halting consternation. Who would assemble it? Operate it? Be responsible for acquiring the necessary corn-popping provisions? I'd thrown a curveball at our daily routine of greens-fee-in, golfer-out, and the box sat in the shop for a week, an unwelcome interloper, until someone finally summoned the courage to open it.

Hours of study had made Gary a master of the point-of-sale system, and John was a natural greeter with an eye for business and bottom line, but anything that involved a screwdriver was left to Jimmy, the retired mechanic, so we waited for him to warm up to our addition that he eventually decided needed a thorough bath. "I don't trust these thingamajigs from China," he said when I found him soaking its every piece in the industrial sink in the kitchen, the one with knobs that turned on in either direction but only stopped at one precise position (turning off the water was like guessing the combination for a safe). After a complete disinfecting, Jimmy assembled a bright red box that sat on our counter, ready to spill bags of burnt corn for movie night. It took another week of trial-and-error to produce anything but smoking black kernels, which required the expertise of our greens crew to remedy. I watched as four adult men stood around a small machine forged of cheap aluminum and plastic, crossing our fingers that we had finally achieved the proper ratio of corn-to-oil-to-temperature, and that our calculations for an ideal kernel agitator speed would prove accurate.

"This is like watching four monkeys fuck a football," Jimmy noted, and we agreed.

As golden nuggets of goodness leapt from the basket down into the hold, we cheered and clasped hands and hugged. Sullivan County, it seemed, was ready for its miracles.

Club championship weekend wasn't ten minutes old when I realized why they hadn't held one in years. We were set for a field of eighteen entrants, a mix of resident and nonresident members, and I'd carefully arranged threesomes and one foursome the previous evening, making out official scorecards and writing names in mediocre script on a real-deal Titleist scoresheet that lent earnestness to our competition. Three of those names didn't show up, but one of them who did, Griff, was already complaining about being paired with Frank. "I'm not playing with him. You trying to kill me, putting me with him? No way, not that asshole," Griff said within clear earshot of Frank, who shook his head and quietly walked over to our fuzzy putting green that was the size of a kiddie pool and was seeing an unusual amount of action with fifteen hopefuls warming up.

I knew nothing of our Liberty members' grudges, nor did I know their playing ability, so I'd arranged the groups by a careful generational mix—some old paired with some young, unsure which was more likely to know the rules of golf but hopeful one might. I'd briefed everyone on the practices of tournament golf—keep your competitor's scorecard, putt everything out, and play the ball down, the last of which was met with protesting groans. "What if I'm in the tire rut on three? What if my ball's on a dirt patch?" I explained that unplayable penalty drops were always an option and got busy making up peaceful pairings. Since no-shows had me reshuffling groups anyway, I put Griff in my threesome and asked Frank to tee off in the first group. He kindly obliged.

Not only had Griff shown up angry about his draw, but he'd parked his truck directly beside the PLEASE DON'T PARK ON THE GRASS sign, again, and when it was time for our group to tee off, I decided to unburden my resentment rather than let it stew for eighteen holes.

As he approached the tee with his driver, I said, "Griff, do you have to park your truck on the grass? There are plenty of spots in the parking lot," and I could hear my plan backfiring before the words left my mouth.

"Oh, is this how we're going to start?" he said. He was a large man in his fifties with heavy hands and wide shoulders, an hour-clocking build that seemed to justify the oversized tires on his mud-splattered four-by-four. He was a longtime member who no doubt had his own ideas about everything we were doing, and he shared them generously.

"If I were you, I'd worry more about there being no ball washers and benches on the course. Where are the trash cans?" he said. "We've got one tee marker. Look at this, it's embarrassing. We can't afford two tee markers? It's ridiculous."

I wasn't interested in explaining our tee marker system or trends in on-course accoutrements; I could recognize the people who walked the world looking for a fight, and long ago I'd decided to refrain from enabling them. I decided that I'd just had the longest conversation I would ever have with Griff, and I handed him my scorecard and wished him good luck. Thank God I'd put Dan Yaun in our threesome, who was a kind enough soul to share a cart with anyone. All three of us hit the first fairway, and off we went.

Pretending that I wasn't bubbling with rage wasn't going to work; I tripled the first hole after flubbing two chips and was quickly three-down to two guys who could play. I knew Dan had game; his name was painted on the board in the clubhouse alongside plenty of Yaun siblings and cousins, but Griff had made a stress-free par on our opener. He had an imperfect but powerful, balanced swing, and my mind summoned visions of club championships past. I wondered where a tongue-lashing about tee markers and losing to the golfer who delivered it would rank in my list of big-day failures.

Rather than fake that I wasn't bothered by getting abused for trying to keep this course afloat and spending months away from my family and dropping pieces of our retirement on a place for Griff to play his golf, I played angry instead of playing sad. Sad, self-loathing golf was my default, where I doubted my swing, my ability, my every life choice until all I could feel was a wilting surrender. But angry golf seemed to inspire a focus that wasn't going to let me off so easily; there were thirty-five holes left and not one I couldn't birdie. Shaun had the greens rolling well and putts would fall. When I showed up for a tournament knowing I was unprepared or afraid of the course, I was dead money, but that wasn't the case today. Starting off with a seven would be an amusing prologue to a story I could hear myself telling tomorrow. Bring on the Trump jokes, I thought; I was going to win the club championship at my own golf course without a drop of diffidence or remorse.

We shared three more pars before Griff dumped a ball in the creek on five, then I eagled the par-four sixth with a drive that pulled up two paces short of the cup. I was six shots up after day one, and twelve shots clear when we finished the following day. I had to present myself with the winning trophy—a nice Sullivan County plaque by Squid Designs—that I put back in the shop and sold two weeks later. I'd been waiting for that evidence of a win for decades, but course management had conquered ego, placing our bottom line ahead of pride.

After day one, I had sorted our contestants into three flights. They had produced a diverse collection of numbers—from tallies in the 70s to the 100s—but arranging them into mathematically accessible groups gave everyone something to play for on Sunday. The flight winners were awarded newly arrived Sullivan County Yeti bottles (the Claret Tumblers, we called them), and each posed for a proud photograph for the website—even Griff, who collected a red jug for the low senior golfer when his final score bested Dan's by five. When I announced his name and he stood up to collect his temperature-maintaining trophy, he nearly smiled and said thank you. He left soon after but first pulled me aside and said that he enjoyed playing with me this weekend, and that he thought that we were doing a good job. And as if to prove he meant it, his tires never touched the grass again.

An approving nod from a demanding member could have been the highlight of Club Championship Weekend, but it wasn't. Nor was me winning a piece of wood that Allyson would have quickly placed atop a pile of miscellany in my office. Rather, it was the small joys of hosting real golf on our golf course. We got to toil on holes we rarely took too seriously. We got to see our last-place finisher come off the course with a wide grin, delighted to have traveled up from New Jersey to play in his life's first real tournament. We got to watch local members and golfers from afar crack open beers together and shoot the shit over paper plates of John's sausages, the grill fired up for a special day, even if John had to cook with a plastic fork because we couldn't find a spatula.

A twentysomething from Brooklyn commiserated with a retired steamfitter about the water on five, and Dan Yaun sipped an IPA and talked about how much fun the weekend had been. "I really missed this," he said, "the competition. I'm glad we have it back." I was worried that our modest gathering of wide-ranging talents vying for water bottles wouldn't feel like a sincere golf event, but approval from Dan suggested that we'd pulled something off.

I sat down beside a doctor who had driven up from Pennsylvania on a motorcycle with his clubs strapped across the back, and I listened to him talk about how well Henry swung the club. Henry's name was the first on the sign-up sheet; he came dressed in his best Sullivan County gear and looked both anxious and excited to find his name inked on an official scoresheet that morning. He'd shot two rounds in the '90s but won his flight, and when he took his life's first golf trophy into his hands and looked at it, for a moment there seemed to be little difference between a Claret Jug and his Claret Tumbler.

I had told Shaun that he had to stick around and show his face at the prize presentations, which I knew was an annoyance after arriving at 5 a.m. on a Sunday to prep the course. But this was the only time we were going to have a collection of members on hand for an official outing, and you didn't host a club championship without giving the superintendent his due. After the prizes had been awarded, I asked everyone to thank Shaun who was sitting on the bench over there, who had not only provided a well-conditioned golf course for our championship, but was the only reason any of us were here right now. The crowd put down their beers and gave him a standing ovation, plus a few hoots and hollers. Shaun shook his head, then nodded a humble thank-you.

I didn't stay late most afternoons, especially on Sundays when the supermarket and takeout spots closed early, but I filled up on sausages and hung around the Adirondack chairs until the last golfer left. Shaun's wife, Marisol, showed up around five to pick him up. They shared one car and she'd been out with their daughter, Adah, all day, who was five years old and headed to kindergarten in the fall. I waved hello to Marisol in the driver's seat. She was soft-spoken around the course but sometimes we'd talk about her job doing remote IT for a bank, and she'd get excited explaining the problems she'd solved that week. You could tell by the way she looked after Shaun and the way he doted on her that they were partners in the most genuine way. The hours he worked at the course were the only ones they spent apart, and while I spoke to Allyson on the phone every night, there was a sturdiness to their life that a roamer couldn't help but envy.

I watched as Adah ran out from the other side of their Jeep and bolted up to the patio to hug her dad. She had black hair to her shoulders and shared her mother's brown eyes and tan complexion. Her sneakers looked like she'd had a good day on the trails with Mom, but she wasn't finished with her fun yet. She wanted to go for a ride down to the trout stream, so Shaun and his family squeezed into a cart and off they went, down the first fairway until they were over the hill and out of sight. There were no golfers out there to interrupt them, and she'd have free run of the rocks and the water, a girl with a backyard the size of a golf course.

TIMES HERALD-RECORD, AUGUST 12, 1946

GOLF CLUB SECTION SOLD FOR HOUSING

Tract at Liberty to Be Used for Subdivision

LIBERTY—Plans for development of a residential area here near the golf course of the Sullivan County Golf and Country Club were announced today by Nial Sherwood, civil engineer here, after his purchase of a tract of land from the club for $14,400.

The new development, to be known as Fairways—taking its name from its proximity to the links—is already being mapped for streets and building lots. It is one of two parcels offered for public sale by the golf club under sealed proposals. There was but one other bid, of $5,000, offered by Morris Rattner, realtor here.

The property, which lies across the road from the golf course, is near the intersections of the Liberty-White Sulphur Springs road and one leading to the station of the New York Ontario Western Railway Company. It embraces area once the site of many old farms of the earlier days of Liberty.

Lots in the new development will be sold, subject to some restrictions, and no business places will be permitted within the area.

AUGUST 2023

SULLIVAN COUNTY GOLF COMPANY
CHECKING ACCOUNT

Beginning balance: $53,513.68

Additions: $30,166.57

Subtractions: $42,433.48

Ending balance: $41,246.77

I took my dad golfing on his ninetieth birthday. It was late May and I came home from the Catskills for a few days to celebrate with him. My brothers and sisters wanted to mark the occasion with a proper party, but as my dad told us, most of his friends were dead. He just wanted to golf and go out to dinner, so I set up a tee time at Rolling Green where he'd played for over forty-five years and where he'd sent me for my first lesson and first loop.

I couldn't begin to tally the rounds we'd shared together. In my summers from high school through college, we played three or four days a week—he'd meet me after I caddied and we'd go around in three hours, then have dinner in the grill, living more like summer roommates than father and son, with Mom spending the season at our little place down the shore. He would head down to be with her on the weekends, but in those eight years of summer evenings spent sharing a house, Dad and I cooked zero meals in our kitchen. Mom would come home in September to find the dishwasher hadn't been run since she left. We got to know the grill menu at Rolling Green pretty well.

A lot of those rounds were quiet affairs where I was grinding for birdies or was grumpy about my score; I remember hardly any of them, really, the way you lose track of one unremarkable day after another, but I knew a time was coming when I'd recall them all as a gift. The sound of our gas cart motoring across an empty course at twilight, the light shortening as we approached September, baseball on the grill room TV as we searched the specials list and complained about the Phillies' pitching. Golf on Dad's ninetieth wasn't a grinding affair and I was careful to notice its every detail and commit them to memory; how many sons were fortunate enough to say they celebrated this sort of day with their fathers? I wasn't going to waste it on testing new swing thoughts, though Dad seemed to have a few and was more focused on the state of our Nassau than any birthday nostalgia.

He'd invited a couple friends, Dennis and Tim, to make a foursome. Both were many years his junior, and I loved how Dad still found golf buddies who were closer to my age than his. Maybe that was the key to reaching ninety—surround yourself with people who weren't just waiting for their tenure to expire. And thank God he did, because on the list of things you want your parents to live long enough to witness— weddings, kids, graduations—in our golf family, a son with his own course ranked high in that inventory.

In August Dad planned an overnight visit with Dennis and Tim and they booked rooms down the street at Sims's place, the Arnold, where they had their own house across the street from the restaurant and tavern. It was an ideal setup, though something about a ninety-year-old going on a golf getaway with far younger guys had me slightly concerned. Would they keep him out too late? Would they want to play more holes than he could handle? Could he get up the stairs in that house? The good thing about Dad, and about being ninety, was that he didn't really give a shit what they wanted to do. When he was done, he was done—whether it was a meal or a party, when Dad stood up, he was ready to go. It drove my mom nuts, a trait I'd inherited as well (and one he'd inherited from my grandfather, who was famous for standing up with a minute left in the fourth quarter) and practiced with impatient frequency. It drove Allyson nuts, too.

I was more excited for him to take the drive than reach the golf course, because it would take him through his hometown of Scranton and wind him through hills sure to loosen memories of his youth. I expected he'd arrive with a catalog of rekindled stories, and he did, even some I'd never heard before. He told John in the shop how he'd grown up an hour down the road and spent the early part of his life at St. Michael's School for Boys, not far from the Catskills. It was an orphanage, though he wasn't an orphan. My grandfather had lost his job and all his money in the market crash that brought on the Great Depression, so the Wharton-trained accountant took a job running a country orphanage where Dad and his brother, Jack, learned to work a farm alongside boys waiting for a family. Last he'd heard the school had been sold, but maybe they'd take a side trip there on the way home tomorrow, he said, and see what had become of it.

I set their group up in carts and pointed them on their way while I finished up my morning fairways. I wanted to join Dad for golf, but after all the swings he'd seen me make, it would be more novel for him to see his son atop a mower, his globe-trotting golfer now showing up at a golf course in work pants and boots. Plus, I wanted to prove this wasn't another one of my how-much-can-I-play-in-a-season boondoggles. I still played nine holes a few times a week, but if he harbored any doubt whether taking over a golf course was for work or fun, I didn't want him going home and telling Mom that I was up here for the latter.

"I couldn't get this kid to mow our lawn, and now look at him," he said to his buddies, and even though I did occasionally mow our lawn (when money was tight), I didn't interject. If this was my golf course, it was his by extension. In some ways, the place felt more like his than mine. If he hadn't taken up golf in the Navy, neither I nor my brothers would have ever played. Growing up in the eighties, you only attempted golf if your parents played or if you caddied, and he'd given me both avenues by picking up a golf club in his twenties. From a Navy course in San Diego, our family's golf story had arrived here in Sullivan County, where his Scranton accent and his recall of every mountain and hotel and town in the Hudson Valley—he'd been to that lake, worked in that town, vacationed on those hills—made him a far better fit up here than me.

I joined them on the back nine where Dad was all energy, his steps lightened by a Catskills clock that, for him, seemed to move backward. He had walked to school beneath mountains like these; he'd breathed this air through the most carefree years of his life. It was funny to think that, as a traveler, vitality and inspiration were always found elsewhere, but watching Dad return to his hills was proof of the power in the familiar. We had dinner at the Arnold that night, and Dad called the trout on their pub menu the best dish he'd ever tasted.

The next morning, they came back early, Dad ready to go around again, and he told me he'd had the strangest dreams last night. They were memories from the farm at St. Michael's, and in one he was picking tomatoes with Jack, his best friend and big brother who passed away when I was still a toddler. In another, he was standing in a wide field and staring at a large, white horse. The horse approached him slowly, he said. He might have been three, four years old, but he didn't move. The horse walked directly up to him, leaned his large head down toward my father's, and put his nose up against his. He had completely forgotten that happened, but it did happen, he said, and last night he relived it like it was yesterday.

I worked the fairways while Dad and the guys played another eighteen on an overcast, empty course—it really was Dad's golf course that day, all to himself—before calling it quits and hitting the road back to Philadelphia. They hung around the Adirondacks for a bit first, and I snuck a picture of him leaning back in one of those chairs, sipping a longneck beer with one leg crossed over the other. And when I look at that image now, I don't know if I've ever seen my father looking quite so relaxed, or quite so happy. He'd played at plenty of special places over a long golf life, but there's something altogether different about courses that feel like home.

I could sense John peeking out the pro shop window, wondering what the hell I was doing. Nothing to see here, I thought, just a ginger from Philadelphia sitting at a picnic table with three ultra-Orthodox Jewish men, only one of whom was speaking English.

What sounded like the beginning of a bar joke was my current best option for saving Sullivan County Golf Club. Strangers and friends had reached out via text and email to ask my plans for the course's future. I had no plan to offer them, but I made a list of those who I thought might have money to invest and didn't enjoy reading business plans. I prioritized those who were golf-crazy and might take a shot on a nine-holer that, as of August, was still operating in the black.

Payroll ate up about $8,000 every week, with taxes, inventory, insurance, and utilities costing another $5,000 each month. In the grand scheme of golf, it was an absurdly meager operating budget, and Shaun was working for roughly one-third of his worth, but he'd volunteered for small wages to keep our experiment afloat. It was working for now, but relying on the charity of one's staff wasn't sustainable, nor was expecting to capture 250 nonresident members every year, folks from Illinois and

Scotland who had sent us their money on an Instagram-inspired whim. The Met Golf Section had put our story on the cover of their monthly magazine and that had helped top up our coffer, but we'd only remain a cause for so long. If we were going to keep Sullivan County affordable and priced according to what we could offer, we either needed to up our offerings or grow Liberty's golf base by 400 percent.

It seemed an impossible scale to level. Our current rates earned just enough to keep our thumbs plugged in the dike. If we raised prices, we had to improve the course and the clubhouse, and if we raised them too much, we'd be robbed of our value cachet and drive away the locals. I'd answered enough emails from Liberty residents inquiring about special deals or lower cart rates to know that ours was a fixed-income community, and that even the gentlest ratchet upward could push golf out of their budget. Yet we couldn't continue with a shuttered clubhouse and collapsing maintenance shed and six working carts and the medieval remains of a basement locker room. If the course and clubhouse cost a million dollars (for 187 acres, it would be a good price), I would then need to pump another million dollars into improvements—at least. And making back two million dollars on twenty-dollar greens fees was a tragic sort of math. I was anything but a businessman, but I could decipher that even with a large, reckless investment, a Sullivan County Golf Club with me as its owner was a financial lemon.

If greens fees and memberships weren't profitable—breaking even on golf seemed possible, even likely, but a surplus felt like fantasy—I considered other avenues for income. Our course used roughly 40 percent of the property, leaving one hundred extra acres that stretched toward an unexplored ridge in the distance, and that land offered possibilities. Add nine more holes and go for eighteen? The forest that enveloped our holes was thick and tall, and clearing it looked like an exorbitant endeavor. Plus, much of that extra acreage was on the side of a mountain or sunk in untouchable wetlands; doubling our golf would be mining for gold dust, where a few specks cost far more to find than we'd recover. And I liked nine-hole golf. I liked it in Scotland and Ireland, and I liked it in Liberty. Since fewer holes meant fewer inputs, less gas, less labor, less cost, the best thing we had going for us was a smaller scorecard. Rather than follow the lead of developers who were adding second and third courses, maybe they should be following ours, growing the game by shrinking it.

Ever since I'd signed my deal with Chris and Sims, I hadn't stopped wondering about the potential of their original plan to develop homes and a hotel on the property. What I didn't like about their drawings was that they interrupted the golf course; what I loved about them was that they had once been approved. The county would welcome the development of holiday homes and rooms for visitors; the Catskills had been built on hospitality and vacation real estate, and we had room for both. Perhaps the solution for our golf club had nothing to do with golf. Unfortunately, golf was the only thing I knew anything about, so I researched home prices and developers and read up on trends in Catskills real estate, where history revealed a pattern striped with a thin glimmer of hope.

I learned how the Catskills' first golden age (or its silver age, as described by historian John Conway) had come about via small mountain hotels catering to fresh-air-seeking clients during the industrial boom of the nineteenth century. Its mid-twentieth-century explosion was brought about by the American Plan and the proliferation of behemoth resorts catering to mostly Jewish families, but Irish and Italian families as well. Following the decline of the resorts around 1965, the Catskills rebounded in the 1980s with the spread of second-home communities, a trend that lasted until roughly the year 2000. This jagged timeline revealed that each age of prosperity lasted roughly twenty years before a twenty-year pause, meaning we might be on the verge of a golden or bronze—hell, I'd settle for tin—age of Sullivan County milk and honey.

I asked a friend to come have a look and tell me if overhauling these acres would have us chasing our tails. I was still a partner in a golf course design firm with Colton Craig, whom I'd met when he was fresh out of design school at Oklahoma State, catching loops at Southern Hills to make ends meet. Colton was an architecture geek who had played every Perry Maxwell course for his honors thesis. (Maxwell is one of the golden-age greats; the father of Oklahoma golf, his name gets overshadowed by the East Coast architects, but his hands touched courses from Pine Valley to Augusta to Crystal Downs, to his own celebrated designs at Old Town and Prairie Dunes.) Colton was a stocky ex-wrestler with an energy and passion for design that had me missing age twenty-three. After he caddied for me in Tulsa, we went to dinner at a Mexican place down the street where he told me he was starting his own design firm and wanted me to be his partner. I explained that I had no idea where a drainpipe or cart path should go and that topography maps, to me, looked like spaghetti, but he said that part of the business was his job, and that he wanted a partner who knew people in golf and who knew what a great hole looked like. I'd been fortunate to play plenty of those, I conceded, and by the time our burritos arrived, Craig & Coyne was in business.

Shaun would later confess that it was the announcement of this partnership on social media that had encouraged him to reach out to me on Instagram. He hadn't read any of my books and didn't subscribe to *The Golfer's Journal*, but when he saw that I was getting into design, he thought I might take a liking to the hills in Liberty and have a plan for improving them. Shaun was something of a designer himself—after work, he'd spend his late evenings sketching golf holes, and he'd text the drawings to me at all hours. He'd rerouted and reimagined Sullivan County a thousand different ways, and his ideas had me dreaming of lottery money so that we might someday turn his sketches into soil.

Our little firm got busy in its first few years. Colton was a hustler with a work ethic that frightened me; he'd send emails at three in the morning and sleep in airports, hustling from one lead to the next. I fed him some of those leads and visited sites when the schedule allowed, places in Florida and Oklahoma where he was building a practice course or doing bunker work or, eventually, designing entire course restorations. Shaun made me promise I'd bring Colton up to Sullivan, so I asked him to make a visit that July and give us a dispassionate assessment of our potential. It's the rare architect who can afford to pass and tell you they find your land uninspiring, but it would take a blindfolded architect to say as much about ours.

Before he left the seat of his rental car, Colton was sold. A quick glance at a property falling off a hillside then turning upward like a tidal wave was enough to get him plotting his pièce de résistance. The three of us walked the woods together for two days, dreaming up golf holes and routing rearrangements that would not only make the course more walkable, but would add more moments of pause and wonder. We had two things to sell up here, I told Colton: fun golf holes and great views, and any change that enhanced either was something we should consider. I told him to make room for some houses, too, because every line he drew cost money, and it was going to have to come from somewhere.

Armed with Shaun's sketches and my guidelines, Colton drew a colorful and comprehensive rendering of his dream for Sullivan County and sent it to us shortly after landing back in Oklahoma. When I saw his email and clicked on the attachment, this accidental journey wherein I was moving through a life in the Catskills with a vague set of intentions—suddenly, it all reverberated with purpose. The outlines of fairways curling toward forgotten corners of the property, a hole that played across our pond in the woods, a putting course and a driving range and a creek-side short course routed around a square that read LODGE, plus little red-and-white blocks for homes and cabins, dotted around our edges like pieces from a game of Monopoly:

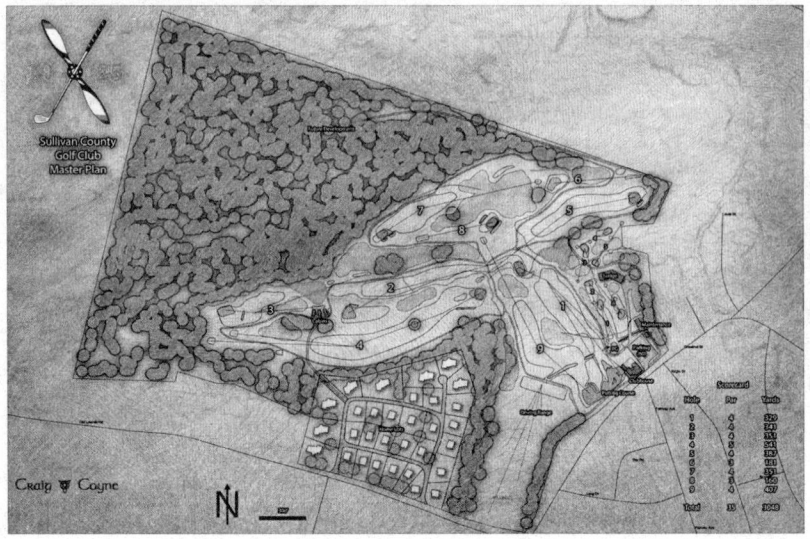

After witnessing what might be, there was no turning back, no settling, no opening a Christmas gift then putting it back under the tree. Our pipe dream was something we could now grasp in our hands, and I was no longer here to just hold the line; I was here to push life into a picture with a chance to do something outlandish, the sort of chance that, in my experience, came along too rarely and should be pursued as an imperative.

Colton rerouted the course so that golfers turned left after the first hole instead of right, reserving the best hillside holes for a more dramatic finish. He moved greens from beside the creek to perched above it and placed tees on ridges we'd found in the woods. A future lodge got Shaun so excited that he sketched out a schematic for a twenty-room inn with modern Catskills touches. Colton said that if he put the course work out to bid (homes and a lodge would come later), he expected the scope of work would come back with a price tag in the range of $750,000.

There's a chance the golf club where you play just spent six million dollars renovating a few dozen bunkers, so if Colton's math doesn't compute, consider that it involved no irrigation system (good enough for Fishers Island, good enough for us) and no sod or seeding. Shaun insisted that any new holes be covered with existing turf scalped from the fairways that would now be driving range (the eighth and ninth, where the underlying clay refused to drain). The job was essentially tree removal and earth moving, and far more of the former than the latter. I'd said we needed to find holes out there rather than build them, and the master plan I sent our first real suitor proved that's what we'd done.

Adam had grown up in nearby Monticello and sent me a note inquiring about my long-term plans for the course. The internet told me he'd done well in real estate in Manhattan, and he was looking for projects like ours where he could invest in his roots. The Catskills had been booming since Covid, he said, and the opportunity was there.

I sent Colton's schematic to Adam and highlighted what would be a new grass driving range—we'd be the only one in the area, and it would likely generate more daily revenue than the course—and noted where Colton had placed home lots with long views of the valley, plus his outlines for glamping and a lodge. Adam said this was exactly what he was looking for and scheduled a visit for the following week. He knew a group of area builders that he wanted us to meet right away.

His Land Rover pulled into the parking lot an hour before his builders arrived—he was excited to see the property and wanted the full tour. He was dressed in loafers and a tailored button-down you couldn't shop for in this zip code, but he was all enthusiasm for everything I showed him. The hills, the views, the quant little clubhouse—it all worked. Authentic Catskills, just what New Yorkers wanted.

When his friends pulled into the lot in a gray minivan, he reached into his back pocket, pulled out a yarmulke, and put it on his head. "These guys are Orthodox, but I told them, this isn't going to be a Hasidic community. They're good builders. Done a ton of work up here."

Adam and I joined the three gentlemen on the picnic bench outside the pro shop. We shook hands and their eyes looked very serious behind small, round spectacles, their faces framed by long, bouncy locks. They wore black pants and starched white shirts, and I explained that I was looking for investors to revitalize the course and develop some properties. I pointed out the ridge behind us, up above number three, as prime home sites that Colton had left off his map since we had no road to access them. But there was an old fire path back in the woods, I explained, and that might be something of a start.

A thin man with a brown beard seemed to be the designated speaker as his two partners only spoke among themselves, reacting to my comments in low-toned Yiddish.

"What is the price?" he asked.

"For the property? I don't own—"

"The homes," he said. "What are you expecting for a price?"

I had no idea, but I told him that 600 to 800k was probably a sweet spot for a holiday home for young New York professionals.

"It's a good price," he said. His partners seemed to agree. "Three bedrooms?"

"Yeah, I think three bedrooms. Maybe four for some of them. I guess it depends on the size of the lots, how good the views are, all that." And to think, people went to school for real estate, and here I was doing a deal pulled directly out of my ass.

The men spoke among themselves, then the speaker said, "I like it. We build nice places for $300,000."

That was quick, I thought. Too quick? Or maybe these guys were that good. I wasn't sure what Adam had in mind for our acres; we had not spoken specifics, but I was getting the sense that he might buy the whole thing and develop the homes himself. He'd spoken about wanting me to be involved in growing the golf, so maybe I'd be the golf partner? This wasn't the setting for exploring those particulars, but if he gave me the money I needed for the golf course and paid Western Sullivan what they wanted for the property, I'd learn Yiddish and intone chants of gratitude.

"Now, the style of the homes," Adam said. "We want something that's modern mountain style. These are for New York families, young couples from the city."

"Yes, they look like Catskills," said our friend. "We make them very nice. Very beautiful."

Adam looked like he had a thought stuck in his throat. He paused, then said, "So, we aren't talking about a community for the Haredim. . . ."

The speaker leaned back, waving his hands at the suggestion. "No, no, no," he said. "We know. But you," he said, pointing at me, "you go for the permit. I go for permit, no way. You go, you get permit."

I wasn't sure what I was agreeing to, but I agreed. Sullivan County government probably deserved more credit, I thought; there were a dozen Hasidic villages within a few miles of the course, so you couldn't say the county had been inhospitable. But I wasn't naïve about the lower Catskills wanting to import visitors beyond the ultra-Orthodox, and I understood the reasoning behind his request. I didn't care what creed our home buyers lived by, so long as they paid asking price and played golf. With real golf clubs.

"This is easy. We do this for you, and you will be very happy," said the speaker, and we all shook hands. The men left, and Adam said he had to run back to the city but would give me a call. As expected, John was waiting inside with a hundred questions that boiled down to whether I was doing a deal to turn the course into an Orthodox summer retreat.

"Don't ask," I said as I walked through the door. "I'm trying to find investors and these guys might be interested. I don't know."

John nodded slowly. "But you're keeping it a golf course," he said.

"Of course I'm keeping the golf course," I said. "That's the only reason I'm here. But we have to get creative. I'm talking to anybody who wants to help."

Adam called to tell me he thought our meeting went well and that he was even more excited about the project now. He had to speak with his partners and come up with a plan, but any proposal would involve me retaining an ownership stake so that I'd stay on to operate the course. As for what kind of course that would be, I had my reservations. He was a real estate guy and could make homes happen, but what would that leave for me and Shaun and Colton when it came time to bring our new putting course and our punch bowl par-three to life? What about the refurbished clubhouse and restaurant our vision desperately required? And that we needed in time for next season? Suddenly, Sullivan County's faraway tomorrow was being decided today, and I feared someone might soon write a check for a vision unlike the one Shaun and I had been texting about at night.

I was grateful for Adam's interest—he'd already given me more time and hope than the first three names on my investor list, guys who said the timing wasn't right but that they were excited to come play the course. And I liked Adam. Beneath the city dealmaker was a kid from the Catskills who wanted more people to enjoy a place he still loved. But doing a deal with a developer I didn't know beyond a few text messages . . . it was a gift horse I was staring straight in the mouth. I didn't want to oversee the golf course; I wanted to give it the chance that Colton's drawings promised. I wanted Shaun to peel fairway off old holes and lay it upon fresh ones. I wanted people to tee off newfound ledges and wonder why they hadn't visited this place before. I wanted to make a mess alongside my friends and watch it grow into something nobody saw coming. And I wanted to spend far too much money on a nine-holer, alongside partners who valued golf shots over kitchen square footage. Adam might indeed be that partner, but I had little time left to figure that out.

It was already August and we had just a few months left to decide whether I would be back up here come April. If he was going to buy these acres, engineering would have to be done and soil tested and plans created and presented to the county—presented by me, apparently, a process I was sure would expose me as a real estate rube. I knew little about the timing and specifics of property development, but if it was anything like development in the story-making world, where someone told you they loved your book and wanted to make it into a television show and then forgot to call you back for six years, I suspected our senses of urgency might not align. I did know two guys who could make things happen quickly up here, and it seemed appropriate to meet them where all of this began.

I waited in the back of the New Munson Diner and watched as Chris and Sims walked through the door, Sims having to stop and say hello at each table before finally settling into our booth. His status as something of a local hero, a Sullivan County kid who had come home to build houses and refurbish hotels and open restaurants, only confirmed my reasoning for the ask I was about to make.

We ordered burgers and wraps and I explained that I was not here to make them an offer on their golf course, nor did I have a buyer lined up—not quite. They'd both been following our progress at the course and Chris would come out some mornings and play early before heading down to their office in Youngsville (like everything in Sullivan County, it was about twenty minutes away), and they were shocked by our membership numbers and noted the crowd of cars in our parking lot when they passed. We were above water, I said, and had proven there was an audience for our golf course. But I laid out the bare economics from my point of view, explaining that I could probably raise enough money to either buy or improve the facility, but not both, and that the only way to go after investment would be to offer a revenue stream outside of golf. We needed a restaurant, and we needed to sell real estate. I knew nothing about either business, but the two men with whom I was having lunch certainly did.

I loathed home-clogged golf holes as much as any golfer, but that wasn't the plan I was proposing. It seemed to me that selling thirty homes built on land away from the course—along the property's most attractive edges—could earn a healthy return for any investors. Golf with a clubhouse restaurant could serve as an amenity to attract home buyers, and if golf and food broke even, everybody wins. It all sounded possible, they agreed, but resurrecting the clubhouse and getting the engineering and planning done for home sites was a significant investment, and they'd sunk as much capital into this property as good judgment allowed. They said I was free to extend our arrangement and run the course under the same terms next year, and maybe the year after, but I'd done my stint as a course borrower, and without a new plan to revitalize the course in a big, expensive way, another term as course mayor would just delay the inevitable.

What if, I suggested, they reopened and ran the restaurant and developed the home sites, and I raised enough money for that to happen? Sims tilted his head, thinking.

"But what would you get out of it?" he asked.

Me and my theoretical partners would become their partners, I said. We'd raise whatever amount of money they thought the property was worth, but none of it would go to them. Instead, we would be 50/50 partners on the project. They'd bring their equity as owners of the land and we'd bring cash, and that cash would go toward revitalizing the course and clubhouse with some left over to get the real estate started.

"Why wouldn't you just buy the course outright and own all of it?" Chris asked.

"Because I don't know anything about the restaurant business. And I can't build houses. And even if I contracted all that out to somebody else, I wouldn't know who to call. I'd call you guys, honestly. It's what you do," I said. "Say I raise a million and we create a partnership that owns everything together—the golf, the real estate, who knows, maybe a hotel eventually—and we put that money into upgrades and getting the planning going, then we have a new course and clubhouse and homes to sell. And we share in all of that equally."

They didn't say no. They didn't leap from their seats and kiss me on the forehead, either, but it clearly wasn't the worst idea they'd been pitched. It solved their most immediate need—to not spend any more money on the golf course they'd bought—and it offered them the upside of forgetting about golf and focusing on the two businesses they'd mastered: hospitality and real estate. It would mean a lot of work on their part; they'd go from being my landlord to being my working partner, and that was the great snag I couldn't unloosen. It would require their team and their skills to make everything outside of the golf go. Golf would remain my responsibility, I explained, and with this year's momentum, we'd proven the course still had legs. I wanted to provide it much sturdier ones, however, so I took out my phone and showed them Colton's plan.

They moved around the images with their fingers. And when Sims finally said, "You think this is doable?" I knew a maybe was in the works. Maybe was all I was hoping for that afternoon, but when Sims confessed that they were in fact looking for a new home for their Italian restaurant, Piccolo Paese, the only place in Liberty where you felt lucky to get a reservation, I thought about raising my goals for our meeting.

Chris said he would need to run a lot of numbers, but he expected that what I was proposing might be possible. Sims noted that this might not require their money, but it would certainly require their time. They'd have to discuss what time they had to offer, but I predicted where they would land. I was proposing a hope they'd already had for the property, and I was offering it to them with frills and partners, served up on a handsome Colton Craig rendering that would be waiting for them back at their office in their inboxes.

"So, who do you plan on bringing in as partners?" Chris asked.

There was, of course, that. I said I had a list, because I did, and I wanted to get Chris's and Sims's input first, because I needed it. This wasn't an arrangement that would interest Adam—there wasn't enough real estate to share between two developers—but a partnership with Chris and Sims would guarantee us a restaurant and a construction site by next spring. As for where I was going to find a million dollars (or potentially more), I could only hope that the other curious folks who had contacted me had stacks of money to which they didn't feel particularly attached.

The safer, wiser route might be to lean on Adam and his partners and try to keep the course afloat until they did their due diligence and sent a large check. But due diligence scared me, and if his partners didn't find the Catskills as worthy as he did, their money might land elsewhere. The deal I'd imagined for Chris and Sims would guarantee us our budget for the golf course, plus homes by the best builders in the area (Allyson enjoyed perusing the real estate apps, and the Foster Supply houses were always the ones she saved). They not only had a plug-and-play restaurant, but their presence in Sullivan County solved my biggest worry about all of this: How would anything get accomplished when I spent eight months of the year in Philadelphia? They spent twelve months of the year down the street. Boots on the ground would be priceless, especially when those boots were known to the politicians and the permitters and had earned the affection of both.

I called Adam and thanked him for his time and interest but informed him I had a potential deal in place that would be more focused on the course and might allow me to get a restaurant in a new clubhouse come spring. He understood and said he remained interested if anything changed. He was looking at some other properties in the area as well, and if there was any way for those projects to align with ours, he wanted to be helpful. I thanked him and we wished each other well. I was confident our paths would cross again. We were hoping for the same tide to lift our boats, and we both had plenty of paddling ahead.

Meanwhile, Chris incorporated Colton's drawing into a thick business plan with graphs and charts and year-by-year projections, and I sent it to the rest of the names on my list while I daydreamed about what it would be like to own part of an Italian restaurant. I'd work the dining room and slap regulars on the back and ask them how they liked the veal. I'd wear long silk ties and run up a tab like Tommy in *Goodfellas*. If I could wrangle a small cadre of folks who saw the potential in our plan and were willing to let us chase it with their money, we could create something that was unthinkable just a few months ago. And we could do it together. Shaun included.

In April and May, Shaun and I had talked a lot about not needing to reinvent Sullivan County, warning each other about turning the club into something it wasn't. I violated that pact almost immediately by lopping off half its name, but we'd otherwise remained focused on maintaining the character, the charm, and the affordability of the place, and all of those pieces were tightly intertwined. But Sullivan County was changing. Golfers in Scotland were wearing hats with our logo and posting the pictures on Instagram. Charles Schwab was coming up here next month to film a commercial about what we were doing and how we were challenging golf's status quo. Shaun was doing interviews with magazine writers and appearing on podcasts, an accidental (and perhaps reluctant) spokesperson for sustainable greenskeeping and rural golf.

On the weekends we'd get a handful of golfers who arrived with a book for me to sign, and they shopped our logo offerings with vigor. John shook his head about the groups from New Jersey and Massachusetts who followed me online and would spend $50 on a hand-forged ball marker and carried their clubs in bespoke leather satchels. For every foursome of locals, we had two who might have played Sleepy Hollow or Baltusrol the day before, and while these universes mixed well—good, cheap, relaxed golf cut across the spectrum—John didn't quite know what to make of the strange sociology that had overtaken our club. When a foursome of hickory players showed up and played in period dress (knickers and ties and wool caps) he was sure I was pranking him. And his name was popping up on podcasts, too—same for Jimmy and Gary— and visitors wanted to meet them ("You're John from the podcast!" was how he was being greeted lately, so he'd adopted John-from-the-Podcast as his new work name). Sullivan County *was* changing because it had to, and though Shaun was our gatekeeper when it came to maintaining our place as an outpost for natural, community golf, he was the biggest dreamer of the bunch.

I'd unintentionally been the snake in the garden in enticing him to think bigger, tempting Shaun with new machines from Toro and pallets of fertilizer from Aquatrols and piles of seed from Hart's Turf Pro. Aquatrols didn't just send us grass food; they took our experiment under their wing, visiting the course in June and July and bringing a team of superintendents and turf scientists both times. Shaun getting to walk his course with Tom Valentine, the Aquatrols portfolio manager whose father and grandfather had maintained the grounds at Merion for a combined eighty years, was a superintendent's waking dream. In our shed Shaun found an old cardboard seed tub with MERION scrawled across it, a remnant from the proprietary strain of bent grass Tom's grandfather engineered at Penn State where they named their turfgrass facility the Valentine Research Center. I watched from a distance as Shaun and Tom got down on their knees alongside six other experts and studied our greens and fringes, and within days of each visit, a fresh pallet of organic turf panacea showed up at our door, along with the sprayers Shaun needed to spread it.

After a morning on our mowers, we sat down one Friday to review where our plans stood. Shaun had been the driver behind almost everything this year; when I had a question or ordered a new product or was presented with a new hire, Shaun was either by my side or first to know. But we had moved into a new phase of financial planning and asset gathering, where I was playing the lead and leaving Shaun to look after the course. I told him about the proposal I'd made to Chris and Sims and showed him the business plan with its three phases of development: Year one, we'd upgrade the course and clubhouse and open the restaurant. In year two, we'd complete engineering and planning for the homes. And by year three, we'd be building homes and would secure funding for a lodge and club amenity center with a pool and a gym. Liberty lacked any place to work out and the community pool had seen better days—Sims was bullish on the potential of memberships that came with such offerings, and maybe we'd have to change our name back to "country club" after all.

It was a big plan to process, and a complete reimagining of the quiet place he'd fallen in love with and had played alone in the evenings, learning its every kick and camber. He studied the plan and turned the page to the map that outlined potential lots, and he pointed to one beside the stream and said, "I want to put our house right here."

Change or die—Shaun knew that better than anyone here. He was the one hotwiring tractors and putting out buckets in the barn when it rained. He knew Sullivan County's every blemish, and the idea that we might finally repair them was better than any pallet of weed retardant. And the golf was going to get better, which is all either of us cared about in the end.

I told him he could definitely have one of the lots—that would be more than a fair finder's fee. I told him that Chris and Sims and I also wanted him to stick around and feel invested, so we planned to make him an owner. Each side of our deal would cut him in for a 1 percent stake, making him 2 percent owner of everything here—the lots, the golf, the restaurant. It wasn't a huge stake, but if we pulled off this plan, his share would have real value.

"I appreciate that," he said. "I really appreciate that." He flipped through pages full of images of what the hotel might look like and what the restaurant might be and how a sample home would show. He studied it all quietly, then said, "Our share would be for Adah. Marisol and I wouldn't touch it. We'd leave it for her to get started in life." I told him that sounded like a great idea.

We talked through the course and some of those numbers. Colton's best bid for the work so far was 700k, not including tree removal. He estimated that we needed fifteen acres of forest cleared for the new holes that were going to fix that death walk up to the third tee (we'd found a connecting par-three in the woods) while leaving space for a driving range, estimating a price for that work at 150k. Chris and Sims needed 350k for the clubhouse and restaurant and a new pro shop in what was currently a breezeway. The present shop would have to be converted into kitchen space—the old space wasn't adequate for any sort of volume—so we'd stud out that open corridor and put John and his team on that side of the building.

I explained to Shaun that if this all went through, I wanted John to have a bigger role in the pro shop. Shaun had been responsible for scheduling the shop shifts and filling in the evening gaps himself, and even though everyone did a little bit of everything at Sullivan County, our superintendent would have enough on his plate if we started digging up fairways. Shaun agreed that John could do more; he lived two hundred yards away and the course was already his second home. And for all the *Hey, Tom*s he fired my way, each proved that he cared and that he was keeping tight tabs on our operation. I'd have to coach him on how to run an outing—we were going to need plenty more of those to hit Chris's numbers—but golf would be in good hands. To prove it, I showed Shaun the picture John sent me that morning: it was our propeller-and-golf-club logo, tattooed brightly on John's upper arm.

"Jesus Christ," Shaun said, laughing. "We better make this work! We're all in on this now."

I looked at the picture again and ran through the numbers in my head, adding 200k for home site permitting and planning, plus a frighteningly modest 100k contingency, and concluded that our de facto pro shop manager had just gotten himself a $1.5 million tattoo.

TIMES HERALD-RECORD, JUNE 26, 1969

THIEF BIRDIES CLUBHOUSE

LIBERTY—Ferndale Bureau of Criminal Investigation agents are continuing their investigation of a burglary of the Sullivan County Golf and Country Club clubhouse.

Authorities said a burglar or burglars entered the clubhouse, on Rt. 52, early Tuesday morning and took about $1,000 in golf balls, liquor, and cash.

Entry, according to BCI agents Ralph Fuente and Anthony Zaccari, was through a small window above the porch level at the western end of the building.

Discovery of the burglary was made at 6 a.m. by Hugh P. Nigro, a member of the greens staff. The clubhouse is managed by Ralph J. Nigro.

SULLIVAN COUNTY GOLF COMPANY

CHECKING ACCOUNT

Beginning balance: $41,246.77

Additions: $16,978.44

Subtractions: $29,703.13

Ending balance: $28,522.08

Fresh ink on his shoulder wasn't the only life change for John. He'd been shopping at Agway and stumbled upon a pen of baby poodles, and while training a puppy might be a bad idea for a guy awaiting back surgery who walked on one and a half feet, he scooped up a white-and-black beauty that he named Ringo who would run John ragged but whose cuteness might have saved our new Sullivan County plans.

I was back from a week in California where I visited with another unlikely friend, Mike Madden, the son of the Hall of Fame football coach whose last name anyone under thirty knew as a video game but perhaps not as an actual person. Ours was an unusual connection; Mike was a Ballybunion member and a lover of Irish golf who had read my Ireland book years ago. He saw on social media that a charity was offering a round of golf with me at Philly Cricket Club (where I'm a freeloader, not a member) and he placed the winning bid (that golf with me was sometimes auctioned off was likely disappointing for all parties—the charities that had to stomach rock-bottom bids, and the winners who discovered that I was only loquacious when paper or a keyboard was involved).

Mike reached out via email, and I didn't make the football connection to his last name, not until Covid interrupted our scheduled round. He lived in California and was planning to fly out to Philly for our golf—he owned Muhammad Ali's training camp in central Pennsylvania, a place called Fighter's Heaven that he'd restored and could visit on his trip, so bidding on golf at Philly Cricket served more than one purpose. But the pandemic scuttled our plans, and when Cricket reopened, Mike's loved ones weren't thrilled about a cross-country flight while the world was still dodging coughs and disinfecting their groceries. He said they'd kept his dad's buses and that he could use one of them to make the drive, and that's when I put the pieces together—he was *that* Madden, whose father had notably avoided air travel, crossing the country from one football game to another in the famed Madden Cruiser.

I was disappointed when the Cruiser didn't pull into the small parking lot at Cricket. Mike had left it up at Fighter's Heaven and rented a car. He didn't think the club would have appreciated a bus, he said, though it probably would have been a hit. He had his dad's large frame if not quite his height, a shaved head and short neck that suggested football was in his blood, but a modest, deferential manner that made him an easy golf partner. He'd been an English major at Harvard where he played wide receiver, and he played his California golf at Monterey Peninsula, a recently restored Mike Strantz that I was itching to visit. We kept in touch, and I scheduled a visit to Monterey when an invite to Cypress Point and a *Golfer's Journal* event at Poppy Hills converged around a golf week that more than justified airfare to San Francisco. We played thirty-six oceanside holes at Monterey Peninsula in one day, followed by eighteen across the hills at Poppy, followed by what might be the rarest golf setting on the planet at Cypress. And by the time I had landed back in Philadelphia, I'd all but abandoned our nine-holer in the mountains.

I'd been ruined by Monterey. Comparing Sullivan County to what many consider America's greatest stretch of golf wasn't a fair equivalence, but my gut didn't care, and the part of me that had championed simple, affordable, public golf went silent. If I was going to own a course, why would I buy one that had no chance of ever resembling the golf I had just played? I got honest with myself: I liked fancy places, and that was okay. I wanted to play them forever and always. I wanted to move my family out to Monterey and beg my way into more rounds with Mike and live an easy California life amid burnished faces and slick greens and caddies shouting wisdom over thundering waves. But when I returned and found Ringo napping in our pro shop, a puppy leashed to our shirt rack, the clouds of delusion blew away. We had a pro shop dog now. We needed to keep having a pro shop.

Ringo woke up and jumped all over me, and missing my dog back home, I sat on the floor and let him lick me from ear to ear. John introduced his new friend, who would keep him company through the winter—he was a bachelor and though his daughter lived at home, she was always out with her college friends, he said. He was glad to have a companion and suggested we open a halfway house out on the course and call it Ringo's. My stomach clenched; there it was, the anxiety of costly projects for which I had identified zero investors. At least not any that could get us within a football field of $1.5 million.

A friend had said he might be in for $20,000 and could rope in a few more friends at that level. A friend who represented the developer behind some of the best golf communities in the country thought our land had potential, but it would take years of deliberation before he could pull the trigger. I spent a week courting another money man who pored over the business plan and toured the course and sent Chris a long set of questions before telling us he was willing to invest $30,000, if only for the fun of it. These were meaningful sums but they were miles away from our starting line, and I didn't have the time or contacts to assemble a squad of a hundred investors, all of whom would require courting and careful attention. Besides, we already had one investor on the hook who was ready to fork over funds with few questions asked: us.

Allyson and I had decided that we would liquidate a large, painful chunk of our retirement if I could persuade a partner to come in for half, or maybe two partners to each join us for a third. Either scenario would eat up several years' worth of her bonus checks, but she loved the idea of selling home sites and owning a lodge and restaurant, and while none of this was a safe way to plan for your seventies, it all sounded like more fun than chasing the S&P. Our preference was for one or two partners who were more interested in doing good by a golf course than reviewing P&L statements; we couldn't juggle fifty who might want to know why we'd spent ten grand on a tractor, or who might push for a better ROI via stiffer membership fees. In the short term, I knew the *L*'s would far exceed the *P*'s, and as we were trying to engineer a complete overhaul in the space of a few months, it was going to be a messy process unfit for MBA metrics. No's were easy to find, and that had me wondering about my predilection toward yes and whether a why-not disposition had finally caught up with me and was ready to teach me a lesson.

The fall months were quiet. A trickle of leaf-peepers came to play their way around our now red and golden hillsides, but by late September, weekday golfers were rare and the weekends weren't much better, as kids were back in school and soccer practice ate up our members' Saturdays and Sundays (the proliferation of full-time youth sports has been a scourge to American golf numbers). Our bank balance remained positive with Mike and Charlie going back to school and dropping off payroll, and we returned to a bare-bones operation of Shaun and Chris on grounds, with John and Gary taking most of the pro shop hours as Jimmy readied himself for a winter in the plow truck. I wasn't sure how long I'd be able to afford Bearded Chris, who would go on seasonal unemployment soon, and if I was going to keep Shaun on a yearly salary, I needed to soon figure out if there was a next year or not.

Our parking lot grew emptier by the week, but we did get visits from a brown van that would park at the far end, from which a short, bearded man in hiking boots would emerge and slip onto the golf course without clubs. He arrived at odd hours, early and late, dodging the pro shop guys, and apparently John had been chasing him all season. Gary informed me that the van I'd spotted belonged to the mushroom man who harvested rare fungi from our tree stumps, and that John was livid that someone was poaching side dishes from under his nose.

"If I ever catch that son of a bitch . . . ," he said. "I've been watching those mushrooms all season and just when they're ready, I go out there and they're gone. He completely cleaned us out."

We debated the legality of the mushroom man's operation. Since he wasn't here to golf, he was clearly trespassing on private property, but as he'd likely been getting away with it for a dozen years or more, it was another hangover from a formerly forsaken course. Park wherever, take your cart wherever, play whenever, and come harvest our tree trunks whenever. If a paying golfer spotted some morels and put them in his bag, so be it, but if he was using our crop for his business, I said we should be compensated. And if one of our staff wanted those mushrooms for himself, as John did, they should be off-limits to nonpaying visitors.

"Exactly!" John agreed. "We're not running a friggin' community farm up here."

There were days when the exchange of Jimmy's cucumbers was the only trade taking place in our golf shop, so I wasn't sure if John's assessment was entirely accurate, but I agreed, and the next time Gary spotted the van, I asked him to politely explain to the man that this was a golf course and private property. John would get his maitakes yet, though we didn't expect it might embroil easygoing Gary in a dust-up.

The following week, Gary found our friend returning from our woods with a plastic bag full of dirty booty, and when he graciously but firmly explained to the scavenger that he shouldn't return, the mushroom man reacted as if he were indeed on mushrooms.

"Go fuck yourself!" was his retort, followed by a diatribe on his right to collect nature's bounty wherever he found it, calling Gary a son of a bitch and proffering an ass-kicking should Gary be interested. He wasn't, and told our harvester that we'd call the cops the next time we saw him. The intruder's mushroom blade remained holstered, and Gary returned to the shop chased by a stream of fungal profanity.

There was a time when such an encounter would have seen me dialing 911, but by October it barely raised a brow. *We need more Snickers bars, the cart path on five washed away. Oh, and the mushroom man hopes we all burn in hell.* The daily reports at Sullivan County could no longer unsettle me, though I was surprised to hear John's news that the turtle eggs had disappeared. No shells, alas; maybe the foxes had their way after all.

In my moments of resigned defeat, when I found foot-long divots in the fairway, those tormenting gouges of dereliction, or when I learned that someone had run over a tee marker and exploded it into a heap of red plastic, I thought back to a day in July, when a group of Monday League regulars was playing on a Saturday afternoon. The fact that they were here outside of a Monday was an encouraging sign that they appreciated our efforts, and when I entered the shop and found a half-dozen post-golf locals sitting around the bar and at the high-tops along the windows, they raised beers in my direction and greeted me with happy faces and hand-shakes, as if we were old friends hanging at our regular spot. Thinking back to where this started—Shaun and I walking through this cold, quiet room of meager potential—it felt like something of a miracle.

The doors and windows were open, a breeze drifting around the space, and Jimmy was arguing about the Jets with a large man named Chauncey who gave up and ordered another round for the room. I'd met them all in the Elks that spring and had assumed they'd be my nemeses over prices and conditions, but here we were, the old gang chopping it up after golf, and when I asked if anyone had a knife so I could open this box of newly arrived golf balls, four blades were produced with rumble-in-the-alley ex-igency (asking for a knife in the Catskills was like asking for a lighter at a NASCAR race). Chauncey insisted I use his; it was razor sharp so I should be careful, he said. He had a mustache that touched his bottom lip and played in a cowboy hat banded with the Stars and Stripes. He sat beside Mike who, unlike Chauncey, didn't pack a knife sharp enough to make sushi, but who never failed to bring along his pug, a well-trained dog who waited for him in the cart while he played. I was glad to see him and sus-pected he was responsible for some of the bright moods in the room—he was the league chairman who loved the game and had been cheering for us ever since league night down at the lodge. Along with Dan Yaun, he was our most reliable ally, and he told me the course was looking great.

"You can tell where the fairway ends and the rough starts," he said. "It hasn't been like that for a while."

Chauncey agreed, and so did Herb, which nearly caused the knife to slip and prune a finger. Herb had been a tough one. He was in his sixties with a tight military buzz cut, and he had worked on a former greens crew here and had strong opinions on what the greens required and where the fairways needed more sun. He said the groundhogs were ruining the tee boxes by burrowing in beneath them, and volunteered his assistance. "I could bring my pistol up here when I'm playing and take care of that for you." I declined his offer, generous as it was. Golfers shooting gophers from their carts sounded like the worst idea ever proffered in the long history of this game. I loved *Caddyshack* as much as the next golfer, but I didn't need to live it.

Herb sipped his beer and groused a bit about the greens being better when he worked here (I suspected his unsolicited expertise was aimed at winning himself a job on the greens crew), but acknowledged they were better than last year. And when I was outside the shop later that afternoon, shuttling carts down to the barn, I overheard him speaking to himself as he walked to his car. "That was a great day," he said to no one in particular, opening his car door, and soon making his way home.

It was a great day. And facilitating one great day for one person, or maybe a few dozen—it felt like enough. Enough to justify Shaun's vision. Enough to prove we were right to still be here. For most of us, great days aren't queued up on our calendars, so while I sat there in a golf cart and felt a satisfaction that warmed the top of my nose and tried to pull water from my eyes, it passed quickly, interrupted by the idea that we needed to keep offering more of them.

More cameras seemed a good start. Marketing folks at Charles Schwab had heard about our efforts at Sullivan, and they offered us a spot in the Challengers series of commercials and short films that highlighted people in golf who were operating outside golf's norms. We were an unusual fit—for a series that featured people who broke from golf's traditional models, I was simply trying to return to them—but I was happy for the publicity and eagerly awaited a filming date in late September.

Our story would air on commercials during PGA Tour events throughout the spring and summer, we were told, which was as exciting as it was terrifying. By May of next year, we had no guarantee there would be a Sullivan County Golf Club, so our hopeful story of revival might have a macabre postscript. No matter; they liked our story and loved the aspirational vibe of our wee golf club—the hills would look great on film, and we scored points for being so far off most golfers' radars. When they arrived, worries about where we'd be next year faded, because Hollywood had come to Sullivan County, and Shaun and I were going to enjoy it.

While most people made short films with their phones now, the Schwab team pulled in with vans of gear and a crew hired out of New York City. This was a proper union shoot, with grips and electricians and a sound department, even a craft services table with drinks and snacks that the pro shop guys designated as that day's lunch. We did sit-down interviews in the old maintenance barn and Shaun answered questions sitting atop a Toro, and in each take I tried to project optimism about our story, but I wasn't going to lie. I told the cameras that I didn't know what the future held for Sullivan County, but we were doing our best to build on this year and survive to our one hundredth anniversary, hoping this place might see one hundred more. It felt like I was preaching a pipe dream, but then my phone rang. I'd put it on silent during filming, but my watch lit up with a call I absolutely had to take.

After our interviews, they filmed us walking the course and improvised tracking shots of my reels spinning while I mowed. They grabbed drone and steady cam footage around the course and clubhouse and waited for sunset's golden hour to grab the last images of the day. The sound tech was putting the microphone back down my shirt for a few final questions when I saw the name pop up on my wrist and I apologized—*sorry, I have to get this*—and jogged back up the first fairway with a wire hanging from my pants because for some reason Bill Murray was calling me on a Tuesday evening in September.

I had not seen him since his visit in the spring, when he'd played through cold orange fog in overalls from Tractor Supply, a golf day he likely only remembered as one he never wanted to live again. I'd texted him a few times over the summer, updating him on our progress and explaining that I was still looking for partners on the course, but our text conversation was one-sided—literally—with my unrequited queries sitting there on the right margin of the screen. The business plan I'd emailed him had similarly failed to elicit a response. I couldn't blame him, considering the place he'd witnessed, and I wished that he'd arrived on one of those July days when the members and guests were happy and playing golf with their kids and their dogs and coming into the shop to pay for nine more holes. But I should have known by now that things with Bill didn't work in a linear fashion. Once you decided you knew his thinking, he made you think again.

After exchanging hellos and disclosing where we were and how much golf we were or weren't playing, Bill said, "I looked at your business plan. So this golf course, it's in an economic opportunity zone?"

I reminded him that it was but that those tax incentives didn't apply to golf courses for some reason (liquor stores, tanning salons, and golf courses are carved out of the EOZ tax code, and I still wonder about the legislative mechanics that arrived at this grouping). He sounded disappointed at that news and said he liked investing in opportunity zones because they were the sort of deals where you slept well at night, putting your money into places where people needed it. I explained that this area certainly needed it—desperately so—whether the tax advantages existed or not (my limited understanding was that businesses in opportunity zones could eventually be sold without having to pay tax on any profits from the sale). He agreed with that point and asked what I needed to keep the course going. I explained the deal I had worked out with the current owners, how we could have a new course and a restaurant and sites to develop as real estate, and I gave him the cost of that arrangement. If he could come in for half, I was good for the other half, and we would be equal partners with the current owners.

"Okay," he said, "I guess that sounds okay."

I was silent for a moment, then I mumbled, "So, you're in?"

"Yeah, I'm in. Okay, I've got to go, this person here needs something, call me later," he said and hung up.

I dropped my phone in the fairway and yelled "Yes!" at the sky. The crew spun around to see what had happened, but I ran in the opposite direction, toward the pro shop where Shaun was waiting for the filming to finish before he left.

I arrived at the door out of breath. I coughed it out: "Bill's in. He's in on buying the golf course."

Shaun's jaw dropped and his eyes opened wide. "Are you serious?" he said.

I smiled and nodded. "I just got off the phone," I said. "We're doing this."

We sort of hugged—Shaun wasn't really the hugging type—then just stood there with our hands over our mouths. Neither of us were particularly skilled at exuberance, and it would take a few days to process what it meant, to connect the absurd string of circumstances that might make it feel real and understand how a few notes exchanged on social media had landed us here:

We owned a golf course.

We owned a golf course with Bill Murray.

We owned a golf course with Bill Murray, and we better not blow it.

SULLIVAN COUNTY GOLF COMPANY
CHECKING ACCOUNT
Improved

I stopped at the bagel shop in Monticello on my way to the hospital. The good place, where the morning line stretched out the door and where they said the bagels were as chewy as anything you could find in Brooklyn. They were usually sold out of Asiago by lunchtime, but it was early so I bought a sack and made my way south toward the medical center where I was sure John was tiring of hospital food.

He'd been bouncing around to doctor appointments all season and waiting for paperwork to go through for surgery on his back. His leg problems started there, the doctors said, and whatever was pinched or broken was keeping him up at nights and left him shuffling from the pro shop out to his cart, the one we kept parked on the grass by the door. John expedited his course of treatment when he tripped over Ringo in the middle of the night and shattered his leg, breaking some ribs and leaving one entire side of his body black with bruises. An ambulance rushed him to the hospital where he was taken into surgery, and while this blow wasn't how any of us had hoped to close his season at Sullivan, it meant John was accidentally on the fast track for more procedures that would fix his back as well. Well, not too fast. He'd be living in the hospital for weeks.

He was sleeping when I arrived but woke up when I placed the bagels on his tray table.

"How you doing?" he said, his voice raspy and dulled by painkillers. He was surprised to see me and tried to prop himself up on his pillows. The jumble of wires sticking out of him looked like the back of an old television set, and I suggested he stop moving. I said I brought him some of the Monticello bagels in case he was getting hungry.

"Ah, thanks, man," he said. "The food sucks. I haven't eaten a thing."

He said his daughter and sister had come to visit him, and that they were taking care of Ringo, which he was happy about. I told him not to worry about anything at the course. Jimmy and Gary were covering his shifts and we were slow anyway.

"I know, man, but I didn't want to miss this staff outing," he said. And that was my first thought, too, when I heard he'd broken his leg—that he wouldn't be able to join all of us for the round of golf we'd been looking forward to all season. We'd all seen one another tee off the first, but we hadn't gone out—greens crew and pro shop—and played the course together. Today was that day, and the best I could do was tell him I'd take videos and send them along.

"It sucks. I was ready to kick everybody's ass, too."

He showed off his scars—his leg was stitched from top to bottom with thick sutures—and shifted his gown to reveal bruises that had coalesced into an expansive map of brown and purple. It was clear he wouldn't be back to the shop anytime soon, and since we were closing the course tomorrow—the 31st of October—I wasn't sure when I'd see him next. He'd heard the good news about us buying the course with Chris and Sims and Bill, so there would be a next season, even if we weren't sure where his pro shop was going.

"Don't worry, you'll be hearing from me," he said. And I was sure I would. I'd gotten used to his nightly texts. Most were about resupplying something—I never ordered enough golf balls to make him happy, taking the cheap route of buying a few dozen at a time—but sometimes he just wanted to see where I was and when I'd be back. Maybe it was the drugs talking, but he said, "You're the only one up there who gets me, Tom. They all think I'm nuts. Nobody listens to me. Ringo's a terrible listener. I try to pillow talk with him, but he just humps the pillow."

I told him I wasn't going anywhere. "We couldn't have made it through this year without you," I said. And it was true. Jimmy had a can-do positivity, but working the touch screen while a line of people waited with credit cards wasn't his favorite part of the job. Gary knew where to find every item on every screen, but he was too kind to bother me about who was complaining about what. John wasn't burdened by such restraint. He shot me straight about all our shortcomings, whether I wanted to hear them or not, and our golf club was better because he did. He looked after the place as if it were his. There were times when I wished he'd remember that it wasn't, but in a labor market where you were fortunate to find someone who showed up half the time, my guys had made me the luckiest business operator in town, and we all deserved a little golf.

I'd been trying to talk Bearded Chris into playing for weeks, but he said he didn't play and that even if he wanted to try, his back was bothering him, so I laid off and said he should still stick around for some BBQ afterward. The cookout was canceled when our chef broke his leg, but Chris still came up to the shop as we gathered for staff day at Sullivan. I put a sign on the door—STAFF OUTING, PUT YOUR MONEY IN THE BOX—and locked it behind me, and Gary, Jimmy, Shaun, and I headed to the first tee. And so did Chris.

The four of us teed off, and while I'd thought I had a golf staff without much golf to them, Gary and Jimmy could both play. Gary had a smooth, rhythmic turn befitting a musician, with a short but poised follow-through. And Jimmy went after it—legs, arms, and shoulders— he wound it all up and tossed it at his ball. The contact wasn't always clean, but it was decisive. Shaun, of course, made it look easy with that ten-finger grip and narrow stance, knocking out drives that weren't deep but always found the proper side of the fairway.

Bearded Chris walked with us the whole way, a can of energy drink swinging from his fingers as he helped Gary find his ball and chuckled at Jimmy's misses. I'd never seen Jimmy angry before, but when he chunked his tee shot on our lone par-three, number four, Gary let out an "Oops!" to which a suddenly red-faced Jimmy clapped back, "Oh go fuck yourself!" He apologized, immediately and profusely. "Golf just gets me so mad, Tom. It gets right under my skin!" I told him it was the same for all of us and we carried on, trying to keep up with Shaun, who always played at a superintendent's pace—fast, let's go, there's stuff to do—even if there was no work left at the end of October.

I'd added some stakes to our game—the winner got first pick of the shirts inside, the samples we'd been using all season and selling online— and the losers would get a shirt, too, just maybe not one in their size. Chris put his money on Shaun, which was an easy, chalky pick, but as I didn't think he'd wear a country club–style golf shirt, it was down to Gary and Jimmy for first dibs. Bigger than winning apparel was the show-and-tell nature of our round. You work at a golf course? Okay, then show us you can play golf.

Between laughs, the golf was quiet. Just heavy breath on the hills and the rattle of golf clubs beneath our shoulders. We didn't rehash missteps from the season or gossip about the members, and I found myself trying to see the course through that original lens I'd brought with me months before, when I arrived in the Catskills as a stranger but would soon leave them as something of a local who knew when the gas station opened and where to get the best pizza and who to ask at the hardware store about cups for a water cooler. I knew who liked to play early and who liked to play late. I could tell you who drank Budweiser and who preferred Coors Light. I knew every page of the menu at the diner, and my watch was tuned to when the ice cream place in Manor closed. I even knew what bugs the trout were chasing, even if that was all I'd learned about Sullivan County fly-fishing this year (Shaun had talked me into hiring a guide and getting a lesson, where we spent the first hour talking about insects and trout's appetites, and the second hour standing in a river and tossing lines at the rocks).

Our place didn't look all that different from March—less snow, obviously, plus some fresh paint and tidier greens and fairways—but you'd have to be a local to notice the changes. What had really changed, almost beyond recognition, were the eyes through which I was surveilling it.

I'd arrived here primed to spot problems and catastrophes, cataloging all of Sullivan County's golf sins. I'd come convinced I knew what good golf was, confident about how it should be produced, organized, and sold. I'd been a logo collector, a top-100 chaser, a links tourist who would spend weeks and piles of money to get a few pictures I could post on social media and inspire golf envy via Instagram. As I crossed fairways with a team of guys who made their existence possible, I knew I'd been a golfer who thought he knew everything, but who didn't know much about golf at all.

I didn't know that the best golf hole was always the one you were playing, because you were so damn fortunate to have it. I didn't know that the best course was always the one you called home, where you arrived and exhaled because you slipped into a skin that felt like your own. The golf world had gotten so noisy—a pro schism over silly sums of money, another faraway resort you had to book today, another bespoke and secret hideaway you might someday find on a map if you begged the right person—and my response to the noise had been to shout along, forgetting that this wasn't a game we played by clicks and rankings and architectural debates. It wasn't hanging in our closets or stitched onto our hats. Rather, golf was right here, beneath our feet, wherever we found a ball to strike and a field to strike it in. And in a few months' time, I had come to love the field I was walking, and the people with whom I was walking it.

I'd worried a lot in April, and in May and June. Was the course good enough? Could we keep it going? What could we afford to fix or add? Would people come? I worried less as the months passed and I learned that none of that was really up to me. We'd put in the hours and effort, and we'd see what the books said come October. And now that October was here, they said we were getting at least a few more go-arounds.

When we got to number nine, our season's final hole, I wondered if I should say something or make a toast or mark the occasion. I was glad I didn't, because as Shaun teed up his ball, he turned and told us, "Fellas, no matter what happens from here on out, we'll always have that year we ran a golf course together."

And then he smacked his driver, and the ball climbed and flew against a backdrop of trees turning orange. We watched, and enjoyed the quiet.

PART 3

LINES IN THE DIRT

The Waldorf Astoria

HAS ARRANGED FOR ITS GUESTS TO PLAY THE
EXCELLENT COURSE OF THE

Sullivan County Golf and Country Club
at Liberty, N. Y.

THREE-HOUR TRIP BY AUTO OVER SCENIC
LIBERTY HIGHWAY — ROUTE 17 TO CHARMING
UNCROWDED MOUNTAIN GOLF COURSE

FOR INFORMATION AND GUEST CARDS INQUIRE
AT INFORMATION DESK

The Waldorf Astoria

GUEST CARD

Sullivan County Golf and Country Club
at Liberty, N. Y.

The privileges of the Golf Course have been granted to

Mr. _____

of _____

Manager

Concierge card circa 1930, courtesy of Dan Yaun

SPRING 2024

There were any number of reasons why buying a home in the Catskills was a bad idea, and I listed them to Allyson on our way to see the house she'd found online: We'd just made a bold wager by buying into a golf club ownership group; the winters up here were long and bleak and a thousand miles from the someday Decembers we'd imagined in South Carolina or Florida; and if the course project went to pot, I didn't want my time here to outlast the golf club's, its fallow or repurposed fairways a daily reminder of our failure. I thought I was playing the realist, but her perspective on spending our summers here wasn't a homesteading fantasy.

"Well, every winter you say we should ski. We can do that here," she said as we drove west from the golf club, through farmland and rolling hills dotted with round bales of hay. "And we're past the point of worrying about the course failing. I don't really see that as an option we should be considering. If we're in for a penny, we're in for a pound."

It was a fair point. "We are certainly in for a pound."

I'd toured plenty of homes with Allyson—Saturday showings were something of a pastime for her—and walked into each with my drawbridge up and battlements armed. There would be no sale today, not on my watch. But there's something about spending a lot of money once that inclines you to do it twice, a floodgates mentality that lends itself to financial audacity, and this house sang to our vulnerability coming off the purchase of the course. Perched atop a hill overlooking wide green fields specked with dairy cows, with a wraparound deck pointed at views across a wide mountain valley, and a pond in the distance that came with the property—I was powerless against the view. Plus a pool out back (a pool *and* a pond—the pond would be good for Bill). It was newly built and modeled as a modern farmhouse, and if I was ever going to be inclined to like a house in the Catskills, I feared Allyson had found it.

A goateed real estate agent was waiting for us at the top of the driveway. We introduced ourselves—Allyson friendly, me aloof—and she asked who the builders were, not that either of us would know them.

"Western Sullivan," he said. "They do a lot of great places up here."

Or maybe we would. "Wow. No kidding," I said. "Can you leave now?"

I was joking, I told him, as I berated myself for not texting Sims about the house we were looking at—maybe we could have lopped off the realtor fees and done this deal on a handshake. Forgive me for being stingy and apologies to my realtor friends, but if there ever was a time to pinch pennies, we were there. We had gotten there a while ago, actually, and had sprinted past prudence like a couple of drunken heirs.

Allyson explained that we knew Chris and Sims's company well, and I refrained from adding that we knew their lawyer even better after a winter spent amassing paperwork for our new course-owning partnership, an arrangement that had recently taken a hopeful turn and left us just enough breathing room for this second-home daydream.

When Bill said yes, it was suddenly all go, and we pushed our chips forward into the course ownership pot. But if I could find one more willing partner, we might be able to cling to some of our savings by investing a gentler sum. I wasn't looking to sacrifice more equity, but money that remained in the bank was worth more than other kinds, even if it only stayed there for a few months before sliding its way over to Western Sullivan Properties. There was a moment that fall—it lasted all of ten seconds—when I thought we'd have more than enough capital to go around, on a Zoom call with Colton who was running the numbers and said the entire course remodel was going to cost 400k. I felt my backside leave its seat, levitating with hope. "Hold on, I forgot to add this column," he said, and in one keystroke we were back to $800,000.

Mike Madden had seemed interested in what we were up to, and he was golf-crazy enough to entertain my pitch. Plus, he visited the area a few times every year as his boxing camp wasn't far away. Mike studied the numbers and ran the idea past his mom and his wife, Susie, and I owe a thank-you note to both. They told him that life was short, have fun, go buy yourself a golf course. It was unfortunate that his dad didn't get to weigh in, because I imagine he'd have been in Sullivan County's corner as well, a former caddie turned football Hall of Famer who loved golf and shared that passion with his son. John Madden had passed away a few years earlier, and I regretted missing Mike's invitations to visit their family's weekly NFL watch parties where his dad would hold court in a barn with a bar and a dozen televisions, and where the buffet was formidable (turducken was just a starter, he explained). When I visited Mike in Monterey, he took me to his dad's favorite restaurant down on the wharf, Café Fina, an Italian and seafood place where they kept his dad's regular table unoccupied and hung his Raiders jacket over his chair. On the banquette next to his corner seat, a small chalkboard clung to the wall with his dad's X's and O's scratched onto the slate, plays he'd dream up or dissect over dinner.

So we were a threesome joining Chris and Sims (plus Shaun, who we all agreed was getting his 2 percent stake), which left some financial breathing room—a few short puffs, really—if we wanted to home shop in Sullivan County. For what we would get here, the price was seductive—the Catskills' slump was a boon for anyone looking to buy, as this property would have cost three times its asking price down in the Philly suburbs. And when we stepped into a living room of walls covered with reclaimed barn wood and wide plank floors and windows to the ceiling that showed miles of hills that could have been Vermont but were only three hours from Philadelphia, we decided that we were.

The house was five minutes from the shops and restaurants of downtown Callicoon, a quant river town set on the New York side of the Delaware, and when we went for brunch at the Creek House that afternoon and met Irish Karen who ran the restaurant with her husband and served a full Irish breakfast on Sundays with bangers and rashers they picked up in New York City every week, I decided I wasn't going to miss our theoretical Florida retirement at all. The house was twenty-five minutes from the golf course, which seemed a comfortable buffer between work and home, and I was going to need it, because the projects we had planned for this year stretched the bounds of ambition. I already felt as if Sullivan County had been touched a few times by the wand of good fortune, but we were now asking for a fountain of miracles, and I feared for the day when we might drink it dry.

I was lucky to have partners who didn't sit around. Working with Chris and Sims meant the clubhouse demo could start tomorrow, and by that Christmas, the place had already been gutted by Sims's brother, Ryan, and his crew. The drop celling had been pulled down, revealing a tall canopy of bright wood that would be refinished and lit with dining room sconces. The former pro shop floor had been tiled and ovens had been moved over from the original Piccolo, its building on the other side of town now up for lease. The breezeway was framed in for a cozy new golf shop, and before our contracts were signed and moneys deposited, the old clubhouse was back on its feet. My hopes that Chris and Sims could get work here done quickly were exceeded by stunning, relentless progress, the likes of which this part of the world was not accustomed to.

Shaun and Colton spent the winter texting drawings for the course to each other while I got busy forming a new LLC to join a new LLC with Mike and Bill to join a new LLC with Chris and Sims. The only people busier than Chris and Sims's builders were our attorneys, and while Bill's initial affirmation was straightforward enough, transforming that commitment into binding legal paperwork was a crusade of text messages and long voice mails. Bill was a busy person and a moving target, so tracking down his social security number and creating a joint bank account and finding the lawyer who would do this deal on his behalf—it was months at sea, waiting for Bill to breach. He eventually gave me the number of a woman who arranged these sorts of things for him—not a manager, but a friend, as he didn't care for handlers and their false urgencies. He'd arrived at a place in his life where he focused on the things and the endeavors that pleased him and didn't suffer fools who thought he should do otherwise. Thankfully, owning a golf course remained one of those things, and by March we had a new partnership formed and funded. Chris sent me the details for our new entity's checking account, and we got busy mauling it, one signature at a time.

Back in November, we charted a propitious start for our course renovation by making a sweetheart deal with a local tree clearing company that saved us 50k off Colton's budget. Tree Champions bid 100k to clear fifteen acres of hillside pines (almost all at the end of their life cycle and ready for the mill), land we'd need if we were going to build two new holes and free up space for the driving range and putting course, amenities I was convinced would grow our audience among locals and aspiring golfers. Sims had plans for a new patio with an outdoor bar for dining, and setting it next to a Himalayas-style putting course would capture the golf-curious and give folks a reason to hang around after golf and dinner. Colton had drawn up a seven-hole short course as well that would loop around our someday lodge, but that spend was for another year. We focused first on clearing and hired Tim and his Tree Champions team who'd outbid their nearest competitor by a cautionary amount.

Tim was fit and young—I'd guess late twenties—and when we met with him that autumn, he was eager but perhaps too wide-eyed about the work. I suspected he was used to pulling down a few maples from somebody's front yard, and without saying it, his excitement for the job suggested it would be their biggest contract to date. But he said they could get it done, on time and on budget, and we weren't in a position to reject a lowball offer. Shaun sent me pictures throughout the winter; they were getting after it. The hillside was looking emptier by the day and it seemed the land would be ready come May for US Pitchcare, the construction company Colton had hired to push dirt and shape new greens. And then May came and I returned to Sullivan County for the season, and neither company was anywhere to be seen.

Pitchcare was a small (and affordable) operation that had been delayed on another project; spring rain had set them back a month, maybe more, but their owner, Conor, came by to make regular visits when Colton was in town. We hiked the woods and the stumps together, reviewing drawings on poster-sized sheets of paper while Colton walked the dirt and spray-painted lines from the end of a striping stick, denoting where fairways ended and began, where cart paths should be rerouted, and where greens would be pushed outward toward new edges. I couldn't make much sense of the schematics, unable to discern which stripe was a hill or a hollow, but orange lines on dirt were obvious and exciting, and even if painted soil wasn't permanent, it felt as if the land were changing with each new mark.

I'd imagined golf course architecture as something of a mystical science practiced by philosophical mages, a slow and opaque artform inspired by heavy books and dusty maps, but it was revealing itself to be dirty work done in boots. The decisions that we pundits debated with awkward passion on the message boards, the small choices we all marveled at and connected to overarching narratives about architectural principles—they happened by a few dots of spray paint and a few strikes of a shovel. As I scratched out spots with my heel and Colton marked them with tiny red flags, we looked more like kids playing with crayons than architects plying their trade, and I recalled my days in graduate school when we'd spend an evening emptying pitchers and arguing over why Leopold Bloom carries a bar of soap in his pocket throughout *Ulysses*. Maybe Joyce just needed a shower, I thought; maybe he had a shopping list on his mind. It might not all be magic, I learned, as we plotted mounds on the places where we needed to hide rocky soil or drainage pipes or stumps that would be too large to grind. And I remembered why renowned architect Gil Hanse called his team Caveman Construction: On one of their early jobsites, Gil's crew was looking to reshape some bunkers in the late afternoon, after the maintenance staff had locked up all the equipment and shovels for the day. His colleague, Bill Kittleman, grabbed a stick and started tearing at the bunker's walls and laughing. "Look at this, we are like a bunch of fucking cavemen out here," he said, "building bunkers with sticks!" If Gil could get it done with sticks, Sullivan County had plenty of those. Way too many, as far as Conor was concerned.

He was confident the scope of work could be completed in three months, but he confessed that he was worried about so much untouched timber. "There is a ton of clearing left to do," Conor said. "It's a good thing our team's behind schedule. If I sent my guys up here today, there isn't enough clear land for them to do much. Are your tree guys coming back?"

It had been the question of the spring and would become that summer's question as well. I felt like my daughter who ordered $5 T-shirts from Chinese websites that never quite reached our mailbox. The slope where the new sixth hole was meant to live looked like it had received half a shave, stumps and split trunks coating the land with an obstinate stubble. Our Tree Champs had gone MIA after two months; the equipment they'd left behind, muddy machines with big tires and empty claws, seemed to suggest their eventual return, but when that might happen, none of us could guess. Tim wasn't answering Shaun's calls or my texts. I resorted to some angry messages that involved legal action—if they held up the construction team, they'd be liable for the cost of paying Pitchcare to wait around—which finally lured Tim out to the course on a Monday morning.

The Tree Slobs are here, Shaun texted. *You want to talk to them?*

I hurried up to the course and found Tim walking the woods on the far edge of the property, land that should have been cleared for our new third hole but hadn't been touched (the thin lumber out there would be harder to sell, and I wondered if they'd bother cutting it at all). He was all apologies, and I found myself sympathizing with his trouble. After watching their operation that winter, Shaun had deciphered that Tim's company was tied to his in-laws' tree business, and that he relied on them for equipment and manpower. Tim explained to me that a recent falling-out among his relatives had forged a nasty family rift, and he was nearly tearful as he confessed that he was struggling to get any work done on his contracts.

I liked Tim—he was young and hungry for the work, and it was clear he was embarrassed by the stall-out at Sullivan County. His frustration seemed as real as ours, and you could see it as he walked our untouched corners, so much wood still overhead and weighing on his shoulders. I was sorry for his family troubles, but I told him that something had to be fixed. We'd already called a few other tree companies, and we'd need our deposit returned if he couldn't finish the work. He understood that his problems weren't our problems and promised he was going to get this job done—if he had to come out here with a chainsaw and haul it all out himself, it was getting finished. His determination felt honest, and I found myself rooting for him in his struggle against untended stumps and unreasonable in-laws. I offered to send a nasty note to his relatives if that helped, which he appreciated and said couldn't hurt, so after I threatened them with a lawsuit (I knew nothing of the how, who, or where of forestry lawsuits, but my message sounded like they were my legal forte), their trucks pulled up the next morning and their machines headed back down our hills. The money we'd saved on hiring them had gone into constructing a bridge that could get those machines over our stream, but no matter—the wood was moving again. And within a few days, that would be an undeniable and unfortunate reality.

During some long winter's nap, I'd daydreamed of golfers and bulldozers playing peacefully beside one another, like deer and brown bears nibbling grass side by side. The passing players would smile and wave to Mr. Excavator Operator as he quieted his engine for their strike, before plowing under the fairway they'd just played. Golfers and sod movers sharing a cold drink at the water cooler, commiserating over the potential our digging had unearthed. All handshakes and thank-yous, a playing worksite of gratitude for the fact that Sullivan County was finally getting some love after all these years.

Sullivan County under the knife, we'd learn, was slightly less dreamy. Other clubs would have closed for the season while work was under way, sparing their golfers from traversing deep tire ruts and playing around six-story piles of lumber that looked like some pagan bonfire was being planned beside our second tee. Ours was an intimate routing where we didn't have much space to hide the carnage, nor could we afford a season without any golf revenue. We'd hope for the best and resort to—*gulp*— temporary greens when we needed them, cutting cups into the fairway and asking guests to putt on tiny, improvised circles. We'd eventually need more of them than I'd hoped; some were necessitated by Shaun stripping sod and transplanting it to our new putting surfaces. Others were born of unforced errors.

The texts came quick and angry that morning. They were capitalized and misspelled, suggesting the fury with which Shaun was trying to fire up his SOS.

THEY DRAGGED A TREE ACROS 3 GREEN!!!! FIRE THEM NOW!!! GET THEM OUT OF HEERE!!!

He was inconsolable when I got him on the phone. "I walked through the whole fucking thing with them. I marked the trees for them to take. The big ones, growing over the fairway. I showed them how to get out and get back down the path. And I show up this morning and they left all the ones I marked and instead they cut down this giant fucker and dragged it right the hell out, straight over the green. They snapped the flagstick in two!"

The damage was worse than he described. Shaun had calmed a bit by the time I arrived, and we drove up to the third hole where a trail of torn leaves and busted branches extended from the green back down the middle of the fairway. I knew our tree guys weren't golfers, but even a passing knowledge of juvenile golf basics—*this is where you hit, this is where you putt*—would have told them they'd chosen an awful path. There was screaming between Shaun and Tim's operator who said he had no other way to get that tree out, which Shaun acknowledged as a byproduct of cutting down the wrong damn tree. My conversation with Tim was slightly more cordial; I tried to imagine a solution rather than rehash the missteps, and I told him repairing the gash dug across our green was a $10,000 job. He nodded at that. Then nodded some more. In his silence there was an acceptance that his final check would be lighter by 10k, and we'd get on with the business of fixing their mess.

We hadn't even brought out the construction team yet, and we were already down to eight and a half greens after Shaun roped off the gash and did his best to level, seed, and sand it with few such provisions on hand. It was indeed a new sort of year at Sullivan County, because while I once tried to escape the drafty weariness of our clubhouse to find peace on our nifty little course, the clubhouse was suddenly our beacon of progress. The signs for our new Piccolo Paese had arrived and were hanging out front, and the new patio was covered with benches and bright outdoor dining tables with yellow umbrellas. A few planters by the restaurant entrance—a door we hadn't even tried to open last year—welcomed visitors through a small gauntlet of fresh herbs, and we even had a smoker in the corner where a partner of Sims's was going to sell barbecue at lunch. We were only a week behind schedule on trying to open for Memorial Day (rebuilding a clubhouse and getting a restaurant inspected and open in five months seemed an aggressive deadline), but the dining room was bright and clean and decorated with old Liberty signage, and the metal-topped bar was long and new and looked out over our practice green where drinkers could wager on Phil's putts for hours on end.

Chris and Sims's team had even refurbished the downstairs locker room that now had freshly painted drywall and a new bathroom with proper, working fixtures. They tossed most of the rusted-out lockers but kept a few along the wall as a nostalgic touch, where member names from the 1950s and '60s still stuck to the doors on yellowing bits of paper. Whoever cleaned this place up and hauled out that unholy latrine,

I thought, deserved medals and commendations for distinguished service to golf.

Upstairs, the breezeway turned golf shop was small but cheerful. We didn't need much, I told Chris, and he delivered on that request. We had a few windows and French doors and some reclaimed tables where last year's leftover merchandise was displayed. John wasn't happy about the desk, however, and when I entered for the first time, I found him sitting behind a small white computer table Chris ordered off the internet. It looked like something you'd put in your kids' bedroom, or that my daughters would dress up with mirrors and use as a makeup station. Seeing John sitting there on a folding chair in the middle of the room behind a particleboard desk not wide enough for his elbows, a big scowl on his face—I was inclined to keep it, a reminder of our humble roots.

"We gotta do something about this" were his first words of our new season, and I laughed and told him he looked cute. I also told him that he looked like half of his former self; he was down at least fifty pounds and said he was walking much better after a handful of off-season surgeries. Gone were the baggy T-shirts and basketball shorts, swapped for khaki golf bottoms and collared Sullivan County gear befitting a man who was, with my encouragement, asserting himself as pro shop leader.

John's stride was more flexible now, if not his disposition. He was honest about it, at least—he admitted he was too old to be anything but himself, and that he wasn't interested in being bossed around at this stage of his life. The requests I'd made of staff couldn't be characterized as bossing anybody—we'd probably be better off if they could—so I knew to whom he was referring.

Atop our list of needs for the new partnership was hiring a general manager to oversee operations—food, golf, and events, now that we had a place to host such things. Chris and Sims could only be here so much, and now that I had a home down the road where my kids were spending their summer vacation, I'd be here less as well (it seemed ironic, but last year, I had nowhere else to go—mow and play golf, or sit in front of the air conditioner in my rental). Trey was a good find. He didn't have much experience in hospitality or golf—his background was mostly retail in NYC—but he'd moved up here with his partner and was enthusiastic for the job. There wasn't a wellspring of administrative talent in these parts, and we felt lucky to find someone with energy and enthusiasm and a head on his shoulders.

John, had he been consulted on our hire, would have voiced a dissenting vote.

It would have been difficult to find two more contrary characters in the Catskills. If John was Brooklyn, Trey was West Village. John's hair clipped tight at the barbershop; Trey's look sculpted at the salon. John blunt and unfiltered and older; Trey deferential and polite and young. They did have one thing in common—they both believed they knew how to do the other's one's job. When Trey walked into the shop with some display bowls and racks, I could tell that golf was going to be our own fortress this year, and that John was going to dig the moat.

"What's this for?" John asked when Trey proudly placed a ball dispenser on the desk. It was one of those wire chute racks you saw at putt-putt courses, from which you choose between red, purple, or blue.

"It's for golf balls. People need balls to play golf."

John shot me a look, then tried to be courteous.

"Okay. We don't sell balls that way, but that's good, we'll find a use for it."

Trey's artisanal bowls might come in handy for ball markers, we decided, and he'd done well with the belt display. We lacked space for hanging belts, so the little box he'd ordered was a nice addition to our blank slate of a shop. I could tell John hated watching me bond with Trey over how to best display our merchandise. Pushing apparel was Trey's bread and butter, and we agreed on the shelf and hanger systems he would order to maximize our square footage. He left with a short list of jobs and said he'd be back to check in later.

"Are you kidding me?" John said. He picked up the ball rack. "The fuck are we going to do with this?"

"He's not a golf guy. That's fine. That's why you're here."

"Yeah, but I'm telling you, if he starts telling me what to do—"

"He's the general manager. He's mostly dealing with the restaurant, but if he needs something from you, you need to help."

John stewed for a moment. "General manager. Right. You know I ran a facility with two hundred employees? The rehab, right down the road, I was in charge of the whole thing. I know what it takes to run a business, and I'm telling ya, this guy don't got it."

"Well, you don't have to worry about that. That's not your call," I said. "Let's keep the golf moving and be nice."

"You know I'll be nice." He smiled. "I'm always nice."

Trey scored an early triumph when he acquired a horse trailer that had been converted into a handsome outdoor bar. The inside was paneled with bright wood and a side panel swung upward to reveal ice chests and a point-of-sale terminal that completed our vision for an après-golf outdoor hang. Still, assimilating into our team would be an uphill hike for Trey. He was order imposed on a troupe used to doing improv. The new guy hadn't sweat with us in the old shop, and he was a year behind on learning this crew's peccadilloes and personalities: who needed to hear things twice, and who didn't want to hear them once. It wasn't his fault nor was it fair, but in this building, he'd forever be the outsider. It was the nature of life up here, where a faint but firm line was drawn between lifers and newcomers. You felt it most acutely in the offseason, at the gas station and in the hardware store, where the lady behind the counter knew everybody's name but yours. You couldn't blame the residents for keeping up their guard; they'd been abandoned by the city folks before. That sting manifested itself in a suspicion of new anythings; it was safer to complain about progress than be disappointed again by progress revoked. I'd felt it at the golf course where the members had to watch me mow grass for months before raising a hand to wave. Flash and promises didn't play here, but a glint of struggle did. It felt a little like the Philadelphia I'd grown up around in that regard—if you could prove you knew the grind, they'd welcome you as their own. Trey was not any of those things. And John was.

He hadn't been born in the Catskills, but John was as local as they came. He'd gone to Grossinger's as a kid on class trips from Brooklyn (he'd sneak out the window at night and jog to Pizza Hut, unsated by American Plan dining) and had been to Paul's Hotel during the twilight years of the Borscht Belt, when it was a Mafia hang set beside a lake in which troubled wiseguys were said to find the water without a life vest. Though he'd stuck around the Catskills to distance himself from his relatives' line of work, he'd first landed here in his twenties for the same reason Shaun discovered Sullivan County—rehab tourism. When he left Brooklyn to get clean, he told his mother not to worry, that he was going to go up there and get better, and someday he would be running the place. It was the hubris of an addict, and recovery was meant to realign such ego and inspire some lifesaving humility. But fair play to John—he got better, got a job at the recovery center, and would eventually manage the facility and oversee a large workforce. We were now experiencing the turbulence of downsizing John from rehab boss to golf club subordinate; year one had been a lifeboat whim, a haphazard stumble toward profitability where our chain of command ended at whoever had the first answer. But now that we were a real business with real resources and real plans, we needed a dose of organizational health that some would be more willing to swallow than others.

The girls came up for opening night at Piccolo, and though the servers struggled (a waitress quit five minutes before her shift, a person-nel adjustment that Sims wasn't mourning), Chef Baco's Northern Italian dishes were medalists. He had emigrated from Croatia so his take on Italian wasn't veal parm and gravy, but authentic Northern tortellacchi and spiedini that came with an anchovy and caper sauce and had to be the tastiest dish this side of Manhattan. John stopped by our table to say hello—his mother's cooking had made him snobbish about Italian food, but he said Baco's menu was bona fide—and Allyson asked him about the tattoo poking out from under the sleeve of his new staff golf shirt (our standards were indeed rising). John proudly revealed the Sullivan County logo that covered most of his triceps, and her eyes opened wide. "That is awesome," she said. "But I thought Tom was joking!"

"Nope. Sullivan County, through and through," John said.

Allyson smiled and said, "Well, you can't go anywhere else now, John. You're stuck with us."

"More like you guys are stuck with me," he said, nudging my shoul-der. "This tattoo's probably the only thing keeping him from firing me!"

We laughed, though my chuckle was a guilty one. I was not plotting John's departure, but I was aware that he'd been butting heads not just with Trey, but with Shaun as well. That winter, the maintenance barn's roof breathed its last gasp and gave way, so Shaun moved his gear up to the back side of the cart shed. There was just enough room for his ma-chines amid a parking puzzle of twenty new E-Z-GO carts I'd leased for the season (new to us, anyway—they'd come off a one-year lease from a walking-only US Open elite, maybe the few carts they kept for golfers with medical accommodations, and getting their leftovers felt like we were dressing up in royal hand-me-downs). It was a crowded and (hope-fully) temporary solution where Shaun and Bearded Chris had to service their machines outside the barn, so our greenskeeping operation took on the appearance of a gearhead campout beside the parking lot. It put golf ops and turf ops into an uncomfortable proximity, and a daily war was waged for access to the barn's one spigot.

In the golf club work hierarchy, turf can be a bit of a bully—*there's no golf without us!*—so when John would send Henry over to wash carts, if Shaun was stressed or busy, he might snap over being asked to borrow his hose because the golf guys had busted theirs. Shaun and John could both run hot, and the ensuing text exchanges (in which I was graciously included) involved a lot of ALL CAPS demands for respect and accusations of disloyalty, to which I would eventually reply: *The next person who texts on this thread no longer works here.* That would settle them down for a few minutes, until they each texted me individually to resume a litany of grievance.

We had barely embarked upon our bold new era at Sullivan County, and the stakes and stress were already exposing our fissures. Shaun and John both knew my threats were idle: I'd quit Sullivan County before Shaun did, and John had more job insurance than that tattoo. When it came to scheduling shifts and ordering inventory and hiring the kids we needed outside, the shop required someone who was always around and looking to lead, and there was only one candidate who lived across the street and excelled at drawing up to-do lists and translating them into orders.

Chris and Sims agreed that my role needed to evolve. More owner, less operator—if Sullivan County was meant to survive, its staff had to learn how to run it without deferring to us on where to park the carts, how to fold the napkins, and what to charge for a T-shirt. It meant encouraging John's leadership without completely dropping the reins. He was happy for more autonomy, and I gave him the emails and phone numbers for our vendors and told him ninety-day terms didn't mean our inventory was free. We argued over whether we needed gloves and rental clubs for lefties—he was right, because we did—but I could trust him to shop prudently on the Titleist website. I could also trust him for the local perspective. He was tied into the Monday Night crew and heard the town gossip. I needed an ear to resident opinion, and while I wished his reports were rosier, he knew why the Liberty crowd wasn't signing up for memberships this year.

"They don't think we're open. They see the trucks and the mess and they don't want to come up here," he explained. "And the league guys, they're not happy about the temporary greens, the crap all over the place. They asked for the restaurant to be open for them on Mondays, so we opened last Monday, and then they complained about the menu and the prices and spent hardly nothing." He could barely bring himself to say it: "They want the dollar hot dogs back."

John's willingness to take the hot dog bullets—it made him truly indispensable. We'd have enough customers to sustain a restaurant for three, maybe four months out of the year—dollar dogs were out of the question, and it hurt my soul that our locals couldn't get that. I'd read the Facebook rants about our annual membership—bumped up to $650, after a million-plus-dollar spend—and wanted to throw up my hands and surrender. I watched the cost of golf skyrocket elsewhere while our paltry prices were met with grief instead of gratitude, and I wondered why we were bothering at all. I wanted to scream that their idea of what golf should cost had already killed the course a handful of times, and that if the people here were going to fight us, we could find more gratifying ways to lose money.

I didn't just need John to keep me tuned in; in those moments, I also needed him to back me off the brink, reminding me that we weren't the first people charged with keeping this club afloat. If the locals had strong opinions about our endeavors, they were earned over a century's worth of care for a place they might now find hard to recognize.

"Listen, when they see the improvements after the work is done, they'll love it and they'll come back," John said. "Don't let the loud ones ruin what's happening here. Some of the guys get it. I've been telling them, just wait, be patient, it'll be worth it. I mean, it is a mess out there. They've got plenty to complain about."

John was right, and the uproar wasn't unanimous. Dan Yaun was excited that his course was getting a facelift, and Mike from the league still played three days a week and told us he couldn't wait to test the new routing. One of the league members stopped me on my way to my car (I dodged the Monday crowd, opting to cover my ears to their input) and thanked me for our efforts. "Rome wasn't built in a day," he said. "More of us get that than you probably think. The grumpy guys are always the noisiest." There was just enough optimism to keep me from asking Allyson to cancel the shades she'd ordered for the new house and put our dream home back on the market. I channeled resentment toward motivation; if we could prove the naysayers wrong, if we could make them love golf holes they didn't want, it would be a selfish satisfaction that transcended bank statements and new bunkers.

Now we just had to do it. The restaurant team had proven that one could pull off miracles at Sullivan County, but I worried that moving dishes might be quite a different contest from moving dirt.

SUMMER 2024

I was confident Allyson wouldn't mind. So much so that I forgot to ask her.

To shave cost off the construction budget, we'd crossed accommodations off our bid sheet, assuming I could borrow a house from Sims to house the construction crew. When all his homes rented for the season and Western Sullivan's inventory all sold, I made reservations on Airbnb for an unknown number of overnight guests—some weeks we'd have five guys on site, some weeks we'd have a dozen—for an unspecific range of dates. June passed before Pitchcare was back on schedule, which meant I forgot about the place with the jacuzzi that I'd rented for them that month, which had the owner wondering why her house looked like nobody had stayed there—because nobody had, I explained. I ended up burning budget on ghost rentals and last-minute leases when the work schedule pushed into August, and rather than ask Chris to waste more money on my schemes for quartering a construction crew, I recalled that there were empty beds in a house down the road that Allyson had just appointed with new bedding and a wraparound sofa from Pottery Barn. So I gave our entry code to a team of sod layers and bulldozer men and asked them to leave their boots by the door.

The girls were back home by the second half of August, busy getting ready for a new school year, and I was only up in Sullivan a few nights every week—it seemed a shame to let the house sit idle. The crew were inconspicuous houseguests who didn't use the pool and made their beds better than I would have, and aside from not quite knowing where their next sleep was scheduled, Pitchcare was a refreshingly professional operation after six months begging Tim to come knock down another tree.

The summer had been a series of threats, work, and stalls on the tree front; there was enough clear land for Pitchcare to get started, but the mule's pace of Tim's team meant we had tree trucks working alongside bulldozers, when the two were never meant to graze side by side. It all left little room for golf, though we still needed to collect greens fees, and my mowing routine had grown less frequent as hairy fairways became the least of our concerns. I showed up when Shaun needed me, but I struggled to steer my way toward the golf course anymore. I couldn't bear the sight of Tim's unattended trucks camped in our parking lot as Pitchcare's dozers grew impatient and started knocking over trees and brush themselves. The only thing worse than the trees they didn't cut was where they left the ones they did. They'd sold the good wood and given up on hauling the rest, so piles of tree trunks lined or rerouted our fairways. Shaun said he could burn it all come winter, but in the meantime, greens fees rightly slowed to a trickle. I considered discounting golf even further, but going lower than $20 for a round seemed futile; might as well just hang out the honor box and shut down the shop.

My Sullivan County honeymoon was officially over when a visiting golfer told me he had been stung by a hornet from the nest in the bunker behind number two, and my first instinct was to tell him he shouldn't have hit his ball there. The hustle and juggle of trying to keep carts moving around excavators had feasted on our morale. Shaun was doing twelve-hour days moving sod from former fairways to new ones, which meant constant watering on a course without an irrigation system. He bought a pump and a hose and the biggest water tank that would fit onto the back of our busted spray rig and repurposed its wheels as a poor man's fire truck. He'd suck water from our pond to fill the tank, then zoom over to the new sod and spray until the tank was empty. From sunup to sundown, he'd fill and water while our pro shop guys grew disheartened from the lack of traffic. Even Henry lost his inspiration, no longer bothering to play in the morning on a course that was down to seven semifunctional holes, and Phil's shadow was no longer crossing our fairways in the afternoon. Putting and chipping to a temporary pin cut into a fairway wasn't worth his two hours, and I couldn't blame him. I was keeping my distance, too.

My first-season routine of mornings spent mowing down the dew and afternoons where I'd deposit stacks of fives and twenties at the bank in town—it was a life hard to recall now amid the dirt and dust and idle carts. I came up once a week and drove loops around the property, steering clear of anyone who looked annoyed or overworked or armed with a question, which meant I kept to myself. Then I spotted a lone worker digging in the lost bunker on number two and wondered if Shaun had hired some extra help while he was on sod duty. The man was tall and wasn't wearing work jeans or a blue Pitchcare shirt. Instead, he was dressed in beach shorts and sneakers and his face, red with sweat, looked a lot like that of an old friend of mine from England. I drove closer and discovered that, somehow, that's precisely who it was.

Julian had joined me on my Irish and Scottish ventures, not so much as a golfer, but as proof that preparing for golf trips was an overvalued undertaking. He showed up for a ten-day hike around Ireland with a pair of tennis shoes, six balls, and a rain-absorbent sweater, and in Scotland he found the golf courses to be long, indirect avenues to British ales and meat pies. We had been bar mates turned best friends back in Philadelphia where he'd landed from Manchester after following a girl to America. He was single within a few years, went back to school at Temple, and met a German girl with whom he started a family; they eventually decided to move back to Europe to be closer to both of theirs. He had been living outside Munich for the last eleven years where, during our infrequent text message check-ins, he'd confirm that he still couldn't speak German. Too proud an Englishman, I suspected, and he was raising his son, Henry, as a proper Liverpool fan. Julian had seen me at my best and worst, at my drunkest and my most sober, and he was the rare friend from my drinking days who didn't drop me for deserting the ranks. We had not seen each other in years, and that he was now standing in a sand trap in Sullivan County made little sense, yet perfect sense. He was an up-for-anything character who wore his life like a loose-fitting shirt, very much like the baggy white T-shirt he was donning today that read: I CAME, I SAW, I SAT DOWN.

He put down his shovel to give me a hug, and I asked him what the hell he was doing here.

"I've been following your posts and thought you could use a hand," he said, wiping sweat from his forehead. "I'm in the States for a few weeks. Didn't know where you might be traveling and didn't want to bother you, but I thought I might find you here. I met Shaun this morning. Nice fellow. I said I wanted to help so he gave me a shovel and brought me out here. Watch out for the hornets," he said, pointing to a hole in the corner of the bunker. "Nasty little buggers."

He'd landed at JFK yesterday and rented a place in Liberty for a few nights. He said he went out on the town last evening, which is not something I'd ever heard of anyone doing in Liberty, and I tried to envision a tall Brit wandering the taquerias and kosher shops in search of a pint. "I found a bar with baseball on TV. Nice people. The wings weren't bad," he said. "The grocery store was interesting. They had a toy section with a rabbi costume for kids. The hat and curls and everything. I was going to get it for Henry for Halloween, but then I thought I might not."

English Julian from Germany finding his way to the Catskills was not a shock; his itinerant nature was suited to such a detour. What surprised me was the idea that my world included this sort of friend, someone unselfish enough to work a bunker on his holidays, who wanted to join my undertaking whether I was there or not. I was surprised by the notion that I might deserve such a friend. I was sure I didn't. I excelled at acquaintances but as my life hopped from one chapter to the next—from school to career, from city to suburbs, from bars to kids, from sloth to golf—former bonds faded, my time and energy too focused on finding new ones. Allyson had been the only constant throughout, and I wondered how a cross-ocean visit to see a mate whose voice one hadn't heard in a decade was a no-brainer for one person, while, to me, it felt like an act of unfathomable generosity well beyond my own resources.

Maybe I was too much of a next-thing type, easily seduced by new places and people. Maybe I didn't have the guts to keep someone close when we disappointed each other, preferring the faultlessness of relationships at a distance. Maybe I was a lazy friend. Maybe I was selfish. I was probably all those things, but if I was going to learn to be otherwise, Sullivan County was my chance. It was a break from the lonely keyboard and connections serviced by thumbs-up emojis. I'd done my best to create a life that didn't depend on others, but that was not an option for the life I'd found here. I now relied on Shaun and John, Chris and Sims, Bill and Mike—and so many others, including an Englishman who didn't know how to dig a bunker but was willing to try.

I might not have been fly-fishing yet, but Shaun was pleased that I was at least reading about it in books by David Coggins, one of which, *The Optimist*, offered a sentence I wished I'd lent to one of my own paragraphs: "Once established, angling can support the weight of a friendship at a great distance." Golf could do the same, and though Julian and I weren't bonded by rounds of golf (he was an infrequent golfer who was just as happy to drop a new ball as find his own), the places the game had taken us had forged something stronger than I realized. We took up like we'd left Ireland yesterday, laughing at the absurdity of either of us attempting manual labor (we'd once tried our hands at hardscaping when my parents needed a new front walk, and what we assembled was a slate-and-mortar atrocity on which no ankle was spared) and waiting for Shaun to come show us how these shovels were meant to work. He eventually drove up the hill with a truck bed of sand, and we smoothed it over the spots where Julian had excavated mud that morning, and suddenly we'd made a bunker out of a sunken brown bed of weeds.

We celebrated our progress by eating barbecue in the Adirondacks that afternoon, and that night I took Julian over to Livingston Manor where one could approximate a night on the town, with good pizza and ice cream and a trip to the brewery that served nonalcoholic beer in cans. We replayed nights with old friends whom neither of us saw anymore, recounting an erstwhile bar fight and supplementing it with punches neither of us probably threw. And we talked about things we couldn't have imagined someday discussing when we were furniture at that pub on Fairmount Avenue—whether our kids actually enjoyed sports, the cost of their impending college choices (free in Germany, so Henry was unlikely to follow Julian to Temple), and an aching right hip that was killing the bottom half of my golf swing. We talked about the golf course, too.

"You finally found a course where neither of us has to pay. It's about time," he said. "Can you imagine? If we'd had our own course, back then? The damage we'd have done?"

"I don't think it would have lasted very long."

"Not long at all," he said. "We wouldn't have made a penny."

Julian stayed in Sullivan County for three days, digging ditches for Shaun in the morning and playing temporary greens with me in the afternoon. On Friday we had lunch at the gas station where I recommended the burger, and when we went looking for a seat, the only open booth squeezed us against the back of a large man in a biker's cut patched with a skeletal insignia. He wore a bandana and sported a beard through which his hot dog barely fit, and I hesitated, wondering if we might be better off eating in the car. But Julian sat down and dug in, and in a moment, the man glanced over his shoulder. Suspicion in his eyes, he glanced at us again. He finally turned around and tapped Julian on the shoulder and said, "Hey, you guys need the ketchup?" which Julian accepted with thanks and squirted on his bun.

"Good people up here," he said. "And this burger is fantastic."

When he left the following morning, there was no grand goodbye, no tears shed, no music played. We half-hugged and said we would see each other again soon, because that, it turns out, is what friends do.

Watching Julian rise early to put in hours at my course was a well-timed shaming that pushed me back out onto the Toro, restarting my semi-regular morning routine. I'd spend a chunk of every afternoon hanging around the Pitchcare trucks and talking with Willie, the shaper and job foreman who I was sure could sign his name with his excavator's blade. He was a master of dirt craftsmanship, and while I could see the shape of golf holes in the earth he was pushing, what I mostly saw were unplayable lies and a clock that was moving too quickly. We'd missed our summer grow-in, which meant we'd have to hydroseed in the fall and hope for the best, which meant we'd have to find the money to pay someone with a tanker full of seed and fertilized slurry. We struck most of the new cart paths off the work list and reallocated some funds.

Colton visited every few weeks to remind me that we were the luckiest guys in golf—the only thing better than owning a golf course was getting to build one, and with his architect's eyes he could see past the acres of dried dirt and the wind-whipped dust and the tree clearance that looked as if it had been performed by hurricane instead of by hand, and still see the dream. I'd found little time to dream of late. After Julian left, I was back to finding beds for the crew and comforting our remaining members and finding out where the hell we'd hid Fred's clubs.

The former state of our locker room seemed an unambiguous announcement that it was off-limits; anyone with reasonable standards for the places they entered would reach the second step and know they had arrived in a forsaken space. Little did we know, Fred had been trudging down those steps last season, storing his clubs in one of the crooked lockers that he somehow accessed by clearing a path through a century's worth of clutter. When he emailed me that June to ask where his locker had gone, the one he'd had for thirty years in which he'd stored an irreplaceable set of beloved Lynx irons, my thoughts bounced from one confusion to the next.

The locker room was not operational; nobody knew he was using it; nobody should have been down there aside from employees or an exorcist; we clearly weren't charging for locker rentals or advertising them as part of a membership, so why did he have a locker? And if he did, where was it now?

The pro shop guys were oblivious about Fred's trips down below. The same went for Shaun. Chris said most of the old lockers were beyond salvaging and had been hauled out and trashed during that winter's demolition. I wrote Fred back, regretting to inform him that his clubs were likely lost to the dump, apologizing but defending our actions by stating that we were under new ownership and the new staff had been left uninformed about his club storage. Even if we'd known, someone leaving their clubs beneath a clubhouse that closed in October and reopened in April wasn't a circumstance we could have foreseen.

I hated the idea of tossing away someone's prized set of sticks, and Fred hated that idea, too—he asked for some sort of reimbursement, a position with which I sympathized, but putting a price on irons from the 1980s wasn't easy math. I contemplated offering him a set of previous generation Titleists that were tuned to my specs and sitting in my garage, but I'd pegged them as our next rental set. I said the best I could offer was a discount on his membership and accepted the fact that we would likely lose his business, which along with most of Liberty that season, we did.

Last year, it would have broken my heart to lose a longtime local, but I was local now myself, and with Catskills residence came a spoonful of jadedness that proved useful in such situations. We couldn't please everybody, and I had warmed to that perspective. Still, I was too quick to paint our Liberty golfers with a brush I should have reserved for the bitter few. Plenty of our players appreciated the fact that we were spending money in their town, even if they weren't going to spend theirs here this season. But some golfers would, and they wrote to me hoping they'd have that chance.

Not far behind Fred's email was another message entirely void of complaint. It bore a simple and small request that did more good for me than for the person who was asking it.

Travis was from New Jersey and he had a son who was spending his summer in the Catskills at a camp for children with severe autism. He asked if he might bring Michael up to our course when we weren't busy. His message was almost apologetic in tone—he didn't want to impose and said he would let other groups play through if they were slow. Michael would probably only chip and putt and hit a few drives, he explained, and if we were too busy to accommodate them, he'd completely understand.

I told Travis that he and Michael were required to come see us this year. Sullivan County was made for stress-free, take-it-at-your-own-pace golf, I explained, and they were welcome any time, any day, whether we were busy or not. We had rental sets if he needed them, and if he arrived when the pro shop was closed, have at it and pay later.

I expect no laurels for inviting a father and his autistic son to our golf course; minimum decency should require no mention, but it was clear from Travis's message that finding quiet tee sheets at courses where they'd feel comfortable was a challenge. Public courses in the Northeast were jammed come summer, and his note reminded me that while we needed to be busy enough to meet payroll, we never wanted to be too busy for beginners or tourists or fathers-and-sons looking for space to be unbothered. One of Sullivan County's assets was feeling like you had the place to yourself, and the trick was sustaining that while remaining solvent. We had the quiet and empty bit down pat; the crowded part would be a fun problem should it ever raise its head.

I found Colton and Willie down in our far corner of the property where a few months before we had walked a forest of thin trees not much taller than our heads, a few of them ringed by piles of rotting apples. We noted that we should leave the apple trees, and we worked our way down to the other side of the pond, balancing our boots along the edge of the creek that leaked from where beavers had dammed up the back side of the water. We located a low-lying pad of mossy ground that seemed dry enough for golf, an empty saucer of turf inviting someone to putt across it. We had no idea how far its center was from the tees we had staked up above, but we didn't care. It was a natural green site beside a creek at the bottom edge of a slanted hillside that could play as a wild kicker, tossing wayward drives toward the pin. We planted small flags around its edges and hoped that someday we'd move enough brush to maybe golf here, and when I drove my cart that direction in August, the hole was cleared and the hillside shaped into smooth, brown soil. Willie sat in the cabin of his machine and nodded at the green Colton was conjuring with orange dashes in the dirt.

Colton and I walked over to the water's edge where the green would end beside a cluster of narrow tree stumps that had been nibbled by our beavers, their teeth marks still visible on small spears sticking out of the dirt.

"Natural hazard stakes," Colton noted, and he showed me where an old tree was clinging to the bank and leaning out over the creek. Its trunk created a short sort of gangplank from the green to the water's edge, and we decided it was a feature worth working into the green's contours. I showed Willie where we could create a hump that ran from the tree's base into the heart of the green; it would bisect the putting surface with a natural hillock that would draw players' eyes out toward the tree and the creek and would look as if it had been formed by roots instead of by dozer. Colton painted the depth and width of our addition, and Willie got busy dropping dirt that he'd smooth into a soft mound that would look like it had been there forever.

Willie was a large man whose frame filled most of his excavator's cabin. His hands were stained the color of soil, and his brow was permanently speckled by wet drops of work. I never saw him take a lunch break and I never saw him leaving or arriving; I rarely spotted him anywhere but seated in front of a dashboard of levers, as if he were sewn to his machine. There was little his excavator couldn't do, it seemed—prying up old cart path, flattening brush, turning over stumps, and smoothing out dirt that was beginning to look like fairway.

Shaun adored Willie for his skill and his diligence and his solutions for our every shortcoming. We all did. He'd walked into wishful thinking, and with the help of a five-man team who didn't take many breaks, either, he'd turned it into what Colton had to remind me we were building—a better golf course, with holes of a quality I'd hoped for but never believed we'd see at Sullivan County. We'd been tossing darts at an idea and flowing money toward an ambition, with only the vaguest notion of how to move from *A* to *B*. And when you worked that way, you either drowned in a mire of good intentions, or got saved by someone who knew precisely where *B* was located and pursued it like a pro. Willie didn't say much, which was surprising on a job with so many obstacles up for debate. He just got on with it, ticking tasks off his punch list until September arrived and suddenly our beds were no longer being slept in. I found our house empty but clean, the bedsheets tucked tightly at the corners. Willie and his team worked on their first day and they worked on their last, then disappeared with their machines, off to the next job, leaving us a golf course that was unrecognizable in the most beautiful way.

We decided our new hole down by the pond would be a par-three, maybe three-and-a-half. Par was a handy but overvalued concept; it was a relatively young idea, as far as golf conventions go, and was invented as a way for golfers to play without an incarnate opponent. Golf was traditionally a game of matches, but when you fancied a casual stroll or couldn't find a partner, you could go out and play against a ghost, the British Bogey Man—cousin to the American boogieman—who had already scored a number listed on your scorecard. Bogey scoring lasted into the twentieth century when improvements in equipment and abilities saw it replaced by lower numbers known as par. It was a way to measure success, and I appreciated it as such, but lending it too much credence when deciding where a green or tee should go seemed like an artless choice. Pick the best spots for both, and while we'd originally planned a longer hole for our new third, we opted for the best patches the land offered and didn't worry about sums and scorecards.

It was a joyful hole; so was the new par-three sixth we'd dug out of the forest where a small horseshoe of a green was backed by a mountain slope that would save long shots and dribble them down to the putting surface. Our new ninth felt even stronger. Sullivan County had formerly finished with a flat, mucky fairway that pointed you toward the abandoned side of our clubhouse where we stacked cardboard boxes and empty pallets, but now you'd come home from a perched tee and drive over the second tee box with a church spire for a target. Your second shot played to a ninth green that rolled into a vast new putting course, a touch borrowed from Oakmont's ninth, where the practice green and target green share one large lot of grass.

Front of mind in Colton's routing was the social experience for visitors; the layout had foursomes crisscrossing on three or four occasions, a hub and spoke concept centered around the water station behind the first green that would make golf here a more connected, communal experience. The course was still mostly dirt—Shaun had located a hydroseeding tank and it was on the way—but the difference between shaped dirt and plain dirt was enough to get our locals looking and wondering and asking when the new holes would be open for play. It was like touring a home that was all studs, just before the drywall had been hung. It might not be finished but you could tell you wanted to live there.

I took pictures of all the work and headed home in late September to show Allyson what Willie and Colton and Shaun had made. I don't think she grasped the victory of each new mound and budding bit of green, but she could tell we'd done a lot of something and said it all looked nice. I studied the pictures, flipping through tee box views pointed at new greens, pausing at views no one had ever seen before at Sullivan County, and it struck me that what we had built was a golf course without a weak note. They weren't all symphonies, but each hole was unique and eye-catching, and taken together, they were the thing I'd selfishly wanted since the day I first set foot on its snowy acres: a course I was dying to play.

I'd always enjoyed a loop around our nine. I hadn't enjoyed the walk up to three very much, and I found a few holes rather boring, but any golf was good golf, and I was glad to be playing. But I'd never imagined our nine-holer as a course I'd choose over a tidy country club or some luscious routing posted on Instagram. And now, I suspected that I might. And thank goodness, because the curious golfers who'd visited us that first year had found a novel place to play, but having explored the story they'd read about on Facebook, they might have little reason to return. We wouldn't have to rely on goodwill or podcast cachet once we got the holes grown in and the construction scars stitched up. That might be next month or next year or the year after, but the drawings we'd all gotten giddy about now lived on our property, and soon we'd be happy to send golfers out to play holes they might long think about, holes they might want to visit again on a course they'd be proud to call home.

FALL 2024

I wasn't surprised that Trey didn't last through the season. He was a nice man with the best intentions, but running a restaurant and a golf club requires a contradictory blend of traits—you need a hawkish gentility and a delicately urgent demeanor, where rigid organization appears effortless and labor looks luxurious. It's not an easy mix and one I'd be too timid to attempt, so there was no blame assigned when we all agreed that he wouldn't finish out the fall at Sullivan County. And there were more changes in the offing: Baco had decided to retire at the end of October when the course and restaurant closed. Piccolo had done decent numbers, but he'd been making fresh pasta for decades and deserved a break.

Without Baco cooking for his loyal following, it wouldn't be worth keeping the Piccolo name and menu, and we'd have to rebrand the restaurant come springtime. It was both a loss and an opportunity—I'd miss the spiedini, but we'd struggled to get diners golfing and golfers dining, and a menu with wings and a burger might lure more visitors inside. The patio barbecue was smoked excellence, but it was cost-intensive, and we learned that only a handful of players wanted to sit down to a half-pound of brisket at the turn, so the smoker would be headed elsewhere as well. There were tweaks to be made, for sure, but considering that it took three of us to burn popcorn a year ago, our new food operation had been a victory. Not a profitable victory, however, and the same could be said for golf.

John had warned me in the spring that we should take our work estimates and double them. I knew about overages and contingencies, but I pegged his pessimism to a Brooklyn upbringing where some of his friends made a living collecting envelopes at construction sites. Some nights after work, we'd have dinner together at the bar at Piccolo, and I'd tease out stories from his *Bronx Tale* childhood. His uncle had been a captain for Vincent "The Chin" Gigante who I remembered seeing in news stories as a kid. They called him "The Oddfather" for roaming Greenwich Village in bathrobe and slippers, trying to confuse his FBI surveillance and lay the seeds for an insanity defense. The Genovese gang wasn't as large as the other families, John explained, but they were the envy of the five families as the most disciplined, most loyal crew, who knew that speaking Gigante's name out loud would trigger a swift whacking. If you needed to reference the boss, you either pointed to your chin or made a cupped *C* with your hand. And you never received his instructions directly. The Chin invented a system of runners where messages were passed off between multiple couriers with contrary information, coded so that only the final recipient knew which message was genuine. In John's case, his uncle was careful as well—too careful for his liking. "He used to ask me to warm up his car in the morning and I'm a kid so yeah, I'll start your car. I had no clue he was checking to see if there was a bomb in it."

We hadn't had to grease anybody to get our machines moving, and I was pleased to tell John he'd been wrong—the work had come in on budget (with a few wish-list projects nixed along the way). Still, we were broke heading into the off-season thanks to an overly optimistic estimate of golf and restaurant revenue. The buffer we'd left ourselves for planning and engineering costs for the home sites had been swallowed by a decline in income and an uptick in labor. The restaurant wasn't breaking even yet—not surprising for a first season, Sims said—and with golfers more interested in playing on grass than dirt, our register in the shop had become a paper holder. The Monday League was still showing up, but some came primarily to nurse a grudge. One week Griff gave John ten bucks and said that was all the course was worth. The next week he paid nothing, just hopped in a cart and teed off. John's texts were ripe with plots for revenge, but I told him to let it go. Their complaints weren't without merit, and though most of them saw the bigger picture for Sullivan County's future, the state of our bank account had me thinking Griff was right to wonder if we knew what the hell we were doing.

It was time to go back to the Munson.

I'm not sure how my life's biggest financial decisions became intertwined with a silver-clad diner in Liberty, New York, but hot sauce on hash browns would forevermore taste like wild fiscal leaps. When a sitdown was required, we only needed to name a time. For a place that sold cheap breakfasts, the New Munson Diner was proving to be a very expensive spot.

I met Chris and Sims in our booth in the back and Chris broke down our *P*'s and our *L*'s—heavy on the *L*'s. We'd burned through the money he'd earmarked for developing the homes, which were our only viable strategy for recouping our investment. We'd had $1.5 million to work with that year and had missed our mark by roughly $150,000. It wasn't a disastrous sum for a startup entity, and on the golf side, a half-dozen outings next year could fill that gap. But to reach next year, there was still payroll to cover and a restaurant to relaunch. Taxes and insurance and utilities didn't stop when the pro shop closed, and as I pushed around my eggs we wondered where we might find a new chunk of cash that would allow us to open the course we'd just built and see Sullivan County reach its one hundredth year.

A loan was discussed but rates were ugly and debt undesirable. Plus, we already had a big borrow built into our business plan for a future lodge and short course. We considered going back to all the partners and asking for more capital, but having just cut checks that year, it seemed short timing to come asking for more. And this partner had no more to offer. We settled on looking for one more investor who would come in for an equal share as the rest of us, which would give us funds to start the home sites plus some operational breathing room as the course grew in next spring. I had a name in mind, though I wasn't sure Chris and Sims would believe me when I said he was interested. It seemed silly suggesting that we should ask this individual to buy into a golf course in the Catskills, but after signing a contract with William Murray, they might be less inclined to think I was bluffing.

Chris just smiled and Sims shook his head.

"Jason Kelce? The football player?" Sims laughed. "What, Tom Brady wasn't interested?"

Contrary to the substance of our breakfast meetings at the Munson, I don't know many celebrities and don't run in those circles. I do play a lot of golf, and during some of that golf that summer, I had played a round with Jason at my home club of Waynesborough. I'd been connected with the Super Bowl champion and future Hall of Famer through some mutual Philadelphia friends; he was trying to play more golf in his new retirement and was kind enough to come on the *Golfer's Journal* podcast, which we recorded upstairs after golf. I probably mentioned Sullivan over the course of our round, but I certainly didn't pitch him on a stake. That would happen a few weeks later, when providence placed me in a foursome with two of his business partners, Stephen and Leif, who helped manage Jason's post-football endeavors. I got the sense that they were looking to diversify their investments, and a slice of a New York nine-holer was about as diverse as a portfolio could get. By that point in the season, I knew the state of our Sullivan County reserves, and somewhere on the back nine I mentioned that we might be looking for another partner. I'd grown accustomed to the signs of a quick pass— the averted eyes, the polite smile, the chuckle and avoidance—but no such signals came from Stephen or Leif. I explained that we had acres to develop for homes and hospitality, not knowing that Stephen had a real estate background, and suddenly I had his full attention. He told me I should reach out if we were serious about bringing someone else on board, and after our breakfast at the Munson, I did.

It was a cold October day when Stephen made the drive up to Liberty—too cold to play the course, which was preferable since it was covered with piles of forest shrapnel awaiting a winter burn. Chris and Sims walked him through their plans for the real estate and showed him the quiet corners where we had plenty of room for homes, and in a short time they were speaking the same language—square footage and subdividing, environmentals and lot sizes. The three of them were entrepreneurs, developers, investors interested in the same things, accustomed to the same risk, eager for the next opportunity. The line between Catskills opportunities and Philadelphia opportunities blurred, and though Kelce had been my lead, it was Stephen's admiration for Chris and Sims's small Sullivan County empire that seemed to convince him that this place might be a good idea. Plus, we could sell Jason's Garage Beer in the restaurant and beef from his cattle on the menu (his family office's interests were broad). And a Kelce joining a partnership with a Madden—how could they say no?

They didn't. Bill and Mike were happy to have Jason on board, and within a few months, we not only had funds to meet payroll and pay our taxes, but Sullivan County now had two owners with two very recognizable faces. The celebrity factor couldn't hurt, I figured, but I didn't expect either to spend a lot of time here, and future success wasn't going to be built on Bill's or Jason's names. That novelty might bring in a few curious fans, but if the goal was never to go partner hunting again, we needed guests to enjoy the golf course and the new range and the putting course. They had to talk about the quality of the greens and the drama of the new layout. We were now in business with Bill Murray and Jason Kelce, but the only name that really mattered at Sullivan County was Shaun Smith.

We played our last round of the season on temporary greens. The wind was cold enough to keep our attention, and the reds and yellows of autumn hillsides were already giving way to brown and bare branches. It was the end of October with little left to mow. The course was sodded and seeded and ready to sleep, so Shaun and I took a loop together where we didn't count any strokes. We took the first divots from new tee boxes. We stopped and looked at places where it was difficult to remember the forest. He'd spent years working his way around dense walls of piney darkness, and now that they were gone, it was hard to imagine they'd ever been there. From the top of the course, we could see a half-dozen greens where you once couldn't see any, with long valleys opened to our eyes and hidden mountaintops now in view. Hitting from rectangles of loose turf, we couldn't judge how our new course would play, but there was no doubt that it was quite something to look at.

When we finished, the lot was empty aside from our cars, and the shop was closed for the season. We sat at the only table left on the patio and didn't speak for a while. We drank from our water bottles and caught our breath from the walk. People loved fall golf for the quiet chill and un-crowded courses and the chance to play in a sweater, but I always found the low light a little sad. It meant the clubs would be sitting in the garage soon, and in those empty golf months, I'd feel something missing. For those of us who defined ourselves—at least part of ourselves—by this game, winter in the Northeast could be a time when you felt unteth-ered. From the chase and the routine, from the chance for golf tomorrow. You'd be a lesser player come April, and like the empty branches above us, would be waiting to start over again.

Shaun looked up and glanced to our left, studying the humps and banks of our vast new putting course. He looked at the new berm that stretched a hundred yards long and separated the first tee and final green from the rest of the course. Colton imagined it as a gateway of sorts, creating a sense of departure and arrival, and he dreamed it up after we played Old Barnwell together that winter, where similar ridges add an old-world touch to the property. Right now, it was just a long mound of dirt, and we had to trust that Shaun's seeding would take hold. Other-wise, it would look like more soil waiting to be moved, a construction job without end.

"This was a lot," he said. "Man . . ." His voice drifted off.

"We'd be sitting in the grass right now, last year," I said. "It's hard to remember what this all looked like before."

"Really hard. I mean, look at all this. It doesn't even make sense when you think about it. People don't do this. Not at a place like this."

He wasn't wrong, and maybe that buoyed our chances. Maybe it didn't. There weren't a lot of mom-and-pop places left in golf anymore, with $20 greens fees and nine holes that weren't trying to be perfect, places that didn't have a tee sheet and called back to a time when you pre-pared a field as well as you could and waited for golfers to find it. While places like ours closed in the face of unflinching economics, Shaun was too big a dreamer to walk that path, and he'd linked up with another one via a social media message that had made both our lives unrecognizable to what they were eighteen months before.

Shaun was a small-town superintendent who now owned a golf course with a movie star. I was a soft-handed writer who now studied weather patterns and coveted the mow lines I saw on TV. And Sullivan County was a forgotten patch of golf holes now healing from the ferocity of a Cinderella makeover. It's one thing to send hope out into the world, but it's quite another to watch it turn real as hills of dirt, to sit down amid its consequences and see exactly what hope had in mind.

Within a few seasons—or sooner—we'd know how fate had judged us, but until then I would try to take moments like these and be proud of my friend. He'd seen something he wasn't ready to abandon, so he didn't. He didn't just wish for another chance for his golf course, but he built one with his hands and his hours and his work. Here was living proof, dressed in black work pants and a grease-stained hoodie, that you didn't have to accept life's impediments as inevitabilities, that belief and tenacity could, quite literally, move a mountain.

That didn't mean we weren't crazy. By any business metric, Shaun and I were fools, but we were fools who had made something, together, and without anyone here to judge our ambitions or our hubris or our indisputable naïveté, a million-plus dollars seemed a small price for the chance to tell a friend, "Look at what the hell we did."

He chuckled. "Pretty wild," he said. "I was talking to Marisol last night. We kind of had a heart-to-heart about all this. The toughest part of this year, it wasn't the work and the watering. That was hard, way harder than I thought it was going to be. But the toughest thing is that I feel responsible for pulling you all into this. Like, if I wasn't so stubborn about this place, you wouldn't have to be up here. Chris and Sims wouldn't be here in the restaurant when I know they've got a hundred other places to be. And all the money people spent. You and Bill and Kelce and Mike. And even the guys on my crew and in the shop—they didn't ask for any of this. I feel like I sold everybody on something. I had this idea and all of these people got wrapped up into it. It just . . ." He paused and wiped his hand across his mouth. "It doesn't feel fair to all of you. Do you know what I mean? Like, I don't know whether I should thank everyone, or if I should apologize for getting them into this."

We were quiet for a little while. There was regret and a little fear in his eyes as he stared down at his feet, scratching the bottom of his shoes on the patio. This wasn't a Shaun to whom I was accustomed. I knew early-morning-energy Shaun. I knew caution-to-the-wind Shaun. I knew big-ideas-we-couldn't-afford Shaun, and I even knew tired-and-angry Shaun—had gotten to know him well this summer. But regret and fear didn't suit him. Addicts don't wear such emotions well—they look more dire, feel more desperate—which is probably how we become addicts. I waited a moment, then I stood up and smiled and told him he was an idiot.

"You could blame yourself," I said. "Or you could remember that everyone here has a job because of you. And they'll have a job next year because of you. And no offense, but Sims and Chris and Jason and Bill and Mike, they're all grown-ups, they could have said no. I'm pretty sure they say no to stuff, a lot. You didn't rope anybody into doing anything. Except me. But I do stupid shit all the time."

He smirked and looked up. "That's true." We stood up and we collected our clubs and headed for the parking lot. Shaun would be back up here every day until April, but I was headed home for the winter with one wish in mind: that where there is bare earth, let there be lawn when I return. And another hope:

"Damn, we have to get this parking lot repaved. It needs to be repainted, too."

"It definitely does," he said. "Put it on the list."

We worked through that list of small jobs via off-season texts: I would remind Shaun about something that needed seed or paint or a nail, and he'd tell me he did it last week. Sims and I settled on a new concept for the restaurant—more casual offerings mixed with the popular dishes from Piccolo, chicken parm and calamari meets burgers and wings, and we'd call the place Otto's after our patron aviator who'd given the course its logo. Allyson's graphic designer sister Cristin designed its new look and menu with an aeronautical theme, adding Otto's Beer Flight to our bill of fare, plus a Paper Plane as our signature drink. Chris's wife, Christine, took over on social media, marketing Otto's launch with videos far snappier than the cut-and-paste posts I'd been using to push memberships. They were trickling in slowly—we had a few die-hard nonresidents eager to see the changes, but aside from a handful of locals, most were waiting to pass verdict on the course come spring. We all were. It was a long winter spent wishing for sod to take root, and it wasn't made any brighter by us taking a whipping on social media.

A follower of a popular parody golf account had posted screenshots of our slim events calendar and our membership offerings, and that account's followers decided to run with it. They reposted Sullivan County to hundreds of thousands of anonymous critics who were happy to pile on, wondering how hapless our club must be to sell an annual pass for $450, labeling anyone who would partake of one as an affront to the institution of golf club membership. Some of it was clever satire of golf snobbery; some of it was plain nastiness. I meekly thumbed my way through the comments, defeated and unwilling to wade into the churlish waters of golf Twitter myself—that chum line needed no more blood— when I stopped on one of the longer comments. I read it that evening, and several evenings after.

• • •

Sullivan County is the latest course on the path of my life's golf journey. This summer, I was able to take my son, who has been severely affected by autism, to SCGC for the first time. This was something I worked out with the owner. In the golf world, it is hard to find a place where my son can play and I am an old school golfer, so I don't want to impose on others, but SCGC is remote enough that we went around in 9 holes with ease. My son can hit the ball off the tee and putt, so it is a mix and match round. We were welcomed by everyone at Sullivan County and between the staff, the food, and the simplicity of the time spent there together, that day it was the best golf club in America.

JULY FOURTH 2025

They were typically younger, sometimes blonder, and they suffered for their tips, dodging passes from overserved foursomes who were sure they'd win the beer cart attendant's heart by asking if she hurt herself when she fell from heaven. We took a different tack at Sullivan County, sending out a sixty-year-old from Brooklyn to tell our guests that they'd never find that friggin' drive but could at least enjoy a beer while they looked for it.

Colleen had been wise to order a cooler bag that fit to the front of John's ranger cart (we rarely used it for any actual course marshaling, but John thought parking a cart by the shop with a ranger flag on it would encourage good manners), and she had been a godsend in our first season post-construction. Our new GM was soft-spoken but firm, young but respected by the staff in both the kitchen and the pro shop. A goal for this year was to synergize our operational islands—golf, turf, and food—into one functioning organization, and Colleen's willingness to collaborate with Shaun and John, whom I'd officially knighted as pro shop manager, was a leap in that direction. Each morning, she and Shaun would update all employees via a company text thread about events in the restaurant and cart path rules for the day (free to roam or stay off damp fairways). It was a small and simple instrument, but it helped quash an us-vs.-them mentality. We had cooks coming into the shop to use their discount on merchandise, and Shaun was taking home bags of takeout from the kitchen. Otto's upscale-pub menu was popular, and my daughter Caroline picked it as her new favorite place to eat. We had Kelce's Garage Beer on tap, and on busy nights I'd step behind the bar and thank everyone for coming and buy a round of drinks for the room. What's the fun of owning a restaurant, I figured, if you couldn't play big shot once in a while?

John had spent the winter remodeling the pro shop, and while I might have been more modest in some of the design choices, I didn't want to temper his enthusiasm for off-the-clock work. He sent me pictures of the redesign in progress—huge Sullivan County decals on fresh paint, a new logo carpet for the entrance, and a ring of logoed trim beneath the ceiling. Without merchandise on the walls, it looked like an experimental chamber built to determine how many propeller logos it took before someone believed they could fly. The walls were painted in stripes of red, white, and blue—our club colors—and though I quietly worried to Shaun that John might be making us a barbershop, when the shirts and socks and headcovers went up, it all came out looking cozy and cared for, words that would not have applied to last year's blank box.

I hoped that giving John more authority would save my phone from small and daily decisions, but those queries were replaced by new ideas and big ambitions—*we need a starter's hut, a halfway house, more hands to work the range*—that I quelled with short and vague replies. But when

John texted me at 10 a.m. on the Fourth of July to tell me the course was packed and that he wanted to fill the cart with beers and waters and go sell them on the course, I was happy to encourage him. After the spring we'd had, such news was sweet and longed-for music.

Aside from good food and an adept GM, Sullivan County's new era began not with a bang, but a soggy whimper. I arrived in April praying for a palate of green but walked into a world of beige and brown. The tree carcasses remained; wind and wet had conspired against Shaun's scrap-wood bonfires, and the driving range I'd spent the winter imagining myself clipping tight rows of divots from was a barren plain of meager sprouts. Shaun wasn't worried—growing season started later in the Catskills. But when it did finally start in May, it wouldn't stop raining. He worried then. We all did.

Not since its opening in 1925 had Sullivan County been in more dire need of good growing days, and the forecast offered us almost none. Bad temperatures, bad light, bad gear—the fairways were too wet to mow, and on the days when a few spots were firm enough for work, the rough mower wouldn't start or the sprayer wouldn't spray. Worst of all, we'd built the new holes during a drought and were now subjecting loose sod to a month of rain. The once forested hillside was showing us all the new ways it wanted to move water, blazing paths we could not have foreseen while shaping greens in the August dust. The fresh stone on our new cart paths washed into roadside clumps, and half our new sixth green was a dark green puddle being fed by a mountain spring we didn't know was there. We had already begged patience last year, telling our members and partners that come June, their course would be a playground from which they'd have to be pulled away. But anyone who visited that spring would have been convinced that we took a whole bunch of money and, instead of burning the wood piles, used wads of cash instead.

They probably would have gotten lost, too. Rather than spend thousands on new hole signage (I'd written that check not long ago, and with our new design, those signs were now obsolete), I took the minimalistic approach to our new layout, buying tee markers numbered one through nine. Play one, then look for two, then three—seemed straightforward enough. This scheme for golf traffic, however, would require our guests to know where to look for those tee markers, and since our routing now went left after the first green instead of right, even locals were looping around in a state of golf bewilderment. The shop guys tried to give clear directions on how to proceed, but most newcomers showed up back in the shop saying they couldn't find the first tee after driving past it three times (it was in the middle of the new putting course, which was a cool concept if not an anticipated one). For six weeks Jimmy, John, and Gary watched golfers drive the wrong direction across our hillsides, returning to report that they weren't sure they played the holes in order, or that they were confident they had only played eight, maybe seven of the holes they'd paid for. Shaun and I thought the hard parts were over, but by the beginning of June, I knew they had returned when I was summoned, yet again, to the diner.

It was like taking swing tips from a beginner, and for the beginner to be right. Chris and Sims had kept their noses far away from golf, deferring to Shaun, John, and me on maintenance and tournaments and everything that hung in the shop, but as Chris slid a pile of papers around his coffee mug and across the table, I was suddenly seated at the center of a golf intervention.

Complaints had been circling around the bar at Otto's—lost golfers, wet fairways, and bare blotches where seed had found no footing—and Chris had taken a ride around the course yesterday, snapping pictures of problem areas and assembling them into a presentation deck of depressing girth. His tone was encouraging—he and Sims both wanted to know what they could do to help—but I couldn't help but feel embarrassed, the golf guy having to explain himself to the restaurant and real estate team. I now knew the pain of every greenskeeper who ever sat in front of a greens committee where the grievances were justified and the explanations few.

They understood that weather had held us back, but Chris wondered if some seed and hay could help mask some of our blemishes. He built houses and that's what they'd do while waiting for a lawn to grow, but coaxing out bent grass was different from residential landscaping, and I shuddered at the prospect of suggesting a coat of hay to my superintendent. I flipped through the pages of unglamorous photography and said I'd take all of it to Shaun for his feedback, though I was sure there was nothing here he didn't know.

"Shaun is basically drinking from a fire hose," I said. "He's got to keep the course in playing condition, take care of all the greens and all the grass out there, and right now he's digging drainage ditches and laying pipe all over the place because the course won't drain."

"But that's sort of the point," said Sims. "People don't see drainage work. They just see dirt and they think the course is still under construction. I know he's working as hard as he can. We just want to help him organize that work into goals that he can accomplish, and we think that we as the owners should have some say in what those goals are."

I couldn't disagree and said we should sit down and talk about all of this with Shaun. With Colleen, too. If we wanted to understand what our greenskeeping team was doing and prioritize their tasks, that communication should begin with our general manager. They agreed, and in a week's time we were all sitting around a long table in Otto's on a quiet and empty morning. When Chris pulled out his pile of papers, I felt my back sliding down my chair, seeking a hole I would not find.

I'd told Shaun about the meeting at the diner and warned him of the issues that had been aired, and while I knew he'd be unsettled by Chris and Sims wading into golf agronomy, the critiques knocked him down. His face sank and his shoulders slumped; he shook his head not in frustration, but surrender. He knew every single flaw on our golf course, he said, and thought about them every minute of every day. "I'm working out of the back of a cart barn with broken equipment and three guys. It rained for a month straight and we've had three grow days when we should have had fifty. It's not an excuse, man. It's just the reality."

By the time we gathered at Otto's, he seemed less defeated, more pissed off. When Chris asked if we could put together a list of aesthetic priorities—visitor-facing things like cleanup and wood piles and dead sod—and check things off that list each week, Shaun snapped back.

"You can't do that."

"Why not?" Chris countered with a little fight in his voice. In our prior deliberations, Chris had been the softer touch to Sims's bottom-line expediency, but today it was clear that he wasn't here just to listen.

"You can't do that because that list changes every day depending on what's working, what the weather is, what the weather was, and what it's going to be," Shaun said. "I come to work every day with a list of thirty things that need to be done. We've got the equipment to maybe do ten of them. And we've got the time and manpower to maybe do three."

"But what about all these areas here?" Chris said, pointing to pictures of yellow sod and bare soil. "Can't we do something to make these look—?"

"Please don't bring up hay and seed," Shaun interrupted.

"Why not? Wouldn't that be better than looking at this?"

"It wouldn't do a thing," Shaun said, "except waste time and money. You want to seed in June? Without an irrigation system? I'd have to spend all my time watering from the truck and meanwhile the greens go dead and I've got to pull Chris off his work to cover mine. I've got Mike and Charlie up to their knees in drainage ditches right now so that we can even get mowers to the greens. And I'm one busted machine away from us not having a golf course. Think about it like this restaurant. I've got one burner and a full restaurant, and if that burner goes, it's lights out."

"Shaun, that's why we're here," Sims said. He'd been sitting back and taking it in but now sat up in his chair. "If we don't have a list of work and priorities, we don't know what you're doing or can't do, and we can't help you."

Shaun looked down at his hands. He rocked back on his chair, a thought in his mind he seemed reluctant to share. And then he shared it:

"Bottom line is, you guys need to step up."

Silence. God bless Colleen, I thought. Someone invited her to an organizational check-in and she landed at a dysfunctional family dinner. Shaun and Chris and Sims all looked at me to say something. I was the golf guy in the partnership and had yet to say a word about our golf operations. But I wore too many hats at this table; Shaun's boss and his assistant, his mower guy and his friend.

Sims finally broke the quiet. "Well, this isn't how I thought this was going to go. And frankly, now I'm pissed off. We came here to figure out a way to help you, Shaun, and I—"

"But you don't—"

"Don't tell me I don't understand. Our other businesses are successful because we have plans and accountability. Every day, I look at what I can do in five days, in five months, and in five years. There are different priorities that go into each of those buckets, and we are going to have that system here. In the restaurant and on the course. And Colleen is here to help us organize it. All we're asking is for you to tell us what goes where so that we're all on the same page. When someone at the bar asks about the driving range, we can tell them—here's the plan. When they ask about the cart paths or the new greens, Colleen or even the bartender can tell them, here's the plan for that."

Shaun was looking up and listening. He was now nodding at what Sims was saying.

"We're not here to tell you what you're doing wrong, Shaun. We know you're overwhelmed. Who wouldn't be? But we have a whole crew of guys we can get over here to help you. We can take things off your plate. We just need to come to some sort of agreement on what needs to be done so we can do it."

It was quiet again before Shaun said, "I appreciate that. I think that sounds like a good idea." After another moment, he said, "I'm sorry, but this is hard for me."

I finally had something to say, a question to ask because I knew the answer. "What's hard about it, Shaun?"

"Just, trying to not feel like I'm being attacked. Because you aren't attacking me. You're not. You're trying to help, and I appreciate that. It's hard for me to accept that without feeling like I've failed. And that's on me."

He turned and looked at our GM. "Colleen, I'm just getting to know you and I'm really glad you're here. I absolutely want to work with you, and it will be a huge help to have someone here who I can tell what we're doing and who can keep us on it. Just so you know why I reacted like that, and you should know this because sometimes I'll react in ways I don't want to," he said. "Not that long ago, my life was very different than this. Very different. I was homeless in the city, bottle for a pillow, and I really don't want to be that again. So no matter what anybody tells me, I get so afraid of disappointing someone that I think I'm disappointing them all the time. And if there's a list of things to do, I just don't want to fail at it and disappoint you."

"Shaun, we're the ones who don't want to disappoint *you*," Sims said.

"I get that. I'm sorry. I do trust you guys. I trust you completely," he said. "I want to have a meeting every week with Colleen and we can review what we're working on and what needs to be done, and if you can send your guys in to take on some of the jobs we can't do, that would be a huge load off."

"Absolutely," Chris said. "That's what we're going to do."

We made a list of projects and tasked them out—Chris's crew would build stairs where the new routing needed them, then dig drainage with something bigger than the shovels Shaun's team had been using. They'd handle the cart paths and let Shaun get back to growing grass. John had a schedule of rotating high schoolers coming in to wash carts and tidy up outside, but most of their time was spent looking for jobs, and now they'd have some—filling divots, raking bunkers, piling up sticks, and pulling rocks from where grass wouldn't grow on the berms. In the meantime, I would order course directional signs to guide visitors from green to tee. (I splurged on a cargo of arrows and engraved instructions; if guests got lost out there now, it probably wasn't safe for them to leave their homes unaccompanied.)

Five-day plan, sorted. Five-month plan: a new work shed for Shaun at the far end of the new driving range, a range where the grass hadn't grown in yet, but where we needed to get visitors paying for buckets. I purchased a dozen mats we could use while waiting for the turf, and we stocked it with range balls imported from Philadelphia (we got a sweetheart deal when Waynesborough members tired of losing wayward drives in the practice range and decided to switch to yellow balls, thus retiring a few thousand white ones we were happy to accept). And in that new shed, more gear for Shaun—a backup fairway mower and top dresser, an aerator and a greens roller, equipment most courses take for granted but that had been daydream stuff for us.

We'd find the money for it, because we had to. There were too many stakeholders, too many people counting on a paycheck, to operate by hope any longer. We'd had one foot in the world of good-enough, the other in not-great-enough, and we all agreed it was time to leap into the latter. No more battling with boxes that couldn't be checked. Shaun would get an office with a whiteboard and the tools to write ambitious things there and cross them off in short time.

At the end of our meeting, we stood up from our seats and collectively exhaled. Sims walked over to shake Shaun's hand, and he said, "No way. We need a hug after that."

And with hugs came sunshine. Over the ensuing weeks, the course dried out, the drainage pipes went in, Toro came by to review orders for next season, and as Shaun predicted they would, the seeds cracked open, and brown gave way to green.

I left Sullivan County to lead a weeklong tour of the Scottish Highlands with a revived spirit. Grievances and souls had been laid bare, and what had been a collection of gangs now felt like a team reading from the same book. For an operation that once couldn't agree on a notepad, much less a book of projects and practices, it seemed Sullivan County was finding its way forward.

It would soon occur to me that it might be time to let it do so on its own.

I would be somewhere north of Inverness when Eastern time would kick in and the texts started hitting my phone. I'd read how Gary had called out because of the rain and John was meant to cover his shift, but Shaun hadn't seen either of them and the sun was out and golfers were peering through the pro shop windows. Or how the carts were covered in mud because we still didn't have a wash pad, which John said Shaun was supposed to build, but Shaun had left that to the pro shop kids while he was busy watering sod. Or how someone was going to break their neck on the stairs up to Keith's old apartment, the only space left to store buckets of range balls. I'd wake to last evening's New York messages and learn that Shaun was tired of John's know-it-all attitude, and that John would no longer abide Shaun's disrespect. Each claimed the other was ruining their progress while I revisited Scottish fairways I had once traveled with the light feet of a young man whose worries didn't extend beyond double-bogey.

Over the past three seasons, I'd been asked a hundred times by curious golfers who might wonder about owning a course or who were curious whether I was up to the task: What's the hardest thing about this new endeavor? What didn't you expect?

The cost, for starters—equipment, carts, fuel, wages, and so many small things (first-aid kit, signage, scorecards) drained money at twice the clip I'd anticipated. Five grand here, three grand there—have a good day at the register, then flush it all out tomorrow on the bare necessities of golf. But money was at least a problem with an overt solution: Make more. Managing people and personalities, on the other hand, was a whole other circumstance for which I was perfectly unequipped.

I had not managed anybody since high school student council, and the stakes of filling the soda machine and putting on the Christmas dance were modest in comparison to the organizational health of a multi-partner golf and hospitality corporation. Sims ran a tight personnel ship over in the restaurant—if you couldn't get it done, you had to go—and was looking for me to do the same with golf. He'd been managing staff for decades and possessed a clear-eyed decisiveness, while I'd gone and made friends with my employees. I'd hoped that an encouraging word could inspire discipline, because I'd entered this business burdened by the need to be liked. I watched those history documentaries at night about Carnegie and Ford and J. P. Morgan, and funny how they didn't lose sleep about someone not smiling as they left the room. I did, and after returning from Scotland and sitting down to talk with Allyson about the things I wasn't able to fix or wasn't engineered to handle, I texted John and Shaun to tell them that I was stepping back from the course. We had a capable GM, I said, so I wished them well and said that Colleen would be their point of contact for the rest of this season.

Shaun called shortly after I hit send. I had expected he would and let the first call go. I picked up on the second one.

"Calm down. You're not going anywhere," he said. My ultimatum had been genuine, but if it held a bit of bluff, Shaun sniffed it out immediately.

He'd work out his beef with John—it had been a stressful weather week, and he apologized for getting me involved. He reminded me that this was our thing, together, and we'd get through it that way. He understood that bulldozers and budgets had made it difficult to recall that all we wanted was a simple spot to play a simple game. We had that now, even if it felt like simple had slipped away.

"Look, you are right where I was two weeks ago, and you brought me back to earth," he said. "We all have our moments. I probably have one every day. Take a breath, look at how far we've come. You sound like I did in that meeting so I know where your head's at. You're feeling overwhelmed. You're feeling sorry for yourself. It'll pass and we'll go out there tomorrow and get after it."

There are few people who can pull me back from my ledges, and I wasn't sure how Shaun had become one of them. I had friends whom I could join for a round or bother for tee times at strange and wonderful places, but they couldn't tell me what I was thinking, or more importantly, what was wrong with it.

A few days later, the three of us sat down on the patio and discussed simple requests. John's came straight out of the boroughs: He could take the heat but wouldn't stand for disrespect. Shaun agreed and asked for clear communication on anything to do with staff, the course, or the equipment. At a course where the range picker doubled as a work cart and one spigot filled our irrigation-on-wheels when it wasn't washing our carts, such communication was overdue. Shaun told John he was great with the guests and that the shop would fall apart without him, and John nodded quietly in appreciation.

Shaun was right and I was glad he said it, even if there had been talk among the partners about whether John was the best fit for our business. John had openly wondered as much to me. He liked Colleen and said he would work with her, but not for her. He'd lived too much life, he said, to take orders from someone half his age who didn't know golf. I didn't expect Colleen to boss him around—it wasn't her nature—but she had to be the point person for purchasing and cash flow and scheduling, and all those daily decisions that had previously flowed back to me. T-shirt orders and approving paint for the locker room—those were GM jobs for which Colleen was paid and qualified to manage. John disagreed and dug in, and I worried that his chain-of-command obstinacy would disqualify him from our vision for Sullivan County's future. While I respected his honesty, it was a forthrightness without bounds. A weariness had gathered around his penchant for pointing out problems, and it had spilled over into the restaurant where his opinions on proper pasta and proper staffing were stirring up resentment.

I preferred solutions to fault-finding, but I also preferred dedication to indifference, and when I stepped back and considered John's motivations, his high-handed frustration grew out of an unwieldy commitment to the success of our business. He was looking ahead to next month and next year, ever concerned about whether we'd reach them. It was care manifesting as pushiness, and it presented a staffing conundrum—what to do about an employee who might care too much? If he acted like he owned the place, it was because a part of his heart did, and I struggled with whether to celebrate such loyalty or let it go for the cause of workplace peace.

He never talked about it, but I knew John had been weathering tough circumstances. He was living alone with Ringo after his daughter had moved out—a move he said he welcomed, but I'm a dad and knew better—and he was selling his longtime home and searching for something smaller. His back had improved after so many surgeries, but he'd just torn his bicep and it seemed his body couldn't catch a break. His big personality would never betray it, but John's life wasn't an easy one, and beneath the bluster I sensed a struggle larger than our little course.

It didn't help that Ringo had grown big and was a jumper; he'd nearly knocked over a dinner guest and would have to be kept at home when Otto's was open. But I'd accept John leaving to let his dog out if it meant I had a guy in the shop who woke up thinking about new ways to save our golf club, and who would serve absolutely any guest to help turn our reputation around.

Jimmy had met a few locals in town who said our course wasn't for them anymore. Too expensive, they said; we'd turned it into a place for out-of-towners. Ours was a singular golf universe where $25 greens fees and $650 annual membership could be considered exclusive, but the municipal course on the other side of Liberty was cheaper, and we'd pushed some of our residents their way. I'd always been a champion of municipal golf, but now I envied their budgetary backstop of county money that seemed an unfair advantage in the race for bottom-dollar golf. The only way to compete was to offer a better product, and we'd made strides in that direction. But we could also make visitors feel like Sullivan County belonged to them in a way a municipal course couldn't. Show up, find your place, find your people. And John proved that's what we offered when two minivans of Hasidic gentlemen pulled into our parking lot on a hot Tuesday afternoon.

Come June, the vans from Brooklyn filled the roads of Sullivan County, as did the walking Haredim whom you'd find hiking the roadsides, far afield from any conspicuous destination. Most didn't drive, I assumed, so they'd hoof it to the shops or synagogues or wait for a passing minivan to come shuttle them home. The two vans that arrived at Sullivan unloaded a surprisingly long line of grown men in ultra-Orthodox attire. With temperatures pushing 90, they had shucked their black overcoats, opting for long-sleeve shirts and shawls that looked like some sort of holy poncho.

John met them at the door where the elder of the group explained that they wanted to rent our carts, to which John explained that these were golf carts and you had to be playing golf to drive them. But where other courses up here might have sent them back out to the road to flag down a ride, John told them to follow him out to the driving range. He was going to teach them golf.

I was home in Callicoon with my family when Shaun sent a picture taken from afar of ten men in religious robes following John across our ninth fairway. Their backs were to the camera, and I could just make out John's lopsided stride, his arms outstretched as he explained something to a group of eager learners. I studied the image and felt like we'd captured our Sullivan County moment. Merion might have Ben Hogan's backswing on eighteen, but a former Brooklyn truck-driving, Mafia nephew pro shop manager teaching golf to the Haredim was our kind of iconic.

I would have paid a hefty sum to eavesdrop on John's lessons that afternoon, but he was so excited to share his coaching foray that I didn't mind hearing it retold as legend. He'd brought out some clubs and a few buckets of balls; he showed them the putting green and the fairway and a tee box—they'd never seen or heard of such things before and they walked them in speculative circles, kids exploring their first playground. He showed them how to hold a club, how to make a small swing, how to avoid getting face-knocked when your friend was swinging. He gave them tees on which to perch their balls, and they studied each as a small and curious gift, a strange utensil of unspecific purpose.

We like to pedestal golf's great coaches who work with names like Rory and Tiger, but there should be a special place in golf's pantheon of teachers for those who take on hopefuls who not only haven't swung a club before, but haven't even seen one. We made a little golf history that day, I think, as John gave golf to men for whom golf was Mars. John said they left happy that afternoon, appreciative of his time and his help. The elder kept asking when they would get to drive the carts; John said a few more trips to the range and they might be ready.

I'd gone back and forth about whether our renovation had been the right choice for Sullivan County. So much dust and so many scars and stumps; we could have just repaved the cart paths and the members might have been happy. But I'd pushed the driving range as essential to growing Liberty's golf audience, and thanks to some willingness and hustle from John, our hope was proved right—we were a golf course for everyone. And best of all, we weren't boring. Not in our wild and tilted layout, not in our idiosyncratic staff, not in the mix of people who found our parking lot. There was a sameness to a lot of golf today—same conditions, same shots, same experiences. You could play a country club in California or Massachusetts and, broadly speaking, have two indistinguishable days.

We didn't have the budget for indistinguishable. Our place offered singularity and inconsistency in ways you'd either find delightful or abhorrent, but Sullivan County Golf Club could promise all comers—owners included—that they would never find it dull.

A few days after the ultra-Orthodox visited our practice tee, I caught sight of an even more surprising driving range tourist. It was late afternoon, and the mats were empty save one man working on a bucket, swinging left-handed clubs that Shaun said he borrowed from the lost-and-found. Any doubts I'd had about our dedication to a driving range went silent when I saw Bearded Chris lashing balls alone. His thin frame in a baggy tank top was silhouetted on the horizon as his clubface struggled for contact. Shaun and I watched from the cart barn, neither of us saying a word, just wide, dumb grins on our faces. He'd hate to know he'd been spotted and probably thought we'd left for the day so he could attempt golf in secret, but watching someone who'd been cutting this grass for a decade finally step off his mower and pick up a club—I think I loved golf more in that moment than I ever had playing it.

· · ·

Henry hadn't been around much this summer. I knew he had outgrown shuffling carts and that he and John weren't getting along as well as they once had; Henry had a better-paying job at the phone store and was juggling shifts between here and there with mixed success. I'm sure John felt like Henry had abandoned him and Sullivan, but he'd just graduated from high school and wanted to have a summer, and I didn't blame him for moving on when he gave his notice. I caught him during his final week and we talked about his plans for the future. Liberty wasn't a town where you took college for granted, and I was happy to hear he was going to do a few semesters at the community college in town, then transfer to the SUNY in nearby Delhi and join their professional golf management program. He wanted to go into the golf business, and I wondered if he might come back here someday as our pro. The position was open and waiting, I told him, and he liked the sound of that idea.

Until then, we'd continue being the best place Sullivan County could be, and on the Fourth of July in our one hundredth year, I arrived to a portrait of it. The parking lot was crowded with the cars of holiday visitors, and John had asked Jimmy to hang around after his morning shift so he could go sell beers on the course. It was a good call; I had been meaning to text Jimmy and ask him to do a double, because I finally could. After much consternation and a half-dozen gun-shy trips to the phone store, Jimmy broke down and bought an iPhone on which he could receive our daily staff updates via text. He could read our messages, he assured me, but replying to them was going to take practice. His first missive to the group read *HhS6*, clarified by a follow-up message that remained a small empty bubble on my screen.

Kids were rolling their balls over the silly mounds we'd built into our putting course, and in the distance, I could see three women taking a golf lesson on the driving range. Dan Yaun's sister Meredith was an accomplished pro and had emailed me to ask whether she could do some teaching this summer when she visited from Florida. I begged her to please do so. She'd won the first women's Scottish Open and coached a college team during the school year—she'd even been a water-skiing champion, which seemed an extraordinary feat for someone from the mountains. Since she'd arrived in Liberty her calendar had been booked solid with lessons, including a few with Gary which did my heart good, seeing my golf staff still loving their golf enough to take a playing lesson after their shift. She'd been teaching adults and kids and newcomers; she would set up foam targets on the putting course and teach children to chip with big plastic clubs. They would laugh and chase after their shots, and if we didn't accomplish anything else this season, kids laughing at their golf looked like success.

A few weeks ago, we'd been close to abandoning one another; today, we were a seamless operation where golfers moved from the range to the putting course to the first tee, then stopped on the patio for Otto's Wings of Glory that I'd put up against any chicken wing in the Catskills. Our horse trailer beer cart was open, and folks were sipping cans in our new rocking chairs between spins around the putting course. Shaun had just finished mowing for the day and came up to the patio benches to join me.

"Crowded today," he said.

"I know. It's really good."

"Really good."

"You hear about Grossinger's?" he asked, and I told him that I had. Our almost-partner Adam had delivered on his intentions to invest in the Catskills. He'd texted a few days ago and the news had just hit the local paper—he'd partnered with a resort group out of Florida and bought the remains of Grossinger's and its golf holes by golden age hero A. W. Tillinghast. Just around the corner from us, the place had once been considered the best golf in the Catskills. Though all the buildings

had been razed and the course had been closed for a decade, the current
owner had kept it mown and saved it from going to seed while he waited
for a buyer. There was a new rumor every month about who that would
be (Tom Doak sniffing around the Catskills was the latest gossip), and
its impending rebirth had become something of a boy-cries-wolf punch
line among Sullivan County's golfers. But Adam got his deal done and,
in the process, might have done more good for us than if he'd bought our
place. Shaun and I agreed—a restored Tillinghast down the road was a
propitious turn for our business. New traffic, more golfers; we'd be an
ideal spot for a bonus nine after a morning eighteen. It was an unofficial
partnership that could turn Liberty into a proper weekend golf destination.

We sat there watching our golf course live and breathe and move
without us lifting a finger. Carts passed us on the way from the ninth
green to the parking lot, faces we didn't know that looked happy enough
with beers in their drink holders and eyes set on their scorecards. Foursomes wiped sweat from their faces and stepped through the door behind us, into the shade of Otto's where there would be golf on TV and
Colleen there to greet them at the door. Ally and Mali (our two best
servers had rhyming names) were working the bar and tables today, so
these new customers would be well looked after and hopefully find their
way back here again.

It's a strange sensation to watch your thing become someone else's, to
do your best with a notion, then hand it over to the world. And when you
see the world enjoying it, you feel something other than happiness. Not a
feeling of being right—right or wrong seems unimportant. It's more like
a connection. Your idea of what a good thing might be matches up with
someone else's, and in that junction is something powerful. It's looking
around and recognizing a part of yourself in everyone you see, and that
feeling makes an otherwise complicated world make sense. Sullivan

County golf had stood for a century, and I'd only been around for a tiny fraction of it, but this faraway place in the mountains felt like a purpose to which I'd be tied for the rest of my life.

Shaun headed home to spend the Fourth with his family, and though I would be coming back up to Otto's for dinner with my in-laws, I was heading home soon to do the same. I wanted to check in on the pro shop first, where I found John and Jimmy deciding how many beers to put in the cart for their next loop around the course.

"This place is fun today, Tom!" Jimmy said. "Man, I love it when we're busy."

I said I loved it, too. The register had been going all morning, he said, and golfers were happy. "The new signs are working. Nobody's getting lost out there, thank God."

"Thank God is right," I said. I told Jimmy and John to keep moving those beers, and I wondered if this holiday might be my own holiday from exiting the pro shop with a problem to ponder. But John gave me a serious look and a "Hey, Tom, before you go . . ." and pointed to the door that foreboded the lousiest of conversations, the ones we had to take outside.

I met him on the paved walkway to the shop and John closed the door behind him. He grabbed my shoulder and lowered his head, pulling us into a huddle, his eyes not meeting mine.

"You know, when I got into this, it was all about, you know, saving the golf course," he said. His voice was unsteady. A man who never searched for words was looking for them, and I worried at what he was trying to say. "But I just want you to know, I think this place saved me."

He coughed and wiped his eyes. I didn't know what to say so I put my hand on his back. I told him we wouldn't be here without him, and I thanked him for being a pain in the ass.

He smiled and nodded. "Alright, enough of that," he said. "We're having a good day, we got more stuff to sell."

"Go for it," I said.

In a few hours, I was back at Otto's with my family to celebrate my father-in-law's birthday. There was no debate over the venue; Otto's was the rare restaurant where both my fifteen-year-old and twelve-year-old approved of the menu, perhaps because they were allowed to order here without a budget. Oysters Rockefeller for Caroline and ribeye for Maggie; their precocious tastes would help pad the morning sales report. I went into a crowded bar and ordered a round on the house, courtesy of Caroline and Maggie, I said, who received a hollering round of applause.

Through the bar window, I noticed someone out on the putting green. I told my table I'd be back in a minute and headed outside.

I had not seen Phil in almost a year, and finding him on an acre-sized putting green when I was accustomed to him brushing putts across our tiny circle in the corner—the new proportions struck me, and with the green all to himself, it looked like something out of a solo putter's dream. I watched him for a bit as he used the hills to roll putts off the bank and trickle them down to the cup, then slowly followed his balls with careful steps, weaving through mounds that came up to his knees.

"What do you think, Phil?" I said, catching him off guard.

"Oh, hey, Tom," he said. "This is something. Don't hardly recognize the place."

"Yeah, we wanted to try something different with the putting green. We modeled it off a putting course in St Andrews. It's not as big as that one, but it's the same idea."

He nodded at my unsolicited insights, then looked out at the course for a moment.

"Looks different out there."

"It's a little different," I said. "But a lot of it we left the same. You should go out there and see it."

"One of these days I will. I'm going to get a cart out and look. The guys are saying it looks pretty good. They said it's getting better every week."

"It is. Every week, a little better."

These hills felt familiar not just to Dad, but also to Mom, whose roots came from towns west and south of Liberty. She was born in Elmira, New York, where her mother passed away when Mom was thirteen. Her father was a coal man and a drinker who never recovered from the loss; Mom and her brother soon moved to Scranton where she shared a narrow bed with her grandmother in a house crowded with newly arrived Irish. Uncles, nieces, cousins from County Mayo—her grandmother took them in as they found their feet, and Mom found her feet working with her aunts in their dress shop, a place called Timely Styles where the coal and iron wealthy browsed, and where her aunts stashed the priciest finery in the back for Mrs. Scranton, heiress to the city's name and its oldest money.

Maybe it was her life as a couture salesgirl that taught Mom how to turn strangers into friends before the door closed behind them. It was a disposition I admired but had not inherited, and the older I got, the more I defaulted to Dad's guarded affability, where razzing passed for affection and hid an undertow of isolation. Mom had no time for that, too busy befriending the nurse, the checkout lady, the bank teller. And Jason Kelce was soon added to her list, hardly an hour into our one-hundred-year anniversary party at Sullivan.

It was his first visit since buying into the course, and we'd spent two months planning a party that would prove that Stephen had steered Jason right. Team Kelce arrived in two SUVs—Stephen and Leif and their partner Cory whom Jason had known since college, plus their social media folks whom we invited to come capture the festivities. His Underdog Apparel team joined us, too—they had made special merchandise for our anniversary, a line of hats, T-shirts, and sweatshirts embroidered with the original Sullivan County Golf & Country Club sign that now hung over the bar. When the inventory arrived, John pulled me aside to tell me they got the name wrong—*What's with "Country Club"?*—but I told him these were throwbacks and would sell, and by the end of that evening, we had just a few T-shirts left.

When they weren't scooping up sweatshirts or shopping at a vintage pop-up stand that Colleen had invited, or trying our long drive contest from the first tee with launch monitors I'd sourced for the party, or tallying a score on the putting course to win an $800 putter Jason's team had donated, our guests lined a buffet that Sims had assembled via his culinary contacts in Manhattan. Carving stations and a crispy roast pig were preceded by a long raw bar of iced oysters and shrimp, plus Paper Planes by the pitcher and cans of Jason's Garage Beer rarely out of reach. It broke both Allyson's and my hearts that she couldn't make the celebration, but tomorrow was the girls' first day of school back in Philadelphia, so my parents and my older brother, Deacon Matt, represented the Coynes. In our family's ranking of priorities and achievements, golf course ownership vs. ordination was a toss-up, and it gave our parents multiple fronts on which to bait a bystander into hearing about their kids—*Do you play golf? Well, are you Catholic?*—but Matt left his collar at home and let me have my moment.

Colton had flown in for the party; same for Mike Madden and his wife Susie who had traveled from California (she was a big fan of *The Office* and was hoping to stop by Scranton on the way back to the airport). Friends from Aquatrols and Toro and the Met Golf Section had all gotten tickets, and Shaun and Marisol were chatting with them while Adah stalked a ball across the putting green, zigging this way and that with a too-long putter.

Bill had even blocked the date on his calendar. He'd been touring Europe with his band that summer (Bill Murray & his Blood Brothers) and I wondered if he could fit us between London and the NASCAR race where I saw he was meant to be the grand marshal in just a few days. He did, and he and his brother Johnny pulled into the parking lot around 6 p.m. in the same Jetta he'd driven to Tractor Supply with Shaun years before, just as the band Colleen hired started to play.

Mom and Dad held court on one of the picnic benches. Mom would typically float from table to table, but her sciatica planted her at a seat where she waved strangers over for a chat. As the party elders, my parents' summons was one you couldn't deny, and as I watched face after face visit with them, I hoped they understood that they didn't have to boast to anyone here that it was their son who owned the golf course. That was common knowledge, not just here but in most of Philadelphia's five counties where they'd walk bookstore innocents over to the golf section and put one of my books in their hands. Plus, given the makeup of our guest list, there was a good chance that the person with whom they were speaking owned some of it, too.

When Jason sat down with Mom, I wandered by and tried to eavesdrop over the music. She told him that they lived near each other back in Philadelphia, and said that his wife seemed like a very sharp young woman. Jason agreed, and Mom said, "Of course we see you on the television all the time. You are one happening person, Jason Kelce. And seeing how you interact with people and treat the people here, and how you talk about your family, I have to say, I admire the way you are living your life."

Jason was probably a man accustomed to compliments, but this one seemed to land. His life must be a hard one to manage, so to hear from a ninety-year-old lady that he was going about it the right way—he paused for a moment and his face softened. He touched my mom on the shoulder and thanked her for saying that. "That means a lot to me," he said. And then she told him that her son Tom owned the golf course.

Earlier that day, a flatbed had pulled up to the course and a woodsman with a skid steer dropped a large stump beside the patio and lit it on fire. The side of the trunk was carved with *Happy 100 to SCGC* and it took a few tries for him to ignite it, but as the temperatures cooled that evening, we took turns standing around a magical chunk of wood that glowed through pre-cut holes, a fire burning deep in its center. Bill was mystified by this artisan bonfire that Sims had arranged, and for a man who knew something about a proper party, it was clear we'd given him a good night. He danced in front of the seven-piece jam band until they turned over the microphone, and the crowd jumped in as he sang "Mustang Sally" and played cowbell to Bachman-Turner Overdrive.

John looked drained after Bill left the pro shop, noting that our stock was suddenly short and that Bill wanted us to order bucket hats. Brother Johnny had to help him carry all his Sullivan County gear out to their car, and after beating up the vintage shop and claiming most of their vinyl, there was hardly room left in their Jetta for their golf clubs.

They'd use them the following morning when we organized nine holes of golf and a lunch Q&A for the party guests. About fifty showed up for golf, and I paired Bill in a group with me and my dad and Colton. Dad teed off the first in front of a crowd. His backswing didn't reach shoulder height anymore, but he still had some pop, and he knocked his drive over the berm and into the fairway. Bill applauded and patted him on the back, and I was still smiling as I teed up my ball and hit it wherever, not really watching its path. Fairway or rough, it didn't matter. I was playing our course with my dad and my friends and thinking about some long-ago advice from my Irish friend Pat Ruddy: *Stay in love with golf. Never stop playing.* I had promised him I wouldn't, and today that was an easy promise to keep.

Our dry summer coated the course in a blanket of beige, but Shaun had run himself ragged keeping the greens wet in anticipation of today, our unveiling to Bill and Jason and Mike. The hardpan tried to hide it, but the forever views and the intersecting fun of the new routing were unmistakable markers of a proper place to play. Tom Valentine from Aquatrols could hardly summon a reaction for Shaun ("I don't know what to say. I can't believe what you got done here"), and since he and his team knew our before and after down to the root, theirs was the only approval Shaun required. They even loved our new sixth hole, the punch bowl par-three that had been designed to gather golf balls down to the green but had mostly gathered critique. Too hard, people said, with too deep grass bunkers and too small a target.

I'd told Colton about the criticism, and as if to offer his own retort, when we arrived at number six, he reached into our bag of shared clubs and borrowed my seven-iron. He stuck his ball on a short tee, eyed the pin tucked back left and took one waggle. Turned his arms and body back, then threw them at the ball—it soared, hit, hopped twice, and disappeared into the cup. We jumped and howled while he just stared at the hole, arms raised in triumphant vindication as Bill hoisted him off his feet. He made the first ace on a hole he designed, while playing it for the first time, in front of Bill Murray. It felt a little like the fix was in—no wonder he'd thought the green was set in the right spot—but there would be no more discussion as to whether the hole was playable.

After golf Bill and I sat on high-top chairs in the dining room and took questions while golfers ate their lunch. Mom and Dad claimed a booth in the far corner with their new pals, Mike and Susie, plus two women I didn't know but whom Mom had turned into lunch buddies. I told some stories of how we all ended up here, dining in a bright, beautiful room that had, not long ago, been a dusty, cobwebbed coffin bracing for demolition. I thanked the people who deserved our gratitude, which was every face in this room: the members, the vendors, Chris and Sims and Sims's brother, Ryan, who so thoroughly transformed this building. Their wives. My wife (thanked in absentia). John and Jimmy and Gary and Bearded Chris, Bill and Mike and Jason—plus his team—and of course, our most senior and most valuable Sullivan County members, Mom and Dad, for whom the whole room stood up and applauded.

They did the same for Shaun when I explained that this project might have many names attached to it, but the one to peg above them all was his. His vision, his work, his stubbornness. He was sitting off to our left, on a bench with his back to the wall, and he didn't stand up when I asked him to say a few words. He lifted a hand and modestly nodded at the cheers. When they subsided, he said, "Thank you, everyone, for being here. It's kind of hard to believe that this is happening, because three years ago, I had this exact dream. I dreamed that we would be sitting here celebrating a one hundredth anniversary. Bill and Jason weren't in it, but it was pretty much just like this." The room laughed and he said, "And now that it's real and this is happening, I'm just incredibly grateful."

There was no better note on which to conclude our talk and turn our attention to fried chicken sandwiches, but Bill raised his hand. He wanted to say something, and the room went quiet.

"You know, Tom here has been very kind to thank all of us. Thorough, too. If you ever win an Oscar, you're ready," he said to me, and the guests chuckled. "But I think he's the one who deserves our thanks." There was a murmur of agreement, and I looked down at my feet, unprepared for what Bill might say. I was an approval-seeker who didn't know how to stomach the thing I sought, dismissing praise as undeserved or disingenuous. But Bill didn't do disingenuous, so I just stared at the floor with my fingers balled in a knot.

"This might sound strange," Bill said, "but I mean it when I say that Tom reminds me of John Belushi."

Awkward laughs from the crowd and some surprised faces, and I looked over to see how my parents judged that comparison. Dad's titled chin was a relief; they had no idea who John Belushi was.

"Belushi was a gatherer. He brought people together, and people followed him. He'd have these big ideas and he would sort of pull you in and pull you along, and because he did, your life would be better for it. I think that's what Tom does and I think that's what he's done here, so I think we should thank him for bringing us here and bringing us along for the ride."

I couldn't look up. I wiped a few tears and sat stuck in my chair, locked in a moment that was long drives to the Catskills and early mornings in the dew. Hard conversations on a patio and easy walks down a mountainside. Muddy knuckles brushing sharp steel, and the shadows of men before sunrise, shapes perched atop machines, hands waving hello in the distance. It was gas station coffee and burnt popcorn, hash browns and hot sauce served in a booth of hope and doubt.

I finally picked up my head and saw a room of clapping hands and smiling faces pointed back at mine. And in the corner, of course Mom was crying, too.

Our friends from the Met Section presented us with a framed parchment on which Sullivan County reaching one hundred years was celebrated in ornate script. We went outside for a picture of it with all the partners. Shaun held the artwork while the other owners crowded around him. There were ten of us in total, more owners than we had golf holes, and Sullivan County Golf Club deserved every one of them.

Left to right: Sims Foster, Stephen Porter, Cory Sims, Jason Kelce, Tom Coyne, Shaun Smith, Mike Madden, Bill Murray, Chris Monello, Leif Edgar

That one-hundred-year plaque hangs in the clubhouse, and you should come see it. Come try the wings and tell us what you think of number six. There won't be a line for the first tee (and if there is, the Adirondacks are comfortable and the putting green has space). Forgive the guys in the shop if they keep you too long, asking your life story or retelling theirs. The winters are long and quiet in Sullivan County, so come summer, conversation with a visitor is welcome currency. It won't cost you much to play our course, aside from some small talk that doesn't matter most places but matters up here.

I'll be there, too, maybe out on a mower or over in the shed, showing Shaun where I chipped another bed knife. If I'm not at the course, I'm probably in Callicoon, where Allyson has a long list of jobs for me to finish—those pictures won't hang themselves—and where yesterday Caroline taught me how to do pool yoga with foam noodles while her sister, Maggie, is off at a Catskills camp she loves, an overnight place that's just two towns down from Liberty, not very far at all from our home.

ACKNOWLEDGMENTS

Before a message from @gorsenod could become fairways and a clubhouse and a new family in the Catskills, it had to become a book first, and that was only possible because an agent at a long-ago cocktail party agreed to read a manuscript. Dan Mandel has been with me through every word and mile since, and in the process has become an accidental hero of Sullivan County Golf Club. So have my editors, Jofie Ferrari-Adler and Carolyn Kelly. Jofie believed in this story and this place from the jump, and he has been an irreplaceable friend and ally. And Carolyn's insights and guidance were a true gift; I am in debt to her talents. Thanks to Michael Burke, too, for such thoughtful inspection.

John Conway's books, time, and expertise were an invaluable resource in my Catskills research, as were books like *The Catskills: Its History and How It Changed America* and *Sullivan County Borscht Belt*, plus the archives of the *Sullivan County Democrat*.

The list of people and companies who took an interest in our little course is too extensive to repeat here, but all the supporters who are named in this story saved a course from closing and a book from being very, very short.

I can only hope that these pages adequately convey my gratitude and admiration for Shaun and our team at Sullivan County. I decline to list them all again here for fear of ranking their value (and for fear of writing some onerously long acknowledgments), but the staff and partners at SCGC have created a place to work and hope with joy and with purpose, and to do so together. And it doesn't exist without its members, both past and present, and our visitors who have given us a morning or afternoon. If you've ever teed it up at Sullivan County, this story is as much yours as mine.

It's Allyson's, too. Maggie's and Caroline's as well. We've got ourselves a golf course, girls. How about that?

ABOUT THE AUTHOR

TOM COYNE is the author of numerous golf titles, including *A Gentleman's Game*, which was adapted into a film starring Gary Sinise, and three *New York Times* bestsellers: *A Course Called Ireland*, *A Course Called Scotland*, and *A Course Called America*. He is the editor and podcast host of *The Golfer's Journal*, and his golf travels are the subject of an upcoming documentary series from the BBC and Paramount. He splits his time between Philadelphia and Sullivan County with his wife and two daughters.